RED WAT

They emerged from the steaming hallway with the jet – smoke-stained, sweating, their uniforms soaking wet – to be taken unawares by the shocking cold night air and the spread of the fire above them. They stared upwards. Gouts of flame were bursting out of several upper windows, and the whole roof seemed ablaze.

'Good grief!' said Taylor. 'Just look at *that*!'

As they walked away, a hot blast of air swept out after them into the street through the front door of number 13.

The second-floor stairs had just collapsed.

By the same author:

Neither the Sea Nor the Sand
Dragon under the Hill
Adam's Tale
Nagasaki 1945
The Edge of Heaven
Royal Wedding
The Year of the Princess
The Murders of the Black Museum
Selfridges
TV-am Celebration of the Royal Wedding
Siren Song
More Murders of the Black Museum

Gordon Honeycombe

RED WATCH

CLASSIC EDITIONS

This edition digitally re-mastered and
published by JM Classic Editions © 2007
Original text © Gordon Honeycombe 1976

ISBN 978-1-905217-31-1

this book is for Stephen
and
for all those who fought the fire
in Clifton Gardens on 13 December 1974

Acknowledgements

All the material in this book is derived from official statements and documents, from my own observations and investigations, and from many conversations with the firemen directly concerned. To all, to everyone named in the text, I would like formally to express my gratitude for the help I was given. I also wish to thank the London Fire Brigade for giving the undertaking their blessing and for assisting me in whatever way they could. My particular thanks must go to Neil Wallington and the men of the Red Watch, Paddington. Without their sustained and whole-hearted co-operation my task would have been much more difficult, if not impossible. I hope this story of their dedication, character, courage and devotion does them and their calling some justice.

Gordon Honeycombe 1976

Contents

PLAN of PART of WORSLEY HOTEL

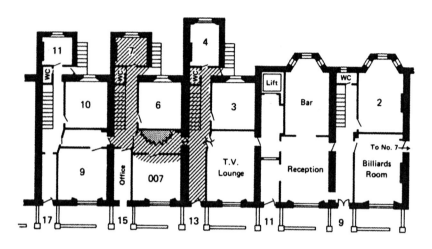

GROUND FLOOR PLAN

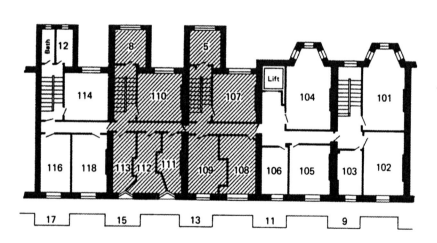

FIRST FLOOR PLAN

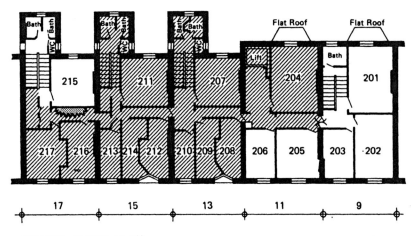

SECOND FLOOR PLAN

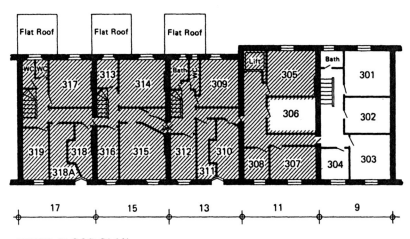

THIRD FLOOR PLAN

Note: The fourth floor rooms in the attic roof above room numbers 17, 15 and 13 (known as a Mansard Roof) are not shown.

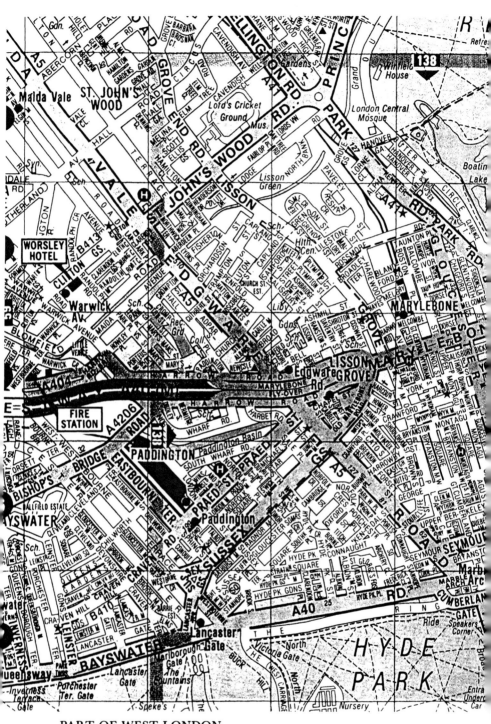

PART OF WEST LONDON
Some of the area covered by A21 (Paddington).

Foreword

When the fire-fighters of Red Watch, on duty at Paddington Fire Station, turned out to a fire-call at the Worsley Hotel in Clifton Gardens on that dark and icy cold early morning of Friday, 13 December 1974, none could have thought that they were about to become part of fire service history.

Within minutes, the four Red Watch crews were at the scene, facing a fire that had already reached nightmare proportions and severity. Reinforcing fire-engines and other crews from fire-stations all over Central London converged on the conflagration at Clifton Gardens, which was destined to become the worst fire in London that year. Thirty fire appliances and 150 firemen were called out to attend the blaze, in which seven people, one a fireman, died.

All fire-fighting, particularly at large outbreaks, is physically demanding and dangerous. But the Worsley Hotel fire posed fire-fighters with a series of very unusual challenges.

The sheer number of residents screaming out from upper floors for rescue, and the rapidly spreading fire situation in separate parts of the building, were serious enough. Parked cars obstructed the roadway in front of the hotel, and there was a shortage of fire-fighting water. The first of the men from Paddington to confront the fire inside the smoke-filled labyrinth of the hotel were forced back by the sudden collapse of stone staircases.

All these circumstances in themselves were not too uncommon for Central London firemen. However, when after an hour, part of the Worsley Hotel's roof crashed down onto a fire-fighting crew working on the second floor, trapping four men in hot, burning debris, the situation suddenly became potentially much worse.

For while the frantic rescue of firemen by firemen amid the unsafe and crumbling structure became a matter of life and death, the fire all around the rescue site on the second floor still had to be brought under control. It was three hours before the four trapped firemen were released: three were badly burned, the fourth was dead.

The full, and true, story of the dramatic and extraordinary events of the Worsley Hotel fire and the few days leading up to it were vividly described in Gordon Honeycombe's *Red Watch*, first published in 1976. The book, the first ever to detail the inside story of firemen's lives and work at a major fire, became an instant best-seller and is now a classic of its kind.

Apart from this, the book also marked something of a watershed. For its publication inaugurated an era in which the public at large began to have a far higher awareness of the work of fire-fighters, and the dangers they regularly face.

In the years since the Worsley Hotel fire, the fire service itself has learnt to project a stronger public relations profile of its role in a modern society where the threat of fire to life and property remains as great as ever. It is also interesting to reflect that although the cause of the Worsley Hotel fire was arson, the incident led directly to a tightening of fire safety legislation covering hostel-type premises nationwide.

More recently, the number of '999' emergency calls of all kinds dealt with by the fire service throughout the United Kingdom has continued to grow, and this has led to more intensified levels of personnel training and preparation, in addition to the development of more sophisticated fire-fighting and rescue equipment. Lightweight breathing apparatus, with radio communications between wearers, infra-red cameras which can see through smoke to detect the source of a fire, and more protective fire-fighting uniforms are just a few examples of modern and welcome additions to a fire-fighter's armoury.

But what has certainly not changed since that fateful night of Friday, 13 December, 1974 is the simple fact that being a fire-fighter still demands a high level of personal courage and selfless commitment which is needed in few other professions.

Regrettably, since that night in 1974, there have been many multiple fire deaths, a number of which have been in hotels and hostels. Even so, I doubt if any of these particular tragedies have contained the dramatic combination of life and death circumstances that occurred at the Worsley Hotel fire. As one of those members of A21's Red Watch who was closely involved 19 years ago in the Worsley fire and in the rescues of two of the four entrapped firemen, I find that the various images of what happened that night in Clifton Gardens are not easily forgotten or suppressed – nor should they be.

Even though I have now been retired from the uniformed fire service for over two years, the sight and sound of an approaching fire engine, with its headlights and blue beacons on and blaring two-tone horns clearing the traffic away from its path, immediately gets my adrenalin flowing, and revives feelings of personal pride and gladness that the fire service is one of the finest jobs in the world.

The crew of the fire engine may be going to deal with a kitchen chip pan fire or with the bloody aftermath of a road accident. Their destination may be to another frustrating and time-wasting malicious false-alarm call. And then again, it might just be to another Worsley Hotel fire which awaits them, ready to test their calling as members of what is, by any comparison, a most noble profession, in which selflessness and bravery conjoin with technical expertise and physical skill.

Neil Wallington 1993

Fireman

by Charles Clisby

Reporter asked me: 'What's it like?'

I shrugged him off: 'I couldn't say.'
You see, I'm not a one for that,
Not one for bragging anyway.

He pressed me hard – and so I tried;
I hoped my tale he understood.
Could it be that telling him
Might do the job a bit of good?

'If you put on six overcoats –
And though you suffered hell from corns
You crammed your feet in army boots –
Wore on your head a crown of thorns –
Lay in a bath, first hot, then cold –
Got out and ran a mile or so –
Into an oven squeezed yourself
And turned to nine the regulo;
If, with a bandage round your eyes,
A wooden peg clipped on your nose,
You then crawled through a concrete maze,
Your feet wrapped round with yards of hose –
You'd get a notion what it's like.'

Reporter laughed: 'It can't be true.'

I looked him in the eyes and said:
'You're right. Five overcoats will do.'

Prologue

Joe Milner supped his coffee and contemplated the forty or so prosperous Rotarians relaxing in the restaurant of the YMCA in Stockwell Road. Tradesmen and businessmen, men of substance and distinction, the members of the Brixton Rotary Club had met for one of their regular lunches and to hear him deliver a post-prandial address in his official capacity as Chief Officer of the London Fire Brigade.

They sat at tables arranged in an E, in a secluded part of the restaurant with all the curtains drawn. The room was very warm, but no warmer than the offices and corridors of Mr Milner's domain – the Brigade Headquarters on the south side of the River Thames by Lambeth Bridge.

The uninitiated were usually surprised to hear Mr Milner's occupation. With his balding head, dark eyes, slight stature and thin, lined face, he looked like an academic, not a man of action – like a man who had learned many lessons from books and not, as he had in fact, from a hard schooling in life.

He felt tired. Since becoming Chief Officer in 1970 he had worked harder and for longer hours than at any period since the war, in which he had fought as one of Wingate's Chindits in Burma. His time was never his own. His slumbers the previous night had been disturbed by a warehouse fire in Bermondsey whose dangerous size had required his attendance, and all that morning politicians and pressmen had been agitating for answers and comments on the firemen's strike in Glasgow and on the situation in London.

He replaced his coffee cup in its saucer and took out his pipe and tobacco. As he did so his roving fireman's eye caught on his left a sign on the wall beyond the Lord Mayor of Lambeth's head – FIRE EXIT. He surmised that the full-length curtains there probably concealed a door or windows leading onto a yard. He had already noted the other exits and instinctively had speculated in an idle moment on the hazards of fighting a blaze in the building. Another sign, on the wall above his head, had briefly amused him. It marked his place at the table – NO SMOKING PLEASE. This request had, however, with due authority been waived by the Rotarians, whose cigars and cigarettes now added a pleasant fug to the convivial atmosphere of the meeting.

As his pipe contributed its own aroma and soothing smoke to the room, he wondered what the assemblage would make of his speech, and whether it would have the desired effect – not on them but on the 6000 firemen in his command.

Copies of the speech, embargoed until 12.30, had already been distributed to the Press. It was now nearly 1.35, and very soon the Club Secretary, Mr Jack Westbury, an alderman and estate agent, would rise and call upon his distinguished guest to address the meeting.

It was Tuesday, 30 October 1973.

The content of Mr Milner's speech had largely been determined four days earlier when the Glasgow firemen went on unofficial strike. Nonetheless it was the first ever strike by firemen in Britain. Conditions of work in Glasgow were notoriously bad – twenty-seven of the city's firemen had been killed on duty in the last ten years. But the strike was basically over a pay rise. Glasgow Corporation had offered the firemen an extra £2.48 a week, to add to their average take-home pay of £28. The men wanted £5 extra. This had been refused; and so on Friday 26 October, only four of the city's 660 firemen had reported for duty, and the fire-stations had been manned by seventy-two Brigade officers, who were joined over the weekend by fire-fighters from the three armed Services. Meanwhile firemen in other cities began a work-to-rule in sympathy with their colleagues in Glasgow or voted to respond to emergency calls only – as did several fire-stations in London. Negotiations for a shorter working week had been going on for two years, since the Cunningham Report in November 1971, and although firemen had been given a small pay rise at the beginning of October, their union thought it was insufficient. The situation in London was aggravated by serious undermanning in fire-stations, by excessive overtime, and by the cost of working in the capital and travelling in and out.

But despite all this and the Glasgow strike, on Monday 29
October, a national conference of the Fire Brigades' Union
decided to take a moderate line. Delegates voted by three to
one *not* to make the Glasgow strike official and to ask the firemen there to return to work. They also urged that the pro-
posals in the Cunningham Report be implemented straight
away. Nonetheless, there was still a possibility, as other cities
began working to rule, that on the firemen's busiest night of
the year, 5 November, the nation's firemen might decide to
stay at home.

It was then that Joe Milner decided, although his role
demanded that he should be publicly impartial, to speak out
and show whose side he and his senior officers were on.

As he turned the type-written pages of his speech phrases in
it struck chords in his imagination, and by the time Mr
Westbury leaned towards him and asked – 'Are you ready,
Joe?' – he was all the more eager to relate what no Chief
Officer had publicly spoken about before, and to make known
what had been unappreciated by the public for too long.

The laudatory introduction over, he stood up, having extinguished his pipe, and without waiting for the applause to
end he began.

'When I am invited to address distinguished gatherings
such as this, I am usually pressed to talk about some aspect of
fire prevention. On this occasion, however, Mr Jack Westbury
made no stipulation about my subject, and with so much
being preached about the pay of public servants in London –
of busmen, policemen, and the like – I couldn't resist the
opportunity to say something about the business of being a
fireman. I therefore asked one of my staff officers to draft some
words for me on that subject. Within an hour or so he put an
almost complete speech on my desk.'

Joe Milner paused, and looked at the typescript on the
table lectern before him. Having begun strongly, he now
lowered the tone of his voice.

'It starts with two quotations. The first is from the 1971
Cunningham Report on which Fire Service salaries are cur-
rently based. It says – "*We conclude that the job of the basic grade
fireman is broadly comparable with industrial jobs in the top SEMI-
SKILLED categories of the LOWER ranges of the skilled trades . . .*"

'The second is a much older quotation – *"A fireman, to be successful, must enter buildings. He must get in below, above, on every side; from opposite houses, over back walls, over side walls, through panels of doors, through windows, through skylights, through holes cut by himself in gates, walls, and the roof. He must know how to reach the attic from the basement by ladders placed on half-burned stairs, and the basement from the attic by a rope made fast on a chimney. His whole success depends on his getting in and remaining there, and he must always carry his appliances with him, as without them he is of no use."*

'Those are the words of Sir Eyre Massey-Shaw, who commanded the London Fire Brigade from 1861 to 1892.'

Mr Milner raised his voice again. 'Does that sound to you like "semi-skilled work"?

'Let me try to describe the reality behind Massey-Shaw's words. Let me tell you what it is *like* to be a fireman in London today. . . .

'The fireman begins each tour of duty by parading in full fire-fighting gear, when he is given precise directions about which appliance he is to ride during his shift. After an inspection, he places his gear on the appliance to which he has been assigned and always in the same place, so that when the calls come there can be no confusion, no hesitation. His routine continues with the checking of the appliance and its equipment. He makes sure that his breathing apparatus fits and is properly adjusted and that his life-support gas-cylinder is functioning. The appliance lockers are opened, their contents are checked, and the position of individual items is noted, so that they can be instantly picked up in an emergency – whatever the time of day or night and whatever the weather. After this there will be what is known as "continuation training" – drills. These are repeatedly practised, until each man instinctively knows his part and the roles of the others on his team and can act speedily, efficiently, and virtually without any directive – as he will have to do, under great stress, when the chips are down.'

Joe Milner saw the next four words in his script, and despite his twenty-eight years of service as a fireman the image they at once evoked, and the sound, gave a new edge to his voice.

'The bells go down. The firemen on duty, whether at drills, lectures, meals or at rest, race to their appliances. The drivers rev up impatiently while the teleprinter chatters out the address of the emergency. Brief directions are given to the driver; the appliance-room doors swing open, and the appliances turn out. Now comes the often hair-raising drive through dense traffic. Speed is vital, but so is safety. Two-tone horns and flashing blue lights help to clear the road and serve also to reassure those in trouble that help is on the way. While the driver concentrates on the route, the others in the crew are struggling into their fire-gear and checking the location of hydrants. The officer-in-charge is mentally running through his topographical knowledge of the area, wondering what kind of property will face them – what particular operational problems the property and the occupants will present. The adrenalin is pumping through each man, keying him up for action, making him ready for some as yet unknown demand on his system. . . . Yet often the arrival is an anti-climax – a false alarm, an insignificant incident. The adrenalin drains away. The men feel washed out, lethargic, though no real effort has been expended. . . . Many times, however, the adrenalin is needed. Some superhuman effort is demanded of them and is always, thank God, forthcoming.

'Perhaps it's a fire in a medium-sized supermarket of four floors and a basement, all of which may be smoke-logged. The officer-in-charge will not yet know exactly where the fire is located within the building. His first task will be to radio for reinforcing appliances and to organize firemen wearing breathing apparatus in the search for any casualties and the seat of the fire. These teams will grope their way forward, keeping close together, so that they may aid each other if trouble comes. They must remember each door they pass through, each turn they make, so that there can be no confusion about the way out. Each foot must be placed carefully, lest floors weakened by fire or rot give way and plunge them into an inferno. Always they are aware of the heat. Its growing intensity tells them when they are approaching its source. And they must always be alert for a sudden build-up of super-heated gases, which may detonate in a flash-over – a ball of flame scorching all in its path. Outside the building, other firemen are pumping water on the flames. Inside, as the search progresses, it may be found that the fire is in the basement.

Tugging with them their heavy, charged hose, the firemen must find or force a way down. On their rumps or bellies now, they will be hot and sweaty – their clothing will be covered in filth and saturated with water. They stumble onto a stairway, and as they go down it the heat-band, a band of high temperature gases which builds up at ceiling level, toasts their exposed skin. Totally blinded by thick smoke, they feel their way down each step, carefully testing each stair-tread before trusting their full weight upon it. Spraying water to cool the atmosphere as they go they reach the base of the stairs. Now they may be confronted with a confusion of passageways. These they must penetrate and explore, only too aware of the dangers surrounding them. Suddenly the fire flares up somewhere in front. Jets of water are directed at the flames, and a dense cloud of hissing, scalding steam envelops them. Isolated from the outside, knowing only their own little part of the whole affair, they hang on – trusting that others are also playing their part, and that their means of retreat are being securely held. . . . Soon, although the minutes seem like hours, they know they are winning. The scalding heat begins to lose its sting. The air at the lowest level begins to cool, and by wiping their goggles and tucking down their heads they begin to see, even though the smoke and steam still linger in a thick layer above. They move on, searching for small pockets of fire. . . . But now they are tired. That remarkable something that drove them on has evaporated. They are wet, chilled, and will be glad to see the outside again. When they are relieved, they drag themselves back through the smoke and scorched passages up into the open air. Once there they will be cold, very cold – very wet, and very exhausted. But they will have that sense of satisfaction that comes from achievement. They have done well – they will know this – and that is enough.'

Someone coughed. A clatter of cutlery in the kitchen impinged on the silent room as the speaker turned over a page before continuing.

'Such a fire as I have tried to describe could, of course, be complicated by people being trapped. Fire, heat and smoke make for some difficulty and discomfort, but for the well-trained crew rescues can be quite a straightforward operation, especially if people are at windows. There are other hazards.

Stone staircases, when subjected to heat then sudden cooling, will almost certainly collapse without warning. Then there are gas-cylinders heated up to explosive potential, chemicals which produce deadly gases, radiation risks – all adding their own complications to the fireman's problems. But above all there is the human tragedy. How much does the fireman see of that! Homes destroyed, burns, injuries, the suffering of children. Sometimes, sadly, we are too late. Or perhaps help was never possible. Then there is the task of picking up the charred body of some unfortunate and wrapping it in a sheet, before taking it to a waiting ambulance outside. There are also moments of sheer satisfaction – to snatch a child from peril and breathe back life into a seemingly lifeless body – to take a whimpering child the pet she prematurely mourns – to be able to tell a distraught wife: "He's all right, dear. We've got him. He's all right." '

The speaker's voice was matter-of-fact, hiding his personal knowledge of such scenes, and of other scenes too horrible to relate. Impassively he gazed about the restaurant before picking up his place on the script and the next point in his thesis.

'There is another role for firemen, not connected with fire, which we term the special service call. I suppose it was inevitable that events would dictate that the Fire Brigade, capable of carrying heavy rescue-equipment and ready for instant turn-out around the clock, would eventually develop into an emergency service able to deal with situations beyond the capabilities of other services. So it is that firemen find themselves waist-deep in floodwaters, rescuing people or pumping out flooded premises. They find themselves faced with the problems of rescue at train crashes, where the casualties suffer terrible injuries. They risk injury to themselves releasing animals that have been sucked into sewage-pits or bogged down in muddy river-beds and threatened by rising waters. They climb trees and houses to rescue cats, and up ladders to release birds entangled in telegraph wires. They crawl beneath underground trains to release the luckless man or woman trapped beneath. They cut, pull, push at metal to get people from their crushed cars. They venture into clouds of ammonia fumes, explosive and corrosive fumes, seeking the valve that will close off the leak. They climb great heights and, perched precariously, cajole and try to persuade some temporarily deranged person from jumping to his death. They release the poor child whose head is stuck in railings. . . . Then there are the lifts which have broken down, leaving the occupants imprisoned between floors until the fireman comes to wind the lift by hand down to a landing. And when, in the factory, people get their limbs caught in machinery, again it's Mr Emergency who comes along to get them out. . . . So it goes on. Each day brings new hazards, new challenges. Today, serving in my Brigade, are many who experienced the Canvey Island floods, the Harrow train crash, the Lewisham train crash, the Southall air disaster, the great and tragic fires of Broad Street, Covent Garden, Smithfield, and a thousand lesser tragedies between.'

A kind of amazement had seized his listeners. They had read about such incidents but had never been truly aware of their real and constant application to the men who manned the red machines. Their sympathetic interest was aroused, and would become highly charged by the end of Mr Milner's speech. His heart was in it, as he said afterwards. But he entered on his final paragraphs with deceptive calm.

'I would like to close with two short examples of true-life drama as seen by firemen. The first is a success story – the second, one which demanded the ultimate from two firemen who took part.'

He gripped the sides of the lectern and raised his voice.

'In 1969, the Brigade were called in daytime to a fire in a hotel in the Bayswater area – at Leinster Gardens. On arrival, the officer-in-charge saw a hotel of six floors, about two hundred feet in length. Smoke was issuing from all floors in the centre of the building. Three people at third-floor windows were calling for help. A ladder was pitched to effect the rescues and a hasty message was despatched for reinforcements. At that moment, as if in response to a command, scores of windows opened all over the building. From the windows smoke began to billow, and frightened faces appeared, calling, screaming for help. A massive rescue operation began. . . . Reinforcing appliances arrived, and the face of the building was soon festooned with ladders – hook-ladders, escape ladders, extension ladders, turntable ladders. More and more firemen clawed their way up the face of the building to the rescue, while others entered the building to fight the fire inside. One by one the trapped people were reached. One by one they were brought down. . . . Panic was averted by firemen calling reassuringly to those who waited their turn, though there were moments when, illogically, people began throwing out suitcases, and hysteria seemed likely to take over. Quite how many were saved was never determined, but conservative estimates say fifty. The important thing is that not a single life was lost. . . .

'A few months before this, another fire raged in the basement of a restaurant. Two firemen in breathing apparatus made their way cautiously into the ground floor of the building. Moments later those outside heard a great roar – saw a flash of flame engulf the ground floor and belch out into the street. In seconds the men outside rushed in and dragged their two friends out into the street. Both men were burned – severely burned. Taken to hospital, they were suspended above their beds, for there was no unburned part of their bodies on which they could lie. For three days they suffered; and then, one shortly after the other, they died. They paid the full price and, some might say, much more. . . .'

Joe Milner released his hold of the lectern, clasped his hands together, and focussed his eyes on the words of his script that said so much, and said so little. His voice broke loudly on the silent room.

'Lest you feel I am only quoting a few isolated examples – here are some facts and figures. . . . In the eight years since 1965, 9 London firemen have been killed and 748 have been injured in the exercise of their duties. In 1972, the London Fire Brigade attended 87 406 calls. They rescued 222 people from fires and 192 animals from the same hazard or from some other. 257 people were extricated from crushed vehicles. 3226 people were released from lifts. On average, the number of calls increases by 10 per cent each year.

'Forgive me,' he said, 'for deviating from the normal type of talk. I felt you would like to know something of what you get, as ratepayers, from your firemen – from every uniformed and non-uniformed man and woman in the fire-stations,

control rooms and workshops of the Brigade. Together they
help to make the London Fire Brigade second to none – and
better than most. Thank you.'

He sat down and picked up his pipe to steady his hands.
The applause that filled the room was sustained and loud.

In the days that followed, the tributes of the Rotarians were
echoed all over the country. There were also more practical
results. On 1 November, union leaders and senior fire officers,
including Mr Milner, met to discuss the London firemen's
claims, and by Friday, 2 November, the basis for a new pay
deal had been tentatively worked out. Three days later, on
5 November, the Glasgow firemen called off their strike and
industrial action in parts of England came to an end –
although some city Brigades continued for a time to work to
rule. After further meetings between union leaders, senior
officers and local authority representatives, an agreement on
rates of pay was reached in London on 16 November and all
industrial action ended. Finally, on 22 November at Black-
pool, union delegates formally accepted the new deal, which
would give the country's 28,000 firemen up to £7.80 a week
more.

The following year a successful recruiting drive was
launched, and many young men decided to leave the hum-
drum nine-to-five routine of office and factory work and be a
fireman in the London Fire Brigade. On the completion of their
eleven weeks of basic training they were sent to one or other
of the 114 fire-stations in London.

Among them were nine recruits who found themselves,
between May and December 1974, posted to one of the nine
fire-stations in 'A' Division – to A21, Paddington.

It would weigh heavily on Joe Milner's mind that the first
fireman to be killed on duty under his command in London
was one of these recruits.

In 1969, the year before he became Chief Officer, six firemen had died – five when an oil-tank exploded at Dudgeon's
Wharf, and one when a burning house collapsed in Shoreditch. Their names were recorded on a roll of honour in the
foyer of the Lambeth Headquarters, opposite the impressive
memorial to the hundreds of men in the Fire Services who died
in the Second World War. The last name on the roll was that

of Acting Leading Fireman Michael William Lee, who was killed in the Shoreditch collapse on 29 September 1969. He was twenty-one.

No name would be inscribed after his for over five years. But in December 1974, there was a fire at Clifton Gardens in Maida Vale, in which seven people died. One of them was a fireman from A21, Paddington – from the shift that happened to be on duty that night, the Red Watch.

The complete list of firemen on the strength of Red Watch, A21 (Paddington) on Tuesday, 10 December 1974

Station Officer Neil Wallington
Sub Officer Paul Taylor
Leading Fireman Jim Griffin
Leading Fireman Ernie Arthurs
Leading Fireman Norman Wooldridge
Fireman Keith Cheal
Fireman Ted Cheer
Fireman Roger Davey
Fireman Bob Dunlop
Fireman Dave Dyer
Fireman Joe Forrest
Fireman Malcolm Garner
Fireman Mick Haskard
Fireman Leroy Hough
Fireman Phil House
Fireman Richard Hughes – 'Winger'
Fireman Malcolm Jackson – 'Jacko'
Fireman Roger Lewis
Fireman Nicholas Martin – 'Pincher'
Fireman Paul Marven
Fireman Pete Morris
Fireman Frank Nice
Fireman Martin Nicholls – 'Nick'
Fireman Keith Orchard
Fireman Hamish Harry Pettit
Fireman Chris Reynolds
Fireman Brian Riley
Fireman Tony Stewart
Fireman Ray Wade
Fireman Jim Waldron – 'Archie'
Fireman Martin Walker
Fireman Dave Webber
Fireman Kevin Wickenden

Tuesday 10 December

At 8.25 a.m. a tall youth came bounding up the final flight of steps of the Underground station and out into Warwick Avenue. But there his precipitate eagerness came to a halt. A cold wind pierced his dark brown sheepskin coat and buffeted his face and hair as he reorientated himself on the pavement, while people on their way to work pushed past him, clutching hats and cases as they dived down the steps. Behind him the Avenue split into other roads on either side of a pile of scaffolding which marked a church under construction. Immediately behind him, on his left, was a tree-lined road of high terraced houses which he saw was called Clifton Gardens. He faced away from it and set off in a south-easterly direction up Warwick Avenue towards his new place of work.

Leroy Hough was nineteen. His day had started at 6.0 a.m., when his mother came into the bedroom he shared with his two younger brothers, switched on the light and shook him awake. Ten minutes later she shouted upstairs – 'Come on! Your breakfast's on the table. You don't want to be late on your first day' – and he wearily dressed in the chilly room before clumping down to the bright warm kitchen. Outside it was still black as night. Neither his brothers nor his two young sisters would surface from their beds by the time he left; nor would his father. Not much was said as he wolfed his bacon and egg in the small dining-room adjoining the kitchen. The radio was on. At 6.30, the news headlines spoke of a bomb explosion that had wrecked a shop in Bath. As he finished off his tea, his mother suggested he should have a shave. So he leapt upstairs to the bathroom, borrowed his father's electric razor and removed the fluff from his face – he still only needed to shave twice a week. At 6.45, he left the house and trekked through the windy lamp-lit council estate to a bus-stop. Some minutes later he jumped off the bus outside Orpington railway station, where he bought a *Daily Mirror*. At 7.20 he got on a train for London. During the journey, a grey dawn slowly lightened the sky, as the winter sun rose behind layers of cloud.

From the small road bridge where Warwick Avenue arched over the Grand Union Canal, whose waters gave the area the illusory local name of Little Venice, he caught a glimpse of the seven-storey practice tower of Paddington fire-station. It loomed up through the trees on his right, beyond the canal basin and above a long terrace of modern council flats. A few yards further on in front of him was a roundabout backed by the gigantic swooping span of Westway. The three incoming lanes were now jammed as usual with stationary rush-hour traffic. But below the flyover the incoming carriageway of the Harrow Road was a moving mass of cars which came zooming up to the roundabout, where they hesitated before dodging around it and on to the Edgware Road.

As Leroy turned right and walked on westwards against this flow of traffic, the trains and tracks leading in and out of Paddington railway station and the goods depot showed through the flyover's legs.

In front of him the road swung past the modern rectangular concrete mass of Paddington fire-station – A21.

It was one of the newest buildings of its kind in London, having replaced the old station in Edgware Road in 1969. Its three storeys, of increasing width and height, were like layered decks, and one tall chimney increased its overall likeness to the superstructure of a ship – appropriately, for that was how senior hands would sometimes refer to it, as the ship; and not without reason, as initially many firemen were recruited from the ranks of ex-seamen. Ex-servicemen in general were preferred as a source of manpower for very nearly a century. It was not until the end of National Service that this unwritten rule was relaxed and the age-limit lowered. However, several nautical phrases and practices were maintained. Each shift was known as a Watch, whose start and finish, and the breaks in between, were announced by the ringing of six bells.

Leroy walked past the forecourt of the station and the five great folding doors of the appliance-room, which were set at an angle to the road to give the fire-engines, or appliances as the Brigade called them, better access to the road. He went up a ramp to a glass door and into the building.

On his right was the glass-walled watchroom, a barren room apart from tables, chairs, two teleprinter machines and a large map of London on a wall which showed the spread of A21's particular responsibility – the station's ground. Its borders were marked by Queensway, Bayswater Road, Regent's Park and Kilburn High Road, and included the largely residential areas of Bayswater, Paddington, Lisson Grove, St John's Wood and Maida Vale. It was in the watchroom that the teleprinter's warning-bell announced the arrival of fire-calls and messages from Wembley control.

Leroy hesitated in the narrow hallway outside the watchroom. The only fellow in it was writing something in a report book. Leroy turned aside and peered through a glass door at the high and wide appliance-room, which was strangely empty of machines. He thought with a tremor of alarm that they must all be out on a job. Then he saw that the machines had been moved back out into the yard to allow a lone civilian armed with bucket and mop to clean the floor. He was far too early. The Red Watch didn't take over until 9.0 a.m.

Despondently, he opened a door and trudged upstairs to the office on the first floor, not knowing what else to do.

He had been there before. The previous Friday after lunch, an all-purpose Divisional van had picked up the new recruits from Southwark and then dropped them off, one by one, at five of the stations in 'A' Division – at Westminster, Chelsea, Euston Road, Manchester Square and Paddington. The latter was the last to be visited as it was the HQ of 'A' Division and the van's base, and it was not until 5.40 p.m. that Leroy was instructed over the tannoy to report to the office. This he did, and was directed across the room to a much smaller office on the other side to see his station officer, Neil Wallington.

Leroy noticed that half of the office wall afforded a good view of the appliance-room below, while a window opposite him overlooked the forecourt and the road leading up to the roundabout. He had an impression of a small desk buried under papers and report books, of walls decked with notices and instructions, and of pieces of equipment heaped on the floor. His impression of the man who briskly concluded a telephone conversation before slapping the phone back on its rest and springing to his feet was confined to his tallness, his apparent youthfulness, his leanness, and his piercing pale blue eyes. Both he and Leroy were in undress uniform, consisting of a dark blue jacket and trousers and a black tie. Leroy's shirt was blue. The station officer's, as befitted his rank, was white, with dark blue epaulettes on which were two white pips in the likeness of pump-impellers.

'Come in. Shut the door.'

Leroy did so, and uncertainly stood at attention, his peaked cap in his hand. The station officer's voice was not unfriendly, but his needle gaze was disconcerting – as was his opening remark.

'Your tie's a bit loose, isn't it?'

'Is it?' asked Leroy in surprise.

'Yes. You're at a Divisional station now, and as such your attire is not all it should be. I suggest you adjust it.'

'Sorry, Guv,' said Leroy, in a marked cockney accent. 'It's the shirt. . . . They gave me one two sizes too big. Sorry.'

Leroy awkwardly tightened up the offending article as the station officer sat down again, seized a biro and suddenly engrossed himself in some notes on a clip-board. Without looking up, he said: 'Sit down.'

Leroy dutifully folded himself on a chair beside the desk. He noticed that under the notes was an open file and some papers that bore his name.

'Right.' The station officer pushed the notes aside, flung the biro on the desk and himself back in his chair. He clasped his hands together and fixed the youth with a beady eye.

'It's Fireman Hough, isn't it?' He rhymed the name with 'enough'.

'No, sir, it's – I'm Hough, sir,' said Leroy, pronouncing his name to rhyme with 'bough'.

'Hough. Christian name Leroy.'

'Yes, sir.'

The station officer dived on the file, glanced through it and then closed it. 'You had a good report from Southwark,' he said. 'You did well. But it's only a start.' He picked up the file. 'There are two kinds of firemen – a fireman, and a *good*

fireman. You'll have to decide which one you're going to be.
Now –' He dropped the file in a wire tray, sat back and folded
his arms. He spoke rapidly, but softly, his voice insisting on
attention.

'I am Station Officer Wallington and I'm in charge of the
Red Watch at A21 of which you are now a member. Or you
will be as from Tuesday. Isn't that so?'

'Yes, sir.'

'For your information, you are joining a Watch at London's
busiest station. Last year A21 had 3471 calls – 300 more than
any other station in the Brigade. And as a consequence, recruits at Paddington can expect to win their spurs very quickly, very quickly indeed – due to the large amount of incidents
requiring our attention.' He leaned forward, his hands on the
desk. 'You will have to familiarize yourself with our ground,
with its topography – the layout of the streets – straight away.
The largest single area of risk concerns the hotels. There are
hundreds of them, full for the most part of foreigners who are
perhaps not quite so familiar with our language and may have
difficulties in escaping from a fire. You follow?'

'Yes, sir.'

'In addition, there are many high-rise buildings, several
hospitals – eleven in all – a mainline railway terminus and
not a few Underground stations, together with thousands of
dwelling-places, mostly bed-sitters, and a certain proportion
of slum-type property. So you can expect to be busy right
from the word "Go". And, since Paddington adjoins A29's
ground – that is, North Kensington – between us we have
more make-ups than any other two stations combined.'

Leroy clutched his cap and shifted uncomfortably in his
chair. The prospect of some activity and excitement as a fireman had been among the reasons that had led him to pack in
his three-year job as a clerk with a firm of tea-importers in the
City where he had felt he was underpaid, unwanted and
exploited. But now he wasn't so sure. He gazed anxiously at
his station officer who, as if sensing his disquiet, leaned forward,
flashed him a smile and continued.

'You may not be aware of this yet, but Paddington has
a certain charisma. In fact the Press office at Lambeth are
always sending people over here – journalists, TV crews,

students and photographers. We don't discourage this, as it's good for the station and the Brigade and good that the public know how firemen live and work. But this charisma I mentioned comes mainly from the spirit of the lads here, from our record – from the fact that we have been involved in many multiple-rescue incidents, such as the fire at the Leinster Towers Hotel, and have won many honours and awards. You see that board over there?' He indicated a framed scroll that was sitting on top of a filing-cabinet. 'It will tell you what awards we've won. Your name could appear there too some day. Time will tell. But from the beginning I will expect you, as a recruit, to make a maximum effort to integrate yourself in the activities of the Watch and aim to achieve the high standards that being a member of the "A" Division demands.'

He paused. 'That's all for now. I'll have a word with you later about the probationary period you're on – after you've got to know the Watch and settled down. Do you have any questions?'

Leroy shook his head.

'Have you been fixed up with a locker?'

'Er . . . no. I don't –'

'Have a word with Jim Griffin, Leading Fireman Griffin. Do you know the station's telephone number? Make a note of it. You know you're due in on your first set of days on Tuesday? Right!'

Suddenly the station officer was on his feet and holding out his hand. Leroy also stood, and took the outstretched hand in his as Neil Wallington gave him a foxy grin and a firm handshake.

'Welcome to the Red Watch, Leroy. I can assure you that you will have a busy, useful, and sometimes hectic life here – but basically a happy one.'

Leroy re-entered the office on the Tuesday morning to find it crowded with four or five leading firemen and sub officers, none of whom he recognized. They must all, he thought, belong to the Blue Watch, who were in the process of going off-duty. The rest of the Watch, unknown to him, were upstairs in the mess, finishing off their breakfast. He hovered in the doorway until a dark thickset man with a cup of tea in his hand asked Leroy what he wanted.

'I'm reporting for duty, sir,' he said apologetically. 'Fireman Hough.'

'Who?'

'He said "How" not "Who",' said another man.

'Hough do you do?' said a third.

'How, Hough!' grunted a fourth with a Red Indian salutation.

He was rescued by the arrival of the leading fireman he had met on Friday, a tall slim man, with his sleeves rolled up, and his thinning hair brushed sideways over his head – Jim Griffin.

'Here's Hough,' said the Blue Watch leader. 'A present from Southwark.'

Griffin smiled slightly. 'Welcome on board,' he said to Leroy. 'Are you looking for your gear? It's upstairs. I'll show you.'

They left the office as someone started singing 'How is the hour' and walked up to the second floor and into a room which was marked 'Car Drivers'. There were four beds in it, each with only a mattress on it, and the room was temporarily unoccupied.

Griffin went to a large cupboard marked Bedding Store and opened it. Inside was Leroy's kitbag and gear.

'Leave the blankets and your bedding in there – you won't need them till Thursday. We're a bit short of lockers and beds at the moment, but we'll put that right later. You can change here. Roll-call's at nine. All right?'

'Yes, thanks.'

Griffin went. Alone, Leroy heaved his crumpled clothes out of the kitbag and slowly dressed himself in his full fire-fighting gear.

He was already wearing the trousers. The undress uniform jacket he had left at home, not wishing to draw attention to himself by wearing it on train and tube. He pulled on the heavy calf-length black leather boots, after shoving his feet through the yellow water-proof leggings that came up to his waist, and struggled into the thick navy-blue Melton of his double-breasted fire-fighting tunic, whose high collar he had difficulty in fastening at the neck. Then he dug out the broad webbing-belt and the axe that hung from it – put them on – with the axe-head upwards on his hip, and lastly fitted the black, laminated helmet made of cork on his head and adjusted the chinstrap.

Once his few and flimsy civilian clothes had been bundled into the cupboard on top of the kitbag, he lumbered unsteadily out of the room, feeling and looking very strange.

His boots skidded on the stairs as he plodded on down to the appliance-room. There he drifted about the bulky red machines – the pump escape, the pump, the turntable ladders – lined up like giant toys facing their exit-doors, ready to take him into unimaginably dangerous situations. Several times, merely to talk to someone, he made forays to accost a passing fireman and inquire where the parade was held or how its start and that of the Watch would be announced. To which the replies were – 'Here' and 'Six bells.'

For twenty minutes he hid himself away among the machines, apprehensive about everything and everyone connected with his new job, and in fearful expectation of his first 'shout' – when the clangour of bells would herald his first trial as a fireman.

No one who noticed him spoke to him, apart from those he approached for information, and apart from his station officer, who walked into the appliance-room, caught Leroy's eye and said: 'Good morning!'

Neil Wallington was on his way to the office. He had parked his Daytona yellow Ford Capri, known by the Watch as the 'Yellow Peril', in the drill yard at the rear of the station, and was crossing the appliance-room when he caught sight of the new recruit, apparently studying the badge of the GLC on the side of the pump. He called out a greeting when the tall lad, looking very lost and uncomfortable in his number one rig, glanced around.

Neil smiled to himself, recalling what he had felt as he waited for his first parade and remembering the interview on the previous Friday, when in order to establish from the start his role as senior officer he had deliberately found fault with the new recruit's dress. He had adopted this ploy before; and the speech of welcome that had followed this had not varied much from the eight others he had given since the recruiting drive began in February that year – as it happened in the very month that he himself had come to Paddington as its new station officer. Leroy, the ninth and newest recruit to come under his charge, brought the total strength of the Watch to thirty-three, a record. But young as Hough was, he was not its youngest member. That honour went to Fireman Keith Cheal, aged eighteen, whom Neil passed on the stairs as he bounded up them to the office.

'Good morning, Keith!'

'Morning, Guv!'

Traditionally, the station officer was called 'the Governor' or 'Guv', even by the older hands. The latest tradition in the Watch was to call the recruits 'Wombles'.

Neil's pleasure at being back on duty again was jolted as soon as he entered the office by the sight of blood. It was dripping onto the floor from Leading Fireman Holmes' thumb, despite the bandage wrapped around it. Holmes was one of the departing Blue Watch. Inquiries revealed that he had been riding in the station ET (emergency tender) en route to a shout about 8.15 a.m. when the driver braked hard to avoid hitting an obstructive car. Holmes' hand had smashed into a wooden support and torn his thumbnail away – as he obligingly showed Neil after taking off the bandage. He was now waiting for an ambulance to take him to St Mary's Hospital in Praed Street.

Neil commiserated with the injured man, greeted Jim Griffin and then the Blue Watch station officer whom he was relieving and went into his office. In a small adjacent room, furnished with a bed and three lockers (one for each station officer on each Watch) he changed into his undress uniform.

The cars on the flyover outside the window were by now moving slowly on towards Marylebone Road. He looked at himself in a wall-mirror and quickly combed his hair forward and then adjusted his black tie.

Suddenly the teleprinter warning-bell rang above his head.

He tensed, staring into the mirror. But the fire-bell remained silent.

He relaxed, as every man in the station did, and carried on with his preparations for parade.

'Red Watch! Red Watch – Shun!'

They stood in a line across the appliance-room in their helmeted fire-gear. The only men in undress uniform were the station officer and the van drivers who stood at the end of the line. They also wore caps. Six bells had sounded a minute before. If the fire-bells rang now, the Watch would break and make for one of the four machines in front of them, most of them having already checked in the daily runners and riders board in the watchroom as to which appliances they were riding.

Neil Wallington faced his men with his acting sub officer for the day, Ernie Arthurs, beside him.

'Call the roll,' he said.

'Answer your names!' said Arthurs, and read them out, each man replying – 'Sir!'

Neil scanned the Watch with a critical eye on the men's turnout and appearance. Leroy, he noted, was now looking even more apprehensive, and his rig was not as well fitting as it might be. One item was, in fact, missing. Something would have to be said about that. Neil considered the other recruits.

Young Nicholls, he observed, had made it after all in time for parade. A message in the handing-over book in the office had said he would be late owing to transport difficulties. But there he was, a tall, slim youth, with deceptively mild eyes and delicate features; he had, however, proved himself to be strong and capable. Then there were Keith Cheal and Kevin Wickenden; the former was the youngest fireman in the Watch, and the latter the smallest. Cheal came from Brighton – a cheerful, adaptable lad, who was manfully growing a moustache in imitation of several of the older hands. Wickenden was bright and gutsy and had already been dubbed the Mighty Microbe and the Merry Goblin by his seniors; he was in fact 5 feet 6 inches, the minimum height requirement for a fireman. Beside him was Dave Dyer, a shy, large and handsome youth, aged nineteen, built like an overweight rugby forward: self-conscious because of this and vulnerable. Yet none of the older firemen ragged him as they invariably did anyone with supposed physical defects or character failings. Nor did they take the opportunity to send up Ray Wade, although his wide and toothy grin inevitably encouraged comparisons with Bugs Bunny. He was twenty-eight, and probably the most amiable and disarming fellow in the Watch; previously, he had been with the London Salvage Corps. He lived at Rainham in Kent, not far from the man next to him in the line-up, Harry Pettit, who came from Rochester. Pettit was twenty-six. Before becoming a fireman he had been an electrician in Chatham dockyard, working on submarines, and came to Paddington in May from the training-school at Greenwich, the first to do so. A very self-assured young man, he was also the best educated of all the recruits and indeed of anyone in the Watch.

Two of the recruits were not on parade that morning. Phil House was away on leave that week, and Tony Stewart, at twenty-nine the oldest recruit – he was ex-RAF – had been detached for duty for two days at A27 (Chelsea).

'Red Watch present and correct, sir,' said Ernie Arthurs, his soft voice belying his dark, florid appearance and fierce cavalier moustache. He was thirty-eight, and like Jim Griffin and Neil himself looked younger than his years.

'Detail the riders,' said Neil.

Arthurs adjusted his grip on the roll-call board. 'Red Watch – stand at ease! Riders for the appliances as follows. In the watchroom, Fireman Dunlop . . .'

He went on to name the five firemen who were on the PE (pump escape); the five on the pump; the three on the TL (turntable ladders); and the seven in the ET (emergency tender).* Then he named the two van drivers for the day, the watchroom relief, and the mess assistant.

Neil watched for any reactions from the men as their duties for that day were officially announced. Only the more experienced firemen would ride in the ET, a red coach-type vehicle carrying a great variety of rescue-equipment stowed in racks and lockers. The ET crew were also all qualified to wear BA sets (breathing apparatus) as they did at any job to which they were called. An officer was in charge of each appliance's

---

*Two firms with long and historic associations with the Fire Service throughout the country made the appliances. A21's PE and pump were made by Dennis, and the TL and ET (made in 1953) by Merryweather.

crew, and the station officer always rode with the pump, the workhorse of the Brigade. Every new recruit was also assigned to it, to gain the most operational experience under his station officer's careful eye.

As Arthurs detailed the men's duties, Neil gazed at them with a customary feeling of pride. Ever since he had abandoned his job as a motor-cycle salesman in Croydon ten years ago and joined the Brigade after a spare-time association with the Auxiliary Fire Service, he had had no further doubts about his vocation. He had welcomed the increasing responsibilities on the fire-ground and in the office that had come with promotion; and from the day he took command of the Red Watch at Paddington his satisfaction at the abilities and achievements of his men had only deepened his sense of fulfilment. He was now thirty-two, married, with a house at Whitstable, and unawares was approaching a time that would test him to the limit, and his men.

'Red Watch detailed,' Arthurs said to Neil, who then gave the command: 'Handlamps!'

Each man detached the thickly insulated yellow torch that hung from his belt, switched it on and directed it at Neil's eyes – so that he could see it was working and that the batteries were not beginning to fail.

He stood before them spotlit by twenty torches, but was not so dazzled that he could not see the one fireman who had failed to bring a torch on parade.

'Fireman Hough,' said Neil to Leroy, who was miserably looking at his boots. 'When you come on roll-call, always bring a handlamp with you. Take it off the appliance you are riding and wear it on your belt – so that I can see you have a working handlamp at the commencement of the shift.'

He raised his voice and said to the others: 'All right!'

They switched their torches off.

'All right,' he repeated to Arthurs. 'Fall them out.'

'Red Watch! Red Watch – Shun!' said Ernie Arthurs. 'Fall out!'

The fire-bell went at ten past nine. Leroy, who was standing by the pump, started and then froze at the sound, his heart pounding.

'It's all right,' said Nicholls calmly. 'It's just being tested.'
Leroy swore in an undertone when the clanging ended, and
took a deep breath. Nicholls gave him a sympathetic smile.

At the end of roll-call Leroy had gone straight to the pump
to get a torch. There Neil Wallington, whose fire-gear was
already on the front seat beside the driver, had briefly shown
him how a BA set was tested and then advised him to leave his
leggings rolled down around his boots outside the appliance
so that he could quickly climb into them when there was a
shout. His tunic, helmet and belt were to be kept in readiness
in the cab. Leroy was introduced to his co-riders, Marven,
Nicholls and the driver, Lewis, who all nodded at him doubtfully, and was told to sit between the first two on the rear
bench in the cab – so that he couldn't, as Neil said, look at the
girls.

'If we get a job, stick behind me,' said Neil. 'Don't let me
out of your sight.'

While Marven made a thorough job of testing his BA set
and while Lewis checked the lights, pressures, mileage, and
diesel-fuel level of the pump, Nicholls, as instructed by Neil,
showed Leroy where all the fire-fighting equipment was
located – the ladders, searchlights and hose-reels, the other
wider hose, the branches and extinguishers, the breaking-in
gear, the couplings, adaptors, dividing-breeches, spanners,
boxlamps and foam equipment.

Soon afterwards Nicholls said: 'Come and have a cup of
tea.'

They went up to the mess on the second floor where most of
the Watch were gathered, sitting around the tables or pouring
out cups of tea for themselves at the kitchen hatch. Leroy sat
with Nicholls at the window, unable to concentrate much on
what was being said to him, being agog at the antics, jokes and
horseplay of the other firemen – most of whom seemed to have
moustaches and hairy arms and a vivid way with words – and
expecting any moment the next heart-stopping summons of the
fire-bell.

'What?' he said, having a notion that Nicholls had asked
him something.

'Nothing,' said Nicholls and looked at him amusedly.

This annoyed Leroy, who didn't like being laughed at, and

he was forming a four-letter word comment on the tea when Nicholls leaned forward and in putting his cup on the table fully displayed the tattoos on his arms. He was wearing a blue T-shirt.

Leroy had half-observed them before. There were four of them, two on each forearm, and included a tiger, a flower, and a winged skull.

'Where did you get them done?' he asked, thinking that Nicholls must be tougher than he looked and must have been in the Navy.

'Oh, in Croydon,' said Nicholls casually. 'When I was sixteen.'

'How old are you now?' Leroy asked.

'Twenty.' He added: 'I'm twenty-one on Friday.'

'Oh, yeah?'

'Friday the thirteenth.'

'Well, I hope it's fucking lucky for you,' said Leroy.

Nicholls smiled; he said: 'Do you want a burn?' He offered Leroy a cigarette.

'Oh . . . Cheers.'

In the meantime, Neil examined the interior of the ET and satisfied himself that the accident to Holmes' thumb had been a thousand-to-one chance. He would not have liked to have the ET taken off the run to be overhauled. As it was, the appliance was a replacement for the station's machine, which was now in workshops. They had had a crisis with all the machines – the TL had only returned to Paddington the day before.

When he went back to the office he grabbed a cup of tea off a tray and telephoned the workshops to find out the station ET's state of repair. There were other phone-calls about standbys, orders of the day, and new equipment. Jim Griffin was writing up the attendance register. Neil got Frank Nice who was making out the weekly list of boots and shoes that needed repair, to deal with an inquiry from the GLC architects' department about some defect in the central heating. Pincher Martin was checking through a file to see what fire prevention commitments there were that day, and Ernie Arthurs was going over a pile of leave-cards – some of the

Watch were already planning their holidays. The last three firemen were all acting up for the day – that is, they had temporarily taken on a higher rank. It was a common practice throughout the Brigade when officers were away on leave or on courses, or off the run with injuries sustained on duty. Acting-up was so usual that Ernie Arthurs had once jokingly suggested that firemen should also be members of Equity.

The ringing of six bells reminded Neil it was 9.30 – time for the start of station drills. He was also reminded by Pincher Martin of another matter, and over the tannoy he told the pump crew to report to the office.

When Lewis, Marven, Nicholls and Leroy Hough did so, he told them: 'Get yourselves ready. Fire-gear and caps, less belts. We're going to do an initial dry-riser test at Wellington Road. We're coming off the run.'

It was Leroy's first ride in a pump. At Southwark, although the recruits had practised with pensioned-off appliances in the yard they had never ridden one nor been to a fire. It was also his first dry-riser test.

He sat between Nicholls and Marven on the rear seat in the cab, his forward view obscured by BA sets hanging on frames between him and the station officer and the driver, Lewis, and his pleasure at going for a ride in the pump was not complicated by it being a shout.

The great steel doors of the appliance-room folded back. With the engine sweetly throbbing the eight-and-a-half ton machine eased out onto the forecourt and then left into the one-way stream of traffic still heading in to the West End.

Nicholls, who was taking seriously his role as Leroy's guide, said: 'This is the Harrow Road.' At the roundabout where the pump turned left again he said: 'This is the south end of Warwick Avenue.' Almost immediately they swung right after crossing the canal bridge and proceeded along a tree-lined road beside the canal. 'Blomfield Road,' said Nicholls. 'It's Edgware Road as far as here,' he explained, getting Leroy to look to his right. 'Then it becomes Maida Vale.'

The pump swung left. In doing so the clapper of the warning-bell on the cab-roof above Neil's head sang out softly.

'Next turning right,' he said to Lewis.

They drove along St John's Wood Road past the high south-
ern stands of Lord's cricket-ground, turned left up Wellington
Road and found the newly completed luxury block of flats
they were looking for on the corner of Acacia Road, opposite
St John's Wood Underground station. It was nine storeys
high, called Birley Lodge, and was faced with yellow brick.

Lewis parked the pump behind the flats.

An FPO (fire prevention officer) from Lambeth was waiting
impatiently for them on the pavement. Together they set to
work.

Their task was to ensure that a vertical pipe known as the
'dry-riser', which extended from an exterior inlet-box on the
ground floor up to the top of the building, was fully operational.
The pipe had outlets on each floor, to which firemen could
couple their hose and quickly charge both dry-riser and hose
with water in the event of a fire.

Generally, since 1939, most new buildings in inner London
of more than four storeys had had dry-risers installed, either
to comply with the law or on the recommendation of the
Brigade. Buildings more than 200 feet in height – about seventeen storeys – would normally be equipped with a wet-riser –
a pipe permanently charged with water.

Marven and Nicholls located a hydrant further down the
road on the opposite side, removed the cover and set up a
double-headed stand-pipe which they got from the pump.
They then connected two lengths of hose to the pipe, laying
them out in the gutter, and as the 75-foot lengths were insufficient to reach the pump, the firemen coupled them to two
other lengths which were connected to the inlet on the machine.
On the other side of it Lewis, assisted by Leroy, did likewise,
taking four lengths of hose across an ornamental lawn, which
was in the process of being laid, to the inlet box on the outside
wall of the block. Meanwhile the FPO had entered the building, and walking up the stairs from floor to floor checked that
the outlets on each floor were closed. When he got to the roof
he fitted a pressure-gauge to the roof outlet, turned the valve
on and signalled down to Neil that he was ready for the riser
to be charged. Neil gave the order for the water to be turned
on at the hydrant. As the hose filled out, Nicholls took a pair
of metal ramps from the back of the pump and laid them over

the two lines of hose on the road to protect them from the wheels of passing cars. Next, Neil told Lewis to open the delivery valves – letting water flow from the pump through the other hoses and up into the dry-riser – and slowly to increase the pressure therein until the pump pressure-gauge read 150 PSI (pounds per square inch).

A bitter wind froze their hands and pinched their faces. The water that spurted out from the couplings was like ice.

While Neil explained to Leroy what was being done and why, Nicholls and Marven stood stamping their feet in the road, answering passers-by who asked, often jocularly – 'Where's the fire?' – with bored and brief denials that there was one.

After six or seven minutes the FPO on the roof gave a thumbs-up signal and Neil called out – 'Knock off and make up!'

Gladly the crew obeyed. Nicholls shut the hydrant down and disconnected the hose, while Marven removed the ramps and returned them to the appliance. Lewis shut the pump down, and uncoupled the lengths of hose leading to the building. Water flooded out of them onto the courtyard and onto the road. Leroy rolled up a length of hose and put it, as instructed by Neil, in the cab.

Nicholls called across to him: 'How are you doing?'

'All right.'

'You know why I'm doing this?' Nicholls asked.

'Doing what?'

'Letting the water run out on the road and not the pavement.'

'You tell me.'

'In case some silly sod slips and sues the Brigade.'

In the meantime the FPO came down from the roof, swearing at the weather, and he and Neil reported to the builders' representative that the dry-riser had been satisfactorily tested. At the pump, the crew were now stowing the rest of the clammy rolled-up lengths of hose in the cab, their hands stiff and frozen.

'Cold, ain't it?' said Leroy.

'Yeah,' said Lewis. 'Colder than the hairs on a polar bear's arse.'

Neil returned and inquired if everything was shipshape.

Lewis answered that it was – except that they were all suffering from a severe lack of therms.

'I'm just as cold as you, gentlemen,' said Neil. 'Come on – let's go and have a look at the show flat.'

He wanted to make a brief inspection of the interior, and this would also give the crew a chance to warm themselves up. They would moreover see for a moment how the other half lived.

The show flat, on a mezzanine floor, had a large living-room and hall, a kitchen, a cloakroom, two spacious bedrooms and two bathrooms, one en suite.

Neil told the other four to wait outside in the hall. He went in and found the vendor's representative engaged in salestalk on the phone. He picked up a brochure about the flats and glanced through it. Then as the telephone conversation seemed like continuing for some time he said: 'Is it all right if we . . .?'

The man waved an assenting hand and went on talking.

'Come on in,' said Neil to the crew. 'Wipe your boots.'

They did so, carefully, on the door-mat, all at once aware of their coarse unwieldy uniforms, and entered the flat with unusual deference, lost in admiration at its sumptuous furnishings, acres of thick cream carpet, gleaming glass, coloured walls, all lit like a commercial by a clear white light from the wide net-curtained windows. Neil told them how much the flat cost – £45 000. None of them would ever be able to afford such a place. Its price was roughly equal to eighteen years' wages.

They gathered together in the fully-fitted kitchen to inspect the cooker, which had both gas and electric rings and an air-filter hood. But they did not remain there long. They felt out of place and abashed. Hardly any of the flats they entered in the course of duty were much like this one. Usually they were the shabby, dark and dingy rooms and bed-sits of the poorer members of the community.

'What do you think of that?' asked Neil as they left the flat.

'Flash place that was, wasn't it?' said Leroy. 'Fitted carpets in the bog! And there was *two* of them!'

'It would cost you half a crown to have a crap in there,' said Nicholls.

'Yeah,' said Lewis. 'But they give you Green Shield stamps.'

'I wonder how long the council waiting-list is,' commented Marven.

'Long enough,' said Lewis lugubriously. 'There must be a load of station officers in line for one of them.'

They hurried down the stairs, and back in the pump their cheerfulness was increased by the warming prospect of a cup of tea and a smoke back at the station.

They returned by a different route, which took them down Grove End Road, across Maida Vale, and so into Warwick Avenue.

On the way the pump went through Clifton Gardens and past the Worsley Hotel.

It was a minute after mid-day when the fire-bell dinned across the yard. The pump crew, now in their denims, had just begun hanging up the lengths of hose to dry in the tower.

Leroy dropped the hose he was carrying and sprang towards the appliance-room.

The other three shouted after him – 'Hey! Where are you going?' – 'That's not for us!' – 'Come back, you silly bugger!' – 'School isn't over yet!'

He halted and turned to face them, utterly bewildered.

'You must work *all* day, Leroy,' said Marven reprovingly.

Nicholls explained. 'The pump's off the run till one,' he said. 'And so are we.'

Leroy walked slowly back to them with downcast eyes. Behind him, in the appliance-room, the ET crew piled into their vehicle, and it sped on its way, its two-tone horn sounding down Harrow Road.

'If you're going to move as quick as that when we get a real shout,' said Marven, 'we *will* be impressed.'

Lewis sniffed. 'It was like a rat up a stove-pipe,' he said.

Earlier, on their return to the station at 11.25 after the dry-riser test, Neil had given them half an hour's break. Stand-easy was officially between 11.0 and 11.15, but as they had not returned in time for it, he told them not to tidy up the pump and refurbish the hose until twelve. So they had spent a reviving thirty minutes in the mess over cups of tea and thick cheese and onion sandwiches and smoked their cigarettes. In the absence on rota leave of the mess manager, Martin Walker, the lunch was being organized by Dave Webber and Keith Orchard, with the help of two civilians. The former was with the ET crew, and accordingly had had to abandon what he was doing when the fire-bell rang for the ET just after twelve and startled Leroy in the yard. It was the station's first shout of the day. The morning had been spent by the ET, PE and TL crews on appliance and equipment maintenance – cleaning, checking and making sure that everything was fully operational.

At 12.20 the ET returned, entering the station through the large gate at the rear of the yard.

By this time the pump crew, after hanging up the hose to dry, had finished getting their machine ready for coming back on the run, and Leroy, curious to know where the ET had been and if it had been in action – though this was unlikely in such a short space of time – wandered into the watchroom.

The duty-man was writing up the emergency tender's return in the log-book, and the driver was recording his mileage.

Leroy picked up the bottom copy of the teleprinter roll which was flopping out of the machine, and began deciphering the indistinct typescript as well as translating its message.

AFA
KENSINGTON HILTON HOTEL
179 HOLLAND PARK AVENUE WII
JB39   D23
D23 PE   P VIA RT
A28 P   TL
A21 ET
I201

'AFA' meant 'automatic fire-alarm'. JB39 was the route-card reference. D23 was Hammersmith fire-station on whose ground the incident had occurred. Its pump escape had been called out, and the pump had been alerted by RT (radio-telephone) – as it must have been out and returning to base from another job – and having informed Wembley control that it was mobile and available, it had been diverted to the hotel. The pump and TL from A28 (Kensington) and A21's ET had also been called, as at least five appliances were always sent to an incident at a hotel.

The next two messages told the rest of the story. At 12.07, the Hammersmith station officer sent a 'Stop' – meaning that the emergency was over – and added that details would follow. This was transmitted to the three stations concerned by Control, who passed on his final message, a detailed Stop, at 12.10. It merely said – *'Alarm caused by AFA'*. Leroy uneasily rattled the money in his trouser pockets, and stared at the appliances through the glass partition. It would be just his luck, he thought, to get called to a hotel fire in his first week, even on his first day.

With an anxious look at the teleprinter, which might spring into life at any moment, Leroy left the watchroom and trailed upstairs, his hands in his pockets.

But before long it was lunchtime. At 1.0 p.m., six bells announced an hour-long break. With the rest of the Watch Leroy collected a plate of steak pie, carrots and potatoes from the kitchen, followed later by chocolate pudding and custard, and cheered up as he tucked into his meal.

'We've a right cunt here,' said Ernie Arthurs, his hands on his hips. 'Governor, what the fuck are we going to do about this knuckle-head?'

'What's the problem?' asked Neil resignedly, looking up from the piles of reports on his desk at Arthurs and Leroy in the doorway.

'Tell him, bird-brain,' said Arthurs.

'I forgot my undress jacket, Guv,' said Leroy, his pale face flushed.

'You forgot it. Well – where is it?'

'It's at home.'

'Where's home?'

'Orpington, Guv.'

'Bloody hell, Fireman Hough!' said Neil. 'It's a fat lot of good in Orpington when you want it at Penfold Street.'

'Sorry, Guv.'

'Never mind the sorries. You'll have to come off the pump and ride something else – that's all. See the sub officer. Ernie – sort him out.'

Neil waved them away. With the end of the lunch-break at 2.0 p.m. he had tannoyed the pump crew to get ready for a fire prevention visit to an old folks' home in Penfold Street. For this they would have to wear undress uniform and caps. Such a visit – to give a talk on fire prevention followed by a demonstration of fire extinguishers and life-saving equipment –was a routine extension of any station's work. Now Leroy, who would have learned something from the visit, could not be taken. Someone else's jacket could have been found for him to wear, but that would have indicated a tolerance of his mistake and thereby diminished his embarrassment. As far as Neil was concerned that was not the way to treat the matter. The boy would have to learn that slackness would not be condoned – and that no fireman could afford to commit errors, however slight.

In the office Ernie Arthurs told Leroy that until the pump returned he would be riding with the TL – 'the big stick' as Arthurs called it. The turntable ladders were also known as 'the flying staircase'. In charge of it that afternoon was Acting Leading Fireman Frank Nice.

Overhearing this information, Neil felt a momentary pang of concern. Proficient though the lanky and affable Frank Nice was, he had only been a fireman for four years. It would have been better if a more experienced bloke had been looking after Leroy – and the huge TL, which was usually only called out for high-up rescue work (its extending ladders could reach the eighth floor of a building) was not the easiest appliance for a recruit.

But there the matter rested. Leroy was sent upstairs to the television room, where Jim Griffin was taking a class on topography, and at 2.15 Neil left with the rest of the pump crew for Penfold Street.

'Now then,' said Jim Griffin and looked at Leroy. 'Where's the Harrow Road?'

With the aid of a slide-projector Griffin had thrown an image of a street plan with no names on it onto a wall. He had then superimposed the road names with another slide for a few minutes, before removing them and quizzing the class.

Leroy suspected a trick. Some of the Watch who were lounging comfortably in their chairs turned their heads to look at him. Everyone seemed to be waiting for him to put his foot in it. He hesitated. Surely the answer wasn't as obvious as it seemed? The more he thought about it, the more confused he became. He smiled at the floor sheepishly and was silent. Griffin pointed at the window. 'It's out there,' he said. No one laughed. Somebody sniffed; and Griffin continued with his questions.

Leroy felt even more miserable, although he tried not to show it. Everyone seemed to be picking on him – yet in fact they all ignored him. Everyone seemed to be eyeing him, assessing him and mocking him behind his back – but the only mickey-taking had in fact been in the kitchen after lunch when the exuberant Chris Reynolds said to him with a John Wayne swagger and a Texan drawl: 'Hi there, stranger! Welcome to Okinawa. And how are things in the cotton country, Leroy? My name is Chris. But the folks in these parts – well – they call me the big C.'

'He *is* a big C,' said someone.

After lunch Leroy had watched the firemen playing snooker in the games-room, which was also, apart from a billiard-table, equipped with table-tennis and a darts-board. Then Nicholls, having been detailed to show him around the station, offered to do so. On the second floor – to one side of the appliance-room roof – were the mess and kitchen, the games-room and a TV room, which was also used for lessons and lectures. On the other side was the firemen's dormitory, divided into sections, and a hothouse drying-room. The wash-rooms, showers and lavatories were also on this floor, as were the junior officers' sleeping quarters – a small bare room with four beds in it separated from each other (as in the men's dormitory) by groups of three lockers, one for each man on each of the three watches. The third floor was taken up by four large penthouse flats, the homes of 'A' Division officers – Divisional Commander Colenutt, Divisional Officer Keable, Assistant Divisional Officers Beasley and Baldwin.

On the second floor were four pole-house doors, guarding the twenty-five foot drop down a shiny steel pole to the appliance-room floor. Leroy declined Nicholls' invitation to descend that way, being disinclined to expose himself to any critical attention unless his descent was caused and covered by a shout. He said very little to the friendly Nicholls, in case he let himself down in some obscure way, and his adopted manner was casual but tough.

They went down the stairs to the ground floor, passing on the way a locked door marked 'Lecture Room', which Nicholls said was the bar.

'Officially it's the social centre,' he added. 'We're allowed to have one because the station is also the HQ of "A" Division. Their offices are in that long low L-shaped building beside the yard. Div Control is here as well.'

'You mean,' said Leroy cautiously, 'that you can have a drink on duty?'

'Oh, yeah,' Nicholls said. 'But only at night. Why not? A couple of halves is all right. It's licensed. Besides, you get very thirsty out on a job. You'll see.'

They entered the uniform room on the ground floor. It was like a changing-room, with nearly a hundred uniforms hanging from pegs above wooden benches. Every man on the three Watches kept his number one rig, his fire-fighting gear, in this room. The array of helmets, belts with axes, and boots, gave actual form to the firemen's seldom expressed perception that they fought a battle against a primeval enemy, fire. Here was their armour – and a sense of that battle in a faint smell of smoke that clung to the tunics.

Leroy's eyes brightened. His spirits were raised by martial fancies, notions of which had partly prompted his enlistment.

'Terrific!' he said.

The teleprinter-bell sounded its warning through the room. He and Nicholls froze, not looking at each other.

'Oh, bollocks!' said Leroy.

Then the fire-bell went.

They were first into the watchroom. The duty-man, Bob Dunlop, switched off the teleprinter-bell while the fire-bell rang on for its full thirty seconds. Then he picked up a microphone and broadcast the teleprinter message all over the station.

'Road traffic accident. . . . Outside . . . Hampstead General Hospital, Haverstock Hill. . . . G26's ground.' He put the microphone down.

'KA34,' he said, and flipped through the route-card box. 'Who's it for?'

'ET of course,' said Nicholls. Dunlop flicked down the switch for the blue light in the appliance-room indicating that the emergency tender had been called, and put away the route-card.

'*They* don't need one,' Nicholls explained. 'They carry their own route-cards.'

Leroy saw on the message that apart from A21's ET, G26's PE and pump and A23's pump had also been alerted. It was 1.49.

Firemen from other crews milled about the watchroom. Some, having satisfied themselves they were not required, returned straight away to their interrupted activities. Others checked over the message or looked at the wall-map, wondering what sort of accident it was.

Within thirty seconds the ET was on its way; and in a few minutes the watchroom was empty but for Dunlop and Leroy, who was waiting to see what drama the follow-up message might reveal.

The Stop came through at 1.55. It said – '*False Alarm.*'

Disappointed, Leroy wandered into the appliance-room to reassure himself that all his gear was where it should be in and outside the pump. Even allowing for some strangeness on his first day he was not enjoying himself as much as he had expected. His first day at training-school had been much more enjoyable and in retrospect his eleven weeks there seemed rosy with humour and effort. The other recruits had been good company, the instructors great characters and some of the funniest blokes he had met. The discipline had not bothered him, nor had the PT, the marching, and doing every drill at a run. He had enjoyed testing himself – climbing the seven-storey tower from window to window using only a thirteen foot hook-ladder – finding his way out of the 'Rat-run' within ten minutes. The run was an obstacle course in a room that had to be negotiated in darkness and artificial smoke. When he was put through it he had had flu and had to come out twice, coughing and choking, his eyes streaming, and feeling very sick. The instructor had told him to go in a third time and complete the course, or resign. Somehow he managed it, drawing on undeveloped resources of will-power and strength, and afterwards felt very proud. He was learning the fireman's most valued quality – respect – not just for others, but above all for himself.

So it was that he had suffered greatly when, a few minutes after the Stop on the shout at Haverstock Hill, he had had to report to Neil and say he had left his uniform jacket at home. Then five minutes after that, he had been further demoralized by Jim Griffin's question about Harrow Road, and he now sat in the TV room in a very depressed state, envying the assurance of the other recruits who were there – Wickenden, Dyer, Nicholls, Cheal, Wade, and Pettit – none of whom appeared to have a care in the world.

Slumped in his chair he remembered with some bitterness the day four months ago on which he had walked through the Orpington shopping precinct and come across a uniformed fireman sitting at a desk surrounded by pictures advertising his trade. 'Shall I interest you?' the fireman said. 'You can try,' said Leroy. 'Forty pounds a week,' said the fireman with a grin; and Leroy had said: 'All right. Tell me some more.'

He was shaken out of his gloom by another question from Jim Griffin.

'Which Underground station did you come in on, Leroy?'

'Warwick Avenue,' he answered without thinking.

'Did you notice the names of the roads as you walked towards the fire-station?'

'Warwick Avenue?' queried Leroy.

Several firemen laughed.

'Any others?' asked Griffin with a slight smile.

'Harrow Road,' said Leroy more confidently. 'Blomfield Road, and . . . Clifton Gardens.'

'That's good,' said Griffin. Someone applauded, and Leroy felt disproportionately pleased.

'Bloody hell!' said Neil.

He had just left the matron's office in the old folks' home in Penfold Street after being told by her that the firemen's visit that afternoon was inconvenient. It transpired that the home's routine had been upset by some incident in the morning and that a chiropodist had decided to make an unexpected visit to the home at the same time as the firemen. The matron felt she couldn't cope with the firemen on top of everything else and asked for the fire prevention visit to be deferred. Neil had mastered his annoyance, controlling a feeling common among firemen that people had little interest in them unless it was in an emergency. He said he would telephone later and fix up another visit. Then he had returned to the pump crew, waiting in the reception area, and told them they weren't wanted.

'Come on,' he said. 'Let's get outside to some fresh air!'

He made what use he could of their wasted visit by taking the crew – Lewis, Marven and Nicholls – on a quick inspection of the building's access-points, configuration and water sources. He then decided that as the pump was officially off the run for the afternoon he might usefully employ the time by showing the crew two of the places on their ground which would present the greatest hazards in the event of a fire. One was the GPO underground sorting-office in Paddington, the other was a company called Palmer Aero Products Ltd, who manufactured aircraft components and whose large factory was across the road from the old folks' home.

They spent over thirty minutes in the factory – with the general manager's permission – examining the various areas of risk: the cyanide salt-baths, the heat-treatment room, the whereabouts of radio-active measuring equipment, the stores of hazardous chemicals. Safety precautions were rigidly observed here, for a fire in such potentially explosive and toxic conditions would not only be destructive but unforeseeably lethal to firemen tackling the blaze.

The crew emerged from the building looking somewhat thoughtful, but they were not the sort of men to brood over the possible dangers in their job. Like all firemen, they were also to a degree fatalistic.

When Neil followed them out of the building, after saying good-bye to the general manager, he found Lewis entertaining a little boy, aged five, who was sitting in the driver's seat with a fireman's helmet on his head. His mother was talking to Nicholls and Marven. She had been on her way home and had stopped so that the child could admire the red fire-engine. Nicholls explained why they were not in their fire-gear, and Marven outlined for her the differences in the appliances.

Neil regarded their unconsidered action with approval – on

a fire-ground the men were single-minded and had little inclination to fraternize with the public.

'Now look,' Neil said, smiling at Lewis. 'I've got enough Wombles in my care back at the station.'

'Well,' said Lewis, 'he's not much smaller than Wickenden and not much younger than Cheal.'

'How's he making out?'

'Still feeling his way – like Leroy.'

Suddenly the radio came to life. On the list of stations prefacing the message was A21.

Neil ducked his head into the cab and closer to the RT as the distorted voice continued.

'From Station Officer Luckraft. . . . Stop for 117 Walm Lane, NW2. . . . Unoccupied house. . . . Three floors twenty-five by thirty-five feet. . . . One quarter of second floor and one eighth of roof damaged by fire. . . . Two jets . . . BA . . .'

'G28's ground,' said Neil.

He glanced at Lewis, not voicing his thought that as A21's appliances with the exception of the TL would seldom if ever be called to a derelict building on G28's ground, the TL *must* have been there – and with it, Leroy.

Neil stared for a moment concernedly at the little boy under the outsize helmet, pretending to be a fireman – his small hands gripping the wheel, his eyes on the road, and his childish voice in a rapture of make-believe imitating the engine's roar and the fire-bell's ring.

'Vroom-vroom! Vroom-vroom! Ding-ding!'

The radio crackled again.

'From Station Officer Luckraft . . . at Walm Lane, NW2. . . . One member of the Brigade injured . . . removed to Willesden General Hospital . . .'

The bells went down in Paddington at 2.47. There was no rush, but in seconds the TV room was empty. Firemen poured down the poles to the appliance-room. Others ran down the stairs. Leroy plunged through the pole-house door, automatically braking with his feet the second before he hit the padded base, and arrived at the bottom of the pole without knowing how he had got there.

He looked for the pump and saw its place was vacant. He

remembered he was now on the turntable ladders. At that moment the yellow light above the machine came on. No other light showed. Only the TL had been called.

Oh, my God, he said to himself, transfixed by terrible imaginings. His legs wouldn't move, wanting to take him in the other direction. But he forced himself towards the scarlet monster, its ladders like a silver dragon's tail laid flat along its back. Dave Dyer and Keith Orchard, the driver, were already in their boots and pulling up their leggings. Leroy followed suit as Acting Leading Fireman Frank Nice ran over to them, clutching a copy of the teleprinter message and a route-card.

'Walm Lane!' he shouted at Keith Orchard, who had started up the TL's engine. 'G28's ground. Fire!'

Nice ran around the front of the machine to get in the Number One's seat. At the same time the great door, at the touch of a button, began folding back on itself, letting in the bright cold light and the wind. Leroy heaved himself into the rear of the cab, where Dyer was already putting on his tunic, and with a slam of closing doors the twelve ton TL edged out of the appliance-room onto the forecourt, the blue lights on the cabin roof revolving and its braying two-tone horn, activated by Nice, already warning the traffic in Harrow Road of its approach.

'Know the way?' asked Nice, pulling down the strap of his helmet. 'The call came from Willesden Green police.' 'The Tube station's in Walm Lane,' said Orchard. 'What number?' They had to raise their voices to be heard above the engine and the horn. '117!' said Nice. He was looking at the route-card. 'Maida Vale – Kilburn High – Willesden Lane!' 'I know the way!' said Orchard.

Nice reached above his head for the leather bell-strap to hammer at the bell on the roof. It dinned out deafeningly above them as the TL towed its long bulk onto the roundabout and then left into Warwick Avenue.

Leroy struggled into his tunic, his hands trembling so much he could hardly do up the buttons, and with the panicking spasms that shook him and the lurching of the machine it was not until the TL was charging up Maida Vale that he was able to fasten his belt. The cab was so wide, that with only him and Dyer in the back he bounced about on the seat as if he were rubber – despite his feet being braced against a support.

'It's not our ground!' shouted Dyer soothingly, opening the window and letting the cold blast sweep around the cab. 'It's Willesden's! Take us a couple of minutes to get there!'

'You all right?' called Nice over his shoulder.

Leroy was fumbling with the helmet-strap under his chin. He meant to shout a confident assent, but when his voice came out with a strangulated 'Yes', he nodded instead.

'When we get there,' called out Nice, 'grab a line or an extinguisher! – if we're needed, that is – and stay with me!'

'Take the water one!' suggested Dyer.

The TL thundered on up Maida Vale to Kilburn High Road, with cars, lorries, and buses pulling into the kerb like frightened sheep. If the lights were at red it slowed down, with bell and horn dinning out together to deter any vehicle from crossing the road. Sometimes, if a build-up of traffic obstructed the way ahead, the TL swerved out onto the wrong side of the road. Nothing was allowed to halt its progress.

In a high state of excitement Leroy held onto the seat and window, wedged against the side of the cab, his senses entranced by the noise and spectacle. The cab's width and its height above the road magnified the TL's all-conquering advance. He had never felt so important, so like a hero riding to the rescue.

Messages came crackling over the radio. But his as yet unpractised ear was unable to interpret them.

He was helped by Orchard, who shouted across at Nice: 'Make pumps *four*! Could be a good one!'

'Could be!' returned Nice.

Leroy's exhilaration quickly waned. His apprehension increased. His imagination, flying ahead, pictured a tall building with tongues of flame leaping from upper windows and the roof – and people screaming, shouting for help. What would he do? In an instant all he had learned in training blew away; his mind went blank, and his palms were sweaty with fear. His eyes strained to see the road ahead and the first orange flames.

What he saw first of all was a policeman, then a pump – then another, and a pump escape. Then he saw the smoke, billowing darkly out of the roof and shattered upper windows of a small two-storey house.

The turntable ladders eased into the left-hand side of the road behind the nearest pump and came to a halt. Frank Nice jumped out.

'Stay here!' he said to the crew, and walked rapidly away. Leroy looked across at Dyer who was casually leaning out of the window. He loosened the straps of a large extinguisher in case it might be needed. In the front Orchard was relaxedly resting his forearms on the steering-wheel.

'Don't we get out?' asked Leroy.

'What?' asked Dyer.

'I mean – do we *stay* here?' Leroy was incredulous.

'Yeah. That's what he said.'

'Relax,' said Orchard. 'Don't look like they'll need us. Looks like they've got it out.'

Leroy peered through the forward window at what he could see of the appliances, hose, firemen, cars, spectators and policemen cluttering the flooded road. He could hardly believe that the energy expended in getting the TL to the fire – and there was, or had been, a fire – was going to prove useless and that he himself, now wound up and ready to prove himself, would not be put to the test. He sat on the edge of his seat, holding the extinguisher between his knees, still in eager anticipation of some action.

He sat like that for several minutes until the RT crackled into life – this time the message came through loud and clear. It was the Stop from Station Officer Luckraft at four minutes past three. The emergency was over.

'Did you hear that?' Orchard called out. 'Unoccupied! Another flaming derelict!'

'Hallo,' he said, some moments later when Luckraft sent his follow-up message. 'Someone's gone and got himself injured. Probably a Womble.'

Leroy leaned back against the cab wall, exhausted. Feelings of relief and frustration fought through him – to be briefly stilled when Frank Nice returned to the TL.

'They've got it,' he said. 'We're not needed.'

'What happened?' asked Leroy.

Nice climbed into his seat. 'Fire in a rear room on the second floor,' he said. 'Went through to the roof. Nothing to worry about. One of the Willesden blokes got injured when he was on a ladder. A slate fell off the roof and split the back of his hand. Lot of blood. But they've got him to a hospital. . . . Okay. Luckraft said we could go. So let's go home.'

The drive back was a very different matter – no bells, no horn, no drama. The TL dutifully stopped at traffic-lights and proceeded at no more than twenty-five m.p.h. To Leroy this leisurely return was a dismal anti-climax, and he sat by the window, the extinguisher still between his knees, feeling altogether deflated. The others, who were now exchanging cheerful comments about pedestrians and motorists – especially the female ones – left him alone. The emergency over, they were basking in the pleasures of a relaxed ride through London.

Leroy was not to know that in more than half the shouts the station had, the crews were never in the event required – as would happen at small fires on another station's ground to which they were called as a back-up in case of need, and at accidents on roads or in houses when the persons involved managed to extricate themselves or deal with the danger before the firemen arrived. Then there were the false alarms. Those classified as being 'Of good intent' were mostly caused by automatic fire-alarms actuating themselves: the Brigade received more than 12 000 such calls in a year. But the main cause of false alarms, classified 'Malicious', were hoax calls. These numbered annually over 15 000. Taken together, the well-intended and malicious calls during the year came to over 27 000. Calls to fires were less than double that figure. But whatever the reason for a call, when the bells went down the firemen had to react with the same urgency and speed.

Leroy's initial despondency on returning to the station was dissipated by a cup of tea – the TL crew arrived back in time for stand-easy at 3.30 – and by the recollected excitement of the ride. It had, after all, been his first shout. For the first time that day he talked animatedly with the others, venturing opinions and not minding the rebuffs.

His sense of well-being increased after the tea-break, when he acquitted himself none too badly in some drills on the pump escape.

Jim Griffin came up to him in the mess at 3.45 and said that he might as well do a drill with the PE crew as the pump was still out on a visit. In the meantime, in the event of a shout, he would continue to ride with the TL.

The purpose of the drill, a slip and pitch to the third floor of the practice tower using the pump escape, was to make sure that firemen could use the fifty-foot wheeled-escape in a rescue attempt as quickly and as efficiently as possible. The PE remained on the run – as all the appliances did during a station drill. If the fire-bell rang, the PE crew would immediately start re-assembling the gear they had removed in double-quick time, in case the call was for them. Leroy would give them a hand – unless the shout involved the TL and him.

Outside, it was still very cold and windy. The setting sun had already vanished behind the high westering flyover in a fierce orange glow like a furnace that illumined the darkening masses of cloud and threw a noose of fire around the top of the tower. In the yard, although it was still light enough to read a number-plate at a distance, the gathering dusk would, in Griffin's opinion, usefully approximate the dark conditions of many a shout.

While the PE crew and Leroy got into their boots, leggings and tunics for the drill, for which they also wore their caps, Griffin backed the PE out of its bay and into the yard, not far from the tower.

Leroy joined up with the others as they walked across the appliance-room. None of them was known to him, but none appeared to be much older than himself. This gave him confidence, as no one would have the advantage of experience; they would work together more or less as equals, as at training-school. He nonetheless decided as a safety measure to put himself at the end of the line and avoid the extra responsibility of being the Number One.

'Fall in over here,' said Griffin.

They lined up facing him and the yard and the sunset.

'Atten-shun! From the right – in fives – number!'

'One!' – 'Two!' – 'Three!' – 'Four!'

'Five!' shouted Leroy.

'Stand at ease!'

Griffin spoke to them more quietly now. 'For the benefit of

Fireman Hough,' he said, 'I want you to slip and pitch the wheeled escape to the third floor. Take your time and explain to him what you're doing.' He looked at Leroy. 'Do you know how to operate the carriage-gear?'

'Yeah – I think so.'

'You see to that then. Fireman Waldron – you can fall out. Wait over there – you won't be needed on this one.'

The four who remained closed up, and Griffin brought them to attention. 'Crew – fall in!' he ordered.

They doubled over to the rear of the PE and stood at attention in a line facing the appliance.

'Crew – mount!'

They ran forward, to left and right of the machine, and climbed into the cab with the Number One in the front. The doors slammed.

Griffin called out: 'You will slip and pitch the escape to the third floor and rest it there. Get to work!'

'Stand by to slip!' shouted the Number One as they piled out of the cab. They raced to the rear.

They pulled the escape's releasing-handle, slid the escape back on its mountings, and bore down on the levers. The wheeled ladders crashed off the PE onto the ground.

'Head left!'

The massive wheels were forced about, and the whole contrivance was pushed towards the tower. On snapped-out orders from the Number One the ladders were swung left again – extended to the third floor – the rounds were aligned at the right height – the carriage was lowered – the escape pushed forward – and the ladders came to rest against the third-floor balcony.

'Blocks down fore and aft!' called the Number One, and chocks were shoved against the wheels to hold them in place. The drill was nearly over.

Griffin approached them, made some comments, and told them to make up – to put the ladders back on the pump escape.

They did so swiftly and then hastily crammed themselves back into the cab, except for the Number One, who ran over to Griffin, stood at attention and said: 'All gear made up – drill complete, sir!'

'Crew – dismount!' ordered Griffin.

The three in the cab got out and fell in with the Number One at attention behind the machine. Griffin walked over to them.

'That was not too bad,' he said. 'This time, I want you to slip and pitch to the *fourth* floor, keeping the same numbers. Crew – mount!'

The four accomplished the second drill successfully, watched by Waldron, and by Chris Reynolds and Pincher Martin from the games-room windows above. They knocked off and made up and fell in once more behind the PE.

In the third and last drill they were joined on Griffin's instruction by Archie Waldron, who as driver also had to operate the pumping-equipment on the appliance. He was twenty-three, pale and loquacious, with wide film-star eyes; the previous week he had been transferred to Paddington from Kensington. He fell in beside the others and all five stood in a row behind the appliance, awaiting Griffin's orders, their faces now lit more by the overflowing light from the line of windows above the appliance-room than by the dying daylight. The watchers at the games-room window had grown, drawn by the autocratic shouted commands of the Number One and by the now theatrical aspect of the scene below in the sunset.

Jim Griffin told the squad to slip and pitch as before and take a hose-reel to work at the third floor.

'Get to work!' he said.

For the third time they dragged the wheeled escape off the appliance, swung it round and pushed it across to the tower, as the Number Two, Waldron, having started the engine, pulled about fifty feet of hose-reel off a revolving drum on the appliance and then set the pump controls at the right pressure.

'Head left again!' commanded the Number One. 'Extend! – Well! – Out in the carriage! – Well! – Into the building! – Down blocks!'

He seized the hose-reel that was passed to him by the Number Three, and having looped it over his right shoulder, ran up the ladders, closely followed by Leroy, who supported the length of hose behind him, keeping it clear of any snags.

They ascended in the approved style – left hand and foot alternating with the right hand and foot.

Once the third-floor balcony was reached, the Number One shouted down – 'Water on the hose-reel!' – and within seconds he was directing a thin jet of water down at the high perimeter wall of the yard. Leroy stood behind him, backing him up, holding the narrow ¾-inch tubing as if it were a full-powered 2¾-inch jet.

'All right!' called Griffin from below. 'Knock off and make up!'

'Knock off and make up!' shouted the Number One.

After they had done so, the five fell in for the last time at the rear of the appliance.

Griffin came up to them and said: 'That was good. You did that well. Any problems, Fireman Hough? Was everything okay?'

'Yes, sir.'

'You're happy. I'm happy. Right then – fall out.'

The five relaxed, exhaling deeply, their breaths like steam in the bitter cold air, their faces shining.

'Archie,' said Jim Griffin. 'Take the PE back inside.' He glanced at the others. 'Have a breather. There'll be volley-ball at 1700 hours,' he said and walked away.

'Great,' said the Number One with a happy grin.

Leroy looked at him wonderingly – he had led them well, working with speed and decision, and was hardly out of breath. In the light from the station windows the set of his features under his peaked cap made him seem like some RAF officer in a war film. All at once aware of someone's eyes on him, the Number One turned his grin on Leroy and reduced it to a smile.

'First day, isn't it?' asked the Number One.

'Yeah.'

'Don't worry. You'll like it here. They're a good bunch of blokes.'

'It's not like training-school,' said Leroy, as they walked back into the appliance-room. The Number One was, he noticed, three or four inches shorter and held himself very straight.

'You mean the drills,' said the Number One. 'No. Here you

don't have to be that fast. You have to be right – to *know*
what you're doing. That's what's important. Who are *you*?'

They stopped behind the pump before separating to get out
of their fire-gear.

'What's your name?' asked the Number One, tilting his
head and fixing Leroy with a keen gaze.

'Well . . . my real name's Leroy. But my mates call me
Lee.'

'Fair enough. My name's Hamish. But they call me by my
second name here – Harry.' He held out his hand. 'I'm Harry
Pettit.'

Neil looked up from the reports on his desk for some respite
and his eyes latched on the volley-ball game in progress out
in the yard. He could see it obliquely through the glass-walled
section of his office beyond a filing-cabinet, and through the
open rear doors of the darkened appliance-room. The yard
had been floodlit for the game, as although it was not long
after 5.15 p.m. night had fallen.

Bathed in a harsh white light, the trousered, T-shirted,
bare-armed figures leaping about the high net were not immediately identifiable. But Neil eventually sorted out who
was playing. It was evidently the usual contest between the
senior hands and the Wombles.

The sight of Leroy's long figure punching the ball reminded
Neil of Griffin's comment that the newest recruit's performance on the pump escape's drills had been up to A21's
standard. This pleased him. He was also glad that Leroy's
first shout had been met and had been no problem. Its details
had been communicated to Neil soon after he and the pump
crew had returned at 4.40 from their visit to the GPO sorting
office in London Street. They had been there longer than
Neil had anticipated. The robot GPO underground railway
that ran seventy feet down from Paddington to Whitechapel
always had a fascination for him – as it clearly also had for
Nicholls, Marven and Lewis, none of whom had seen it before.
GPO officials had explained how the electric, fully-automated
trains loaded with mailbags were controlled, how the conveyor-
belt system worked, also what safety precautions were taken
and what fire-fighting equipment was available.

The pump was now back on the run, and Leroy was back in its crew.

Neil briefly considered the possibility of there being another shout. They had only had three so far that day, two involving the ET and the other, the TL. It was likely that in the hour between 5.0 and 6.0 – when people were coming back home – there would be another one or two calls.

Chris Reynolds' voice could now be heard in the volley-ball game raised in loud derision. Neil guessed that Reynolds was having a go at one of the Wombles, probably Leroy. Their best defence was to grin and bear it – for the humour was never malicious – unless they dared or had the wit to respond in kind. A Womble was best advised to be silent or, in the often-quoted words of Leading Fireman Norman Wooldridge, that it was 'far better to keep your mouth shut and let people think you're a cunt, than open it and remove all doubt'.

A spectacular leap in the volley-ball game by Harry Pettit reminded Neil of a matter concerning Pettit that needed verification.

He tossed the pen on his desk and went into the brightly lit office, where Ernie Arthurs and Frank Nice were tidying up. Jim Griffin was making an alteration to the roll-call board.

'James,' said Neil. 'Who have you put on standby to-morrow?'

'There's Stewart at Chelsea,' said Griffin. 'Again. And Pettit at Kensington.'

'That's fine. Pettit's got his DO's interview with Mr Keable on Thursday at 18.30, so keep him off standbys that night.'

'Well, in fact it's Ray Wade's turn for standby on Thursday night.'

'Good. Let's leave it like that.'

Neil then returned to his office and telephoned the GLC architects' department to confirm something he had just re-membered – that the work of resealing the office floors had been set in motion.

The volley-ball game out in the yard came to an end as he was on the phone, and the floodlights went out.

Not long after, some of the firemen, mainly recruits, began dropping in on the office to find out in advance what their duties were the next day. Conversation became general; the last half hour of a Watch was always the most relaxed and informal as the time for going home approached and the likelihood of a shout decreased.

Neil distinguished the voice of Fireman Hough, and having concluded his telephone calls, leapt up and went into the office.

'What's this?' he demanded. 'Did I hear you asking to go?' Leroy smiled at him defensively.

Jim Griffin said: 'He's got someone on the White Watch to relieve him – Fireman Lettington.'

'Already?' Neil exclaimed. 'You've only been *here* a day!' he said to Leroy. 'And you're skyving off early already!'

'It's this mate of mine,' said Leroy. 'We was at the same school. And then he joined the Brigade on the same day, though I didn't know it till I met him at training-school. He's come in early – it's his first night. Is it okay if he rides for me?'

'Providing you've complied with Brigade order 44/4 (3)a,' said Neil.

Leroy looked dismayed. 'Crikey, Guv. What's that?'

'That, my dear Leroy, sets out your mutual responsibility to amend the nominal-roll board on your appliance. Have you done that?'

'No, Guv.'

'Well – providing Lettington sees to the pump board, and the duty-man knows, you can go. Don't forget the routine next time.'

'Okay, Guv,' said Leroy. He smiled and nodded. 'Good night.'

'Cheerio.'

Neil turned to Jim Griffin and said: 'I wonder how we've gone down with him on his first day.'

'He seems to be settling in quite well,' said Griffin.

'I hope so,' said Neil. 'He looks a useful lad.'

He went into the little bedroom beside his office, went next door and washed his face and hands. Plastic venetian blinds over all the windows concealed the night and the traffic going home on Westway. He dried his hands, returned to the bedroom and rummaged through his civilian clothes in his locker, sorting out a clean shirt to wear when he left. But even if the relieving station officer arrived well before 6.0 p.m.,

when the White Watch officially took over, Neil would stay
on; for he liked to see the Red Watch off duty and to hand any
outstanding problems to the oncoming station officer over a
cup of tea.

He was thoughtfully combing his hair in front of the mirror
when the teleprinter-bell above him pealed out its warning,
and was followed at once by the louder, urgent fire-bell.

'Bugger it!'

He joined in the hurried exit from the office and the rush
down the stairs. It was twenty to six.

'Fire . . .' said the duty-man over the tannoy. 'Ladbroke
Lower School . . . Lancaster Road . . . North Kensington's
ground. . . . PE and pump.'

Leroy had walked as far as the roundabout when the high-
pitched notes of a two-tone horn behind him brought him to
a sudden halt. He looked around, his pulse quickening, his
mind ablaze. In the overhead white neon light of streetlamps
and the higher orange glare of the lights on Westway, a fire-
engine swung out of the station's forecourt and up the road
towards him, its headlights flaring. He saw it was the pump
escape, whose crew he had joined for drill, whose ladders he
had climbed. Its horn was doubled by another as the pump
came out of the forecourt in pursuit. As they passed close by
him, their horns and bells dinning out a warning to the traffic
ahead, he glimpsed the men in the cabs getting into their gear.
Someone who noticed him raised a hand. Then the red
machines, after surging around the roundabout, went storm-
ing down under the arches of Westway, their horns and flashing lights rebounding off its concrete supports and walls.

He stood motionless, his hands in his sheepskin jacket,
facing the way they had vanished, until the horns completely
faded away. He was swearing softly to himself, cursing his
luck that he was not riding with them to the fire.

*

Leroy got home about 7 p.m., had his tea and then went by
bus to a pub, The Five Bells, at Chelsfield, where he played
darts with his friends until closing-time. He returned home and

went straight to bed, tired out after the strain of his first day at A21.

Neil and the pump crew were back at the station by 5.55 p.m. The shout at Ladbroke Lower School proved to be a false alarm and was classified as malicious. He had a cup of tea with the White Watch and left the station about 6.45 p.m. He was in bed by 11.15, after reading a book and watching *News at Ten.*

The White Watch had five shouts that night – none on A21's ground. They were all before midnight and of minor concern: a faulty electrical fitting, a woman shut in a lift, a rubbish fire, a slight traffic accident, and a bus whose engine had caught fire, to which the TL, the PE, the pump, the ET and the pump again were called out in turn. After midnight the White Watch spent an unusually undisturbed night. But in the early hours of the morning, between 4.0 and 5.0 a.m., freak storms hit parts of London, Sussex and Kent. Great gusts of wind, torrential rain and claps of thunder startled people awake.

At dawn, the temperature fell to freezing-point, and a strong south-westerly wind continued to blow.

Wednesday 11 December

In the darkest half-hour before the dawn, Ray Wade set off for work in his white Cortina, accompanied by a fireman from A25, Alan Williams. They left Rainham in Kent soon after 6.30 a.m. and then picked up Harry Pettit, as arranged, by the clock-tower on Star Hill. After driving on through Rochester, a fourth fireman from A26 was added to the carload on the outskirts of Strood. They then continued on up the A2 to London.

They had been travelling to work in this way for several months. All four were family men, in their late twenties, and all four were recruits. Harry was the senior in this respect, having joined the Brigade in May, although he was the youngest of the four. Ray had joined in June, and the other two a fortnight later. They had all been posted to the Red Watch at their respective stations, and as they kept on meeting on railway platforms on their way to and from work, they had decided to share the rigours of travel, and the expenses, by taking it in turn to drive to London. This week it was Ray's turn. Harry was the only one without a car – however, on Thursday he was taking a driving-test.

The test was one of the sporadic topics of their conversation on the long dark run, while the east imperceptibly lightened behind them, slowly deadening the streetlights. The previous evening's TV programmes, last night's storm, the high winds and the morning's bitter cold also brought forth some comments. For a while they discussed the Brigade's pension scheme and what financial returns and safeguards their families would have in the event of their own injury or death. They talked about this dispassionately, but not at length, as they were still drowsy and disinclined for the kind of searching argument that Harry liked to provoke.

They crossed the river at Lambeth Bridge soon after sunrise

– not a hundred yards from the Brigade headquarters where Ray, as a small boy, had stood outside the yard watching the drills and annual displays the firemen had given there years ago.

His memory of the Brigade displays, of the sight and sound of fire-engines, had lain dormant for many years. But when he was nineteen it was revived by the conversation and character of a fireman who happened to live next door to one of his mates. The man impressed him, and he suddenly realized that what he had lacked in his present unproductive, monotonous job in a warehouse, he would find as a fireman. He applied straightaway and had no difficulty passing the basic entry qualifications, i.e. – between eighteen and thirty-one years of age – at least 5 feet 6 inches tall, with a chest measurement of 36 inches or more and an expansion of 2 inches – and apart from being in good general health, he did not need to wear glasses. But when he was put through the simple follow-up tests on education, health and strength, he failed in the latter. He had to lift a certain weight by winching it up to a certain height in thirty seconds. His time was thirty-one. Nothing daunted, he re-applied, passed all the tests – and then was failed on his interview. This rejection hurt him – he *wanted* to serve, to be of use, and in particular to be a fireman.

For several months he became a lorry-driver and found no pleasure in it. On his father's suggestion he then joined the London Salvage Corps. They were run by the insurance companies, their object being to salvage what merchandise or equipment they could in any major fire in and around London. Their depot was in Aldersgate in the City. They also cleared up after any blaze they attended and if necessary secured and guarded premises damaged by fire. Ray was with them for five years.

Soon after joining them, he married. He eventually settled in Rainham, and it was not until after the birth of his sons that he applied for the third time to the London Fire Brigade. 'Third time lucky,' he said to his wife – and it was. Nine years after his first application Ray was accepted; and on leaving the training-school at Southwark he was posted to A21.

Before he and Harry reached Paddington that Wednesday morning, the other two firemen had to be dropped off at A25

(Westminster) and at A26 (Knightsbridge). Harry remained in the back seat, and as Ray drove on up Park Lane to Marble Arch he gazed out over the frosted acres of Hyde Park, whose bare, wind-swayed trees were now burnished by the rising sun.

'It's been bloody quiet,' said Harry.

'What?' said Ray, with a glance in the driving mirror. 'The station?'

'Hardly any shouts,' Harry went on. 'We only had one for the PE yesterday – and that was a hoax. How can people be so bloody irresponsible?'

'You did a good drill yesterday,' said Ray, with a grin at the mirror.

Harry smiled. 'I had a good crew. . . . That big new kid wasn't bad – Leroy – calls himself Lee, by the way. And Archie's not such a nutter as they say. Where did he come from?'

'Archie? A28 – Kensington.'

'He told me he was a Liberal, an actual member of the Party. I had to laugh. Of course they're *all* nutters – so it figures. But at least it shows he's not apathetic. There's something he believes in. . . . What do *you* believe in, Ray?'

'Me? What I'm doing. The job. The wife and kids. What else is there?'

'That's what I'd like to know,' Harry said.

Harry was Ray's mate. This was an assumption easily made by the Watch, who saw them arrive at work together, leave together, and seek out each other's company more often than not at stand-easy – at least when Harry was not in a quiet corner reading a book. It was nonetheless an assumption that caused Ray a lot of gratification. The fact that he was two years older, and an inch taller, were to him about the only conceivable advantages he had over Harry, who was in Ray's opinion much more knowledgeable, except in some practical matters. There was just one feature of Ray's existence that Harry had admitted envying – the fact that Ray had twin three-year-old boys. Not that Harry had ever seen them – neither had been to the other's home or met the other man's wife – but Harry was devoted to his own little boy, who would be two in February, and he wanted more sons. What he and Ray had in common – apart from certain beliefs, which Harry was better able to express – was their working-class backgrounds. Yet this had not prevented Harry from trying to improve himself. He had taken eight 'O' Levels at school, become a senior electrician in Chatham dockyard, and was now taking a correspondence course of 'A' Levels in Literature and Mathematics – besides studying for a degree in Archaeology. He was also a sportsman, playing football with a local team, the Redwood Rangers, until he joined the Watch, and had developed a strong social conscience. For weeks while the populations of Bangla Desh and Ethiopia starved, he had deprived himself, his wife and baby son of all sweets, puddings and other unnecessary delicacies and sent the money that would have been spent on them to Oxfam. In his job, the damage done to people's homes by fire and water openly filled him with concern, and as a general rule, in word and deed, he would take the side of the underdog.

All of this was viewed by Ray with silent admiration. But what was even more amazing, considering Harry's background and employment in a dockyard, was that he never used four-letter words, didn't smoke and hardly ever drank. Harry was simply one of the finest blokes Ray had ever met – he was a gentleman – and he was also Ray's mate.

They arrived at the station a little before 8.30 a.m. Ray manoeuvred his Cortina into the small car park beside the Divisional offices. Then he and Harry strolled through the appliance-room to the watchroom, where the day's duty-man, Keith Cheal, was filling in the roll boards for the individual machines from the roll-call board. With a look at the latter they saw that Harry had been put on standby at A28. He would have to report to Kensington by 9.30 a.m., and would probably remain there all day.

'Bleeding standby!' said Ray.

He was more displeased than Harry, whose sense of curiosity welcomed the chance to meet new situations and people.

'It's all right,' Harry said. 'I might see some action there. What are you on?'

'The PE,' said Ray morosely.

He walked around the teleprinter table to look at the personnel board on the wall – to see which member of the White Watch at present on the PE he might relieve. Their names were on white studs stuck on the board beside the appliances they were riding. The off-duty firemen's tags, in red and blue, were grouped together to one side.

'Oh, well,' said Harry, 'I better get changed. . . . Have you ever been at Kensington?' he asked as they left the watchroom.

'No,' said Ray. 'But with you and Stewart on standbys this week, I bet I'm the next to go.'

'Oh, Christ,' groaned Neil. 'The bloody TL off the run again!'

'I'm sorry, Neil,' said Station Officer White of the White Watch. 'But that's the way it is. The rear axle-lock cable, the nearside one, is defective. Nothing too serious. And the mobile repair van's on its way. All right. Here are the keys. I've checked the petty cash.'

'Thanks, Graham,' said Neil, taking possession of the station keys. He picked up the diary and examined the entries for Wednesday.

'Bloody hell!' he exclaimed. 'The pump's got a dry-riser – the ET's got to go to Wembley for a decontamination drill – and with the TL up the creek I'll only have the PE on the run this morning!'

'Well, that's one out of four,' remarked White with a smile. 'That's not a bad average.'

'Never mind, Guv,' said Ernie Arthurs. 'We can always sling a couple of hook-ladders on top of the van, if things get rough.'

'Are you ready to ride for me?' asked White.

'Yes,' said Neil. 'I've got my gear on the pump.'

'Right. I'll be off.'

White went into the station officer's bedroom to pick up his pipe and tobacco, and his cap. He was one of the few firemen who came to work in uniform.

Neil dropped the diary on his desk, sat down and began flipping through the various papers in the 'Items Pending' tray. He saw amongst other things that HQ at Lambeth would have to be telephoned about the requirement of a second cleaner at the station – standards were falling below par – and that in the afternoon three pumps from other stations were coming to Paddington to take part in a BA drill in the basement Smoke and Humidity rooms. This meant that the ET, which was also involved, would be off the run again. He noted in the diary that the pump, which he was riding and whose crew included Leroy Hough, had to do *two* dry-risers at Porchester Square. It was going to be a day full of awkward administration, to add to the unknown demands of shouts.

'Cheer up,' said White, emerging from the bedroom. 'You're only here till six o'clock – then it's my turn again.'

Neil sighed. 'Well, I hope it's all sorted out by then, Graham. As if we didn't have enough headaches! Did you have a busy night?'

'Very quiet,' White replied. 'Nothing after midnight. . . . Enjoy your problems. Cheerio!' He raised a hand and left Neil on his own and in command of the station.

It's too quiet, thought Neil.

He glanced out into the appliance-room. There hadn't been a decent fire for a month – nothing that could be called a really good job. It had been the same, he remembered, before the blaze at the Leinster Towers Hotel. His eye switched to the framed scroll of honours and awards on top of the filing-cabinet. Chris Reynolds had been commended for his part in the Leinster job. But the last fireman of the Red Watch to win an award had been Frank Nice, back in 1972, and there were no entries for any Watch at A21 after November 1973. Neil wondered if his name would ever appear there. But the circumstances in which it might do so were too remote to contemplate.

He returned his gaze to the appliances below him, distracted by someone's loud whistling of a pop song. Neil could not see who it was, but knew who it was likely to be.

Dave Webber ran up the stairs to the second floor, whistling the tune of 'Get Dancing'. In the absence that day of Martin Walker, who was still away on rota leave, he was mess manager again, and was therefore not required to parade with the others at 9.0 a.m. He already knew that he was on the ET – having checked this in the office the day before – and so, after parking his battered old blue Consul in the yard as the car park was full, he came straight upstairs to the dormitory to change.

'Morning, Harry!' he said, bursting into the second and

middle section where he and five other firemen each had a
bed.

Harry, in his undress uniform, looked up from stowing his
overalls and some books in his kitbag. On the inside of his
locker door was a colour photo of his small son.

'Where are you off to?' Dave called out, flinging his sheep-
skin coat on the mattress and unearthing a pair of overalls and
a T-shirt from the general confusion of clothes and uniforms
in his locker. On a shelf below his bed-gear were some science
fiction paperbacks. On the door was a photo of his fiancée, Sue.

'Kensington,' said Harry. Dave heard him shut his locker
door and turn the key. 'Standby. What are they like?'

'Not a bad bunch,' said Dave. 'You'll fit in okay.'

Harry came out from behind the lockers, his cap on his
head, his kitbag over his shoulder.

'You're looking rather smart, my son,' said Dave in a gruff,
mock-military growl. He paused in unbuttoning his shirt.

Harry smiled. He was five years older than Dave, who
although just twenty-one had already been a fireman for more
than three years.

'Thanks. Don't forget to count me out for dinner.'

'Okay, son,' said Dave, as before. 'I've got you.'

'See you.' Harry walked away.

Dave changed into his overall trousers and put on a white
T-shirt with '*Sahara Desert Canoe Club*' written across it.
After peering at himself in a mirror and flicking his fine fair
hair into some order he breezed along to the kitchen, where
the station's civilian helpers were washing up and tidying away
the White Watch's breakfast.

After opening up the Red Watch store cupboard, Dave took
out the necessary amounts of tea and sugar, and began preparing the first of the day's large pots of tea for the Watch.
The pints of milk he fetched from a fridge, and put them on
the kitchen hatch alongside a trayful of cups. As he worked
he whistled or sang loud accompaniments to the records being
played on Capital Radio.

Dave was one of the brightest characters in the Watch,
young as he was, and one of the ablest firemen. His fair com-
plexion and slightly less than average size belied a natural
strength of will and body, and his brash extroversion con-

cealed a degree of sensitivity and reserve. As with several of his colleagues – Reynolds, Garner, Dunlop, Dyer and Marven – Dave's father had also been a fireman, at the former Lambeth control. This fact had at the beginning of his service given Dave, whose upbringing in the East End had toughened and matured him beyond his years, a careless over-confidence: he already considered himself to be one of the lads and though a rookie was always answering back. The senior hands took him aside and talked to him reprovingly but to little avail. Facetious remarks about his hair growing over his collar and the fact that he had started wearing hippie beads made no impression. Unrepentantly and scruffily up-to-date, Dave carried on whistling, mimicking, joking and jigging about the station at stand-easy as if he were, as Griffin said, 'a supercharged monkey'. It was not until Neil chose to up-braid Dave in a comic but shaming fashion in front of the others that he began to modify his behaviour. He suddenly realized he valued the other firemen's respect and wanted it to be mutual. Within days he had his hair cut, and determin-edly putting his change of style to practical use, he was now working for promotion.

At 9.0 a.m. six bells announced the start of the Watch's duty with roll-call in the appliance-room. At the same time Dave's assistant for the day, Keith Orchard, rusty-haired and unusually soft-spoken for a fireman, arrived in the mess, bear-ing five loaves and a bag of onions.

'Morning, Ginge!' said Dave.

'Morning, Wobbly,' said Orchard.

'Bleeding late again!' said Dave, initiating a ritual bout of amicably abusive pleasantries that continued until they were joined in the mess, within minutes of the end of roll-call, by a noisy crowd of tea-drinking, cigarette-smoking firemen, ex-uberantly sociable at the start of their working day. Conver-sation, such as it was, was largely limited to recent shouts and Brigade matters.

A bevy of Wombles sat by the window. The smallest of them, Wickenden, prompted a comment from Lewis, who said – 'You'd think that the Brigade when they dropped the height-limit to allow dwarves in would have provided us with orange-boxes by the cabs.' Reynolds was boasting that he used to be the

school champion at putting the shot. 'You couldn't put a baked
bean!' Dave remarked. Pincher Martin, acting up as leading
fireman – he was Number One on the TL that day – took away
a trayful of cups of tea for his superiors in the office. Dave
noticed that the new recruit, Leroy, was recklessly raising his
cockney voice in loud dispute with Cheal. 'Listen, kid,' said
Reynolds. 'Cool it. While you was at school flicking ink-
pellets round the classroom, *I* was saving lives!' Harry Pettit
was not in evidence – he must have gone straight to Kensington
after roll-call.

At 9.30, a further six bells cleared from the mess the pump
and ET crews, who went off to get into their fire-gear for their
respective dry-riser tests and decontamination drill. The PE
and TL crews had been detailed to spend the morning on the
cleaning and maintenance of their machines, and those of
them who were not in their overalls disappeared to change
into them or fetch their jackets. Dave, being with the ET
crew, left the cleaning up of the mess, the preparations for the
cheese and onion coffee-break at eleven and the arranging of
lunch to Orchard and Nicholls.

'Don't burn the water!' Dave called out as he left.

'Go on – get lost,' retorted Orchard. 'And I hope the
roentgens get you!'

At 9.45 the pump and the ET left for their different destina-
tions – Neil with the former and Jim Griffin with the latter.

Ernie Arthurs, Acting Sub Officer for the day, was left in
charge of the station and of a much depleted Watch. Only
four firemen were left to clean up the PE and the TL – Ray
Wade, Cheal, Wickenden, and Dunlop.

They set to work, taking their time, for they had all
morning. Ray attended to the pump escape. Washing it inside
and out, polishing and cleaning the bodywork, wheels, lights
and bell, was for him a pleasurable exercise, despite the frosty
air and freezing water. He liked making sure the machines
functioned properly and were spick and span, and he concentrated on the job in hand, saying little to the others. Once the
teleprinter-bell rang out in the silent appliance-room, but
only to warn of a message coming through. Ray paused and
looked up, as if sniffing the air for smoke, and wondered what
Harry was doing.

'Gentlemen! I'm Sub Officer Whitty from the Ops room at Lambeth, and I'm here today to instruct you on the procedure that has been adopted to decontaminate men whose lives have been put at risk by some chemical accident or by a fire involving chemicals. Because the use of chemicals is so wide-spread these days – and on the increase – the Brigade are more than ever likely to be called to incidents involving chemicals. We have to adopt some procedure to meet such emergencies, and what you are about to see is that procedure.'

The speaker was a broad young man with a ginger moustache, dressed in his fire-gear and cap. He stood, holding his notes, on a twelve-foot square of polythene sheets spread across one of the bays in G30's appliance-room. Facing him in a half-circle were A21's ET crew and three pump crews from 'G' Division.

To one side were the three other sub officers who would demonstrate the drill: the 'assistant director', who was dressed in full fire-gear, helmeted, and wearing a face-mask with air filters, and two 'operatives', also masked and enveloped in yellow, hooded protective suits with green gloves.

The large anonymous figure in what looked like a frogman's suit who stood beside them was Chris Reynolds, completely hidden behind a face-mask connected to a BA set and inside a rubbery one-piece Draeger suit, which was diagonally zipped up the front. His helmet perched incongruously on his head.

It had been too windy for the demonstration to be held in the yard. Even so, the plastic sheets on the appliance-room floor jerked and flapped where they were not pinned down by tripods carrying a line of orange tape that enclosed the decontamination arena.

Dave Webber had never seen the demonstration before. Nor had any of the ET crew. Besides Dave and Reynolds they included that day Garner, Hughes, Davey and Nice. Jim Griffin was the Number One. Despite the gusting wind, freezing their faces and hands, they concentrated on what might one day be a matter of life and death for any ET man, all of whom would be expected to deal with an emergency involving chemicals when wearing a Draeger suit. The ET carried two such suits, each worth £300.

Jim Griffin's choice of Reynolds as the contaminated person had caused some banter earlier on, especially while Dave, Hughes and Garner helped him into the suit inside the ET. Reynolds had alternated comic Mr Universe poses with those of a fashion model, and on leaving the ET had not been able to resist a John Wayne walk as he crossed the yard. But now he was as seriously attentive as the others to what the Ops sub officer had to say.

'The most important point I can make is simply that one part per million in air of some chemicals can kill instantly.' Whitty snapped his fingers. 'Like *that*! So make no mistake – it's *imperative* that the proper sequence of actions as laid down in these notes is carried out to the letter. And that's why I'm reading from them – to obviate any mistakes.'

He had to raise his voice as the engine of G30's TL was revved for a few seconds. The station was also a Divisional HQ, like A21, and in addition contained on an upper floor the nerve-centre of Wembley control, where all the 999 calls made in north-west London, from Twickenham to Walthamstow, were received, noted and then transmitted to a fire-station nearest the emergency.

After making some more introductory remarks and explanations, Whitty described the equipment that would be used. It was laid out at the rear of the van, and included a cylindrical vacuum-cleaner. The largest item, a portable generator, had already been set up some distance away – to reduce its noise – and floodlights had been positioned overlooking the polythene sheets.

He then explained how a decontamination area was selected and prepared, and outlined the roles of himself and his three assistants.

'Right!' he said. 'Get the generator going and the lights, Brian. Pete, bring the wearer into the area, facing me. The rest of you, spread yourselves around so you can see what's happening.'

He himself moved to one side. In the middle of the floodlit arena Reynolds bowed coyly to left and right, acknowledging imaginary applause.

'Okay, let's go,' said Whitty. 'Check the cylinder pressure.'

One of the yellow figures did so as Whitty explained why –

having to speak louder now above the noise of the generator.
'This is done to ensure that the wearer has enough oxygen
in his set to last out the decontamination procedure.'

He glanced at the check-list. 'Place wearer in a kneeling
position.'

Reynolds knelt, and on the instruction – 'Vacuum from
head downwards' – an operative set to work with the vacuum-
cleaner extension, running the brush over the front of the
Draeger suit, mainly over the BA set and about the zip. It was
potentially a comic sight, but no one smiled.

Whitty went on reading from his check-list.

'Remove helmet and slacken face-mask straps – Remove
Ceag lamp – Release the body-belt, complementary and
shoulder straps – Operate the by-pass valve gently to flush
and partially inflate the suit – Instruct the wearer to withdraw
his face from the mask into the suit, keeping his head well
forward.'

The helmet and lamp were put on one side.

As the BA set was lifted up and over Reynolds' head, he
worked himself down inside the inflated suit.

Dave allowed himself a slight smile at the apparition of the
swollen, headless Draeger suit swaying on the plastic sheets.
Then his view was partially obscured by one of the operatives,
who vacuumed down and around the suit's diagonal zip. At
the same time, the assistant director walked into the arena on
a four-foot wide strip of plastic which he laid down in front
of him like a carpet. He brought with him a spare pair of boots.

'The director's assistant, wearing mask and gloves and carrying a mask for the wearer, lays out a clean path – he doesn't
roll it – into the zone, enters on it and prepares to put the
mask on the wearer.'

What followed, said Whitty, was done to ensure that the
wearer came into no contact with any part of the suit's contaminated exterior, nor breathed any dangerous fumes.

'Unzip the suit!' he said, and explained – 'This allows the
wearer to withdraw his head from the suit. The director's
assistant immediately puts a mask on the wearer, taking care
not to touch the outside of the suit. . . . The operatives then
pull back the suit, turning the inside of the suit outwards, to
avoid the *outside* of the suit touching the wearer as he emerges.

The director's assistant slips the braces and steadies the wearer while the suit is removed.'

At this point Reynolds was helped to his feet. The suit, turned inside-out, was pulled down to his knees, and he removed his hands from the gloves which were being held by the operatives. One of them then held onto Reynolds' boots as he climbed out of them, supporting himself by putting his chalky hands on the assistant director's shoulders – after which he stepped into the spare pair of boots provided.

With a smirk of satisfaction Reynolds, his T-shirt and trousers covered in chalk from the suit's interior, followed the assistant director along the 'clean path' and out of the floodlit square, while Whitty read out the next moves in the procedure, describing what the yellow-suited operatives were now doing.

'Zip up the suit, and with the set still attached, gather the four corners of the top plastic sheet containing the suit, set and contaminated equipment, e.g. the helmet and Ceag lamp, and make it into a bundle. . . . Place this in a plastic bag, secure and label, stating the chemical involved, the Hazchem code, and the station. . . . Repeat as above until all wearers have been disrobed.'

Sub Officer Whitty entered the square and as he did so told the director's assistant to 'knock off the generator and the lights'. He faced his audience of the ET and pump crews and smoothed his moustache with his fingers.

'Well, as the weather's not too good today,' he said, 'we won't continue with the disrobing of the operatives. But it is done by one operative standing in a plastic bag while the other operative vacuums him down and then undresses him.'

'Mmn. Nice!' said Dave.

'Yeah,' said Whitty with a tired smile. 'We do it all the time. Anyway, the procedure continues roughly the same as for a wearer – the director's assistant disrobing the last operative. Right.' He looked at them sternly. 'This is a training-session, and we can laugh. But on the real thing, nobody does. Okay. Any questions? Or do you have any suggestions? The procedure's open to improvement and if you've got any ideas about that, speak out.'

The crews shifted their feet, stamping them on the ground,

and rubbed their cold hands. The station yard was now empty of drill squads, who had gone to their mess for the mid-morning break, undisturbed by any shouts.

'How do you cope,' asked Jim Griffin, 'with decontamination in adverse weather conditions? You can't always do it outside.'

'Well,' said Whitty. 'As I said at the beginning we have to consider several factors before setting up a decontamination zone. One of them is the weather. If it's raining, it's possible that the chemical may react violently to water. So obviously the decontamination would have to take place under some shelter, in any covered place. Even when it's windy, like today, it's easier to work under shelter.'

'I've got a question,' said Reynolds.

'Let's hear it.'

'What about if –? What if he's injured – the bloke in the Draeger suit?'

'There's nothing laid down for that as yet. As I said before, you've got to adapt your actions to the circumstances. If the person concerned is in a bad way – with broken limbs or bleeding badly – then sod the procedure. We'd just rip up the suit and get him out. It's no good going through the whole procedure if he dies in the process. I've personally been on a dozen decontaminations – for real – so far, and I can tell you now that on each occasion every man has been as concerned as we are that he's decontaminated properly.'

'Would you have an ambulance standing by?' asked Dave.

'No. That's not part of the procedure at present.'

'But you might need one if things go wrong. I mean, the contaminated bloke might have to be carted off to hospital double-quick to save his life. Shouldn't an ambulance always be in attendance?'

'Yes, it should. That's a good suggestion, and I'll take it up with my superiors at Headquarters. After all, an ambulance automatically attends many types of calls, and this *should* include chemical incidents.'

There were few other questions. The crews were too conscious of various physical cravings, mainly for warmth and a cup of tea, and their concentration had dulled. They had dutifully stood in the appliance-room for well over an hour now.

'Right,' said Whitty finally. 'We've gone into stand-easy, so we'll move upstairs and if you've got any other points you'd like to raise, we can chat about them over our tea. Thank you.'

Suddenly all was activity, orders and conversation, as the station officers reassembled their pump crews.

'ET crew!' said Jim Griffin. 'Over here. We'll go and have a cup of tea now. Does anybody know where the messroom is?'

'Follow those lads going up that way,' said one of the 'G' Division station officers.

'Right, lads!' said Griffin. 'Come with me.'

'Here!' said Reynolds. 'Hang on. Who's going to get my boots for me?'

'Come on, you big fairy!' said Griffin. 'Get your gear on and follow us up.'

'Oh, but sir!' protested Reynolds with well-assumed indignation. 'The yard's all *wet*! And look at my *socks* – they're full of *holes*!'

'So is your head,' said Garner.

'Yeah,' said Nice. 'It needs an airing.'

'So do his feet,' said Dave.

'He doesn't need weed-killer,' said Garner. 'All he's got to do is walk around his garden without any socks.'

'Oh, go on, Winger,' pleaded Reynolds. 'Be a sport and fetch my boots for me.'

'No, thanks, Chris,' said Hughes.

'Pathetic, isn't it?' commented Griffin. 'You know, Reynolds, you looked a bloody sight better with that suit on than with it off. Come on.'

'Oh, fellows!' cried Reynolds. 'Have a heart!'

'He's got legs like number seven irons,' Nice remarked.

'You know his boots are bigger than the box they come in,' said Dave as the ET crew walked away, unmoved by Reynolds' entreaties.

'Rotten devils!' he yelled. Then with a happy grin he staggered back to the ET on his heels across the windswept yard.

Ray Wade sat by the window in A21's mess, studiously making a cigarette for himself from the tobacco and papers he carried in a small tin box. Like most of the Red Watch he rolled his own cigarettes. Opposite him Cheal and Wickenden were chatting brightly over their cups of tea. There was no one else in the mess – apart from the workshops crew who had inspected and repaired the TL. It was now back on the run. Orchard and Nicholls were in the kitchen; the few other firemen at the station were in the office.

A chilly breath of the wind outside stole in by the window-frame and fanned Ray's hands as he lit the cigarette. He inhaled, gazing out at the barrier of Westway, feeling unusually dispirited and tired. He glanced at the other two. They were discussing the practicalities of living out of London. Young Cheal, who lived with his family in Brighton, was assuring Wickenden that the distance from work was no drawback. Little Wickenden, who at the moment was living with his parents and brother and an Alsatian dog in New Cross, had apparently just arranged a mortgage on a semi in Herne Bay. Aged twenty, he was going to get married the following year.

'You thinking of going down to Herne Bay?' asked Ray. 'You'll be all right down there. But you want to get rid of that old rat-trap of yours – that rent-a-heap. It'll never make the journey. The wheels will fall off.'

'Old Nell?' replied Wickenden. 'She's beautiful! Never let me down yet.'

'Ah,' said Ray. 'That's only because you've got a magnet on the back picking up the bits. What we ought to do is get a minibus and travel up together – all of us from down that way – you, me, my mates, and Harry.'

'I was fixing to come up with Norman,' said Wickenden. 'He's at Faversham.'

'Oh, yeah,' said Ray. 'Oh, well – suit yourself.'

He gazed out of the window again, musing how capable and responsible the youngsters were nowadays. Ten years ago, when he was their age, he had been a bit of a tearaway. After work, he and his mates, who were all motor-mad, used to meet in coffee-bars before racing their cars up and down the Old Kent Road or doing a burn-up round the Elephant and Castle. Once they had shot down to Hastings for some fish and chips. Another time he had set up a record by driving from the Hastings clock-tower to the one in Eastbourne in nine and a half minutes. Dressed in Bonnie and Clyde gear, complete with red carnations, they had gone to dance-halls like the Locarno and Lyceum and had a good night drinking and chatting up the birds. At weekends they went swimming or to stock-car meetings and ended up in strip clubs, having a laugh. Now that he was a family man those days were over: he only went out with his mates on Friday nights, and then just for a drink. But the young lads these days seemed not to do much more – despite the greater licence they enjoyed.

How *did* they enjoy themselves now? he wondered. Harry would have something to say about that, thought Ray.

He stubbed out his cigarette in an ash-tray. He began to feel more cheerful, for he was naturally optimistic. All he needed, he thought, was a shout to brighten his day.

Out in the yard a single toot on the horn announced the return of the pump from the dry-riser tests. It glided out of sight below him into the appliance-room.

Three of the station's four appliances were now back on the run – the pump, the PE and the TL – which meant that the chances of the Red Watch having a shout had now increased.

'Fire!' said Dave. 'Cecil Rhodes House . . . Goldington Street . . . by St Pancras Road. Oh, fuck it,' he said. 'That's Euston's ground. I was hoping it would be for *us*.'

On the other side of the windowed wall the words he had been reading on the monitor screen paused, before continuing with the route-card number and the details of A23's appliances called to the fire.

He and the rest of the ET crew were standing in a small corridor on the second floor of G30 (Wembley). A wall with three large windows in it separated them from the control room, one of three (the others were at Croydon and Stratford) that dealt with all the 999 calls to the London Fire Brigade.

At the end of their half-hour break Jim Griffin had thought it would interest them to see the new system of dealing with calls that had just been installed. It had only been operational for three days. One of the nine uniformed firemen and firewomen on duty in the control room had been detailed by the Officer of the Watch to put the ET crew in the picture. He had the single tape on his shirt epaulettes of a leading fireman, a rank that was known there as Control Officer II, or 'Conoff Two Denbeigh' as he introduced himself.

He had been explaining to them how the new system, called VDU (visual display unit), worked when a buzzer announcing an incoming call rang out, cutting across the general hum of voices and machines. At the same time a red light came on above a huge map of London on the far wall which showed the disposition of every station and the appliances available. On other boards the whereabouts of senior officers and appliances off the run was shown. With Conoff Denbeigh's help the ET crew had been able to follow roughly what happened next.

There were three desk-units in the room like switchboards, each of which included an electric typewriter with a monitor screen above. When the buzzer sounded a girl wearing earphones took the 999 telephone call which had been routed to the Wembley control room by the GPO, and immediately started typing out the relevant details of the emergency. Everything she typed appeared on her screen and on all the monitors in the room. If she or the caller made a mistake or a correction, she pressed a key that would alter, add to or erase anything that had been typed.

Once the nature of the emergency – fire, road traffic accident, person shut in lift, flooding, etc. – had been established and the full address had been given, a conoff two, also hearing the caller's voice through his earphones, was able to flip through an alphabetical card-index system on drums looking for the name of the street, while the girl on the switchboard noted the caller's telephone number. Having found the street the conoff read out the details on the card giving the route-card number, the station concerned, and the number and type of appliances that would attend a fire in that particular street. The card also listed the six nearest stations, should more appliances be needed in a make-up, and the nearest special appliances, like ETs, TLs and foam-tenders. The necessary information was duly typed out below the caller's phone number, together with the operator's initials and the time the message was received.

At a touch of a button the complete message was then transmitted to teleprinters in the relevant station watchrooms, and the fire-bell was automatically actuated. The whole process took about twenty seconds.

'Previously,' Conoff Denbeigh had said, 'the fire switchboard operator had to write everything down on Form 19 before typing out a teleprinter message. This took time, and could result in some errors being made. For instance, the operator might misunderstand what the card-index operator told her or what the caller said, or misread her handwriting, or make spelling mistakes which would again take time to correct. The station would only receive the message as fast as the operator could type it. And as nobody was specifically ever trained as a teleprinter operator by the Brigade and had to learn the job *here*, typing with two fingers, you'll appreciate why you sometimes had to hang about a bit in the station while the message was transmitted.

'It's all different now – as from this week. By the way, we're the first to get VDU.' He grinned. 'And I'm glad to say it's contagious. Croydon and Stratford will be getting it very soon.'

Conoff Denbeigh was a large, youngish man with thinning ginger hair. While he and the ET crew waited for the follow-up message from A23's station officer – 'Must be Shiner Wright in charge,' said Griffin – Denbeigh continued with his talk.

'Of course,' he said, 'although *our* end of it is much improved, we're still not much helped by some members of the public. There's the bloke who rings up from Enfield and thinks he's talking to Enfield fire-station and he'll say – "Quick! There's a fire down the road from you around the corner by the pub." He doesn't know he's talking to *us* at Wembley. . . . Then there are people who get in such a state that they can't say anything, don't know what they're doing, and forget their own flaming addresses and phone numbers. Sometimes you get a foreigner you just can't understand. I remember this Irishman who told us there was a fire in Tattygalairy, which we thought was some village in Ireland. Turned out he meant the Tate Gallery. . . . Some people get very distressed or angry and abusive when the operator has to say – "Would you repeat that?" – "I'm sorry, I didn't hear that" – "Could you spell that for me?" It's not easy for the operator. And you still get the odd ignorant person who dials 999, shouts "Fire!" and puts the phone down, thinking that's all they have to do. . . .

'You can help to cure this. Whenever you have the chance, tell people that if they ever have to dial 999 they should tell us *exactly* what the trouble is and exactly *where* it is. In that order, and as clearly and concisely as possible.'

'What happens when *we* acknowledge a call at the station?' asked Roger Davey.

'When you do that, and press a button, a light flashes at this end – which lets us know you've got the message and are on the way.'

'Howling down the Harrow Road,' said Dave.

'Listen a moment,' said Denbeigh. 'That's A23 reporting back.'

The unmistakable accents of Shiner Wright, Euston's station officer, could be heard coming through a loud-speaker at the radio operator's desk on the other side of the partition. Through the window they saw the operator flick down a switch and pick up a hand-mike.

'Alpha 23/2, from M2FN – go ahead. Over.'

'M2FN from Alpha 23/2, from Station Officer Wright. Stop for Cecil Rhodes House, Goldington Street. . . . Alarm caused by burning rubbish.'

The operator called up Wright, who was speaking via the RT in his pump, and read over the message, adding at the end after glancing at a clock: 'Time of origin, 12.04. Over.'

'M2FN from Alpha 23/2 – mobile and available. Over.'

The radio operator acknowledged this. He put his mike down and passed the message he had written out on a Form 12F to one of the switchboard operators, who typed it out and transmitted it back to A23.

'Yet another load of rubbish for Euston,' said Frank Nice to Hughes.

Although the ET crew knew how Stop messages were communicated, the actual receiving of one in the control room was a novel experience. At the same time they could well imagine the scene at the other end, with the disgruntled Shiner Wright sitting in the cold cab of his pump, disgustedly looking at a heap of smouldering rubbish and swearing at the kids who had most probably set it alight.

'Can we put our station bells down for a laugh?' Reynolds wanted to know. 'And get that Pincher Martin running about?'

'Be sensible, Reynolds,' Griffin said.

'Oh, go on!' retorted Reynolds. 'There's nothing else going on at A21. What do *you* do here when there's nothing happening?' he asked Denbeigh. 'Play cards?'

'Play cards?' repeated Dave. 'They got *women* here, haven't they? What do you think they do? Cor! I rather fancy that redhead!'

'That's all you ever think about, Webber,' Reynolds said disgustedly. 'You randy little sod. They're intellectuals here – not common like us.'

'Speak for yourself,' said Nice.

Reynolds ignored him. 'I bet they sit around with their crèmes-de-menthe watching BBC2 on their monitors. Don't you?'

'Never watch BBC,' said Denbeigh.

'Can you get it on those things?' asked Reynolds. 'Could you actually get BBC if you wanted?'

At this moment one of the more senior officers at Lambeth HQ entered the corridor – DACO (Deputy Assistant Chief Officer) Charles Clisby.

'Now then!' he said. 'I won't have you speaking in a frivolous fashion of the first fucking step forward in mobilizing appliances since the fucking war!'

Charles Clisby was a character, and liked to live up to his reputation. On this occasion, to mark his visit to Wembley and the suburbs of London he had a straw in his mouth.

He was a tall, lean man with a military manner and thin moustache. His voice was as clipped as his close-cropped greying hair. He was second-in-command of Planning and Development and in his spare time wrote verses about historical events and about the Brigade. He had gone that morning to Wembley to see for himself how his pet project, to which he had devoted himself for two years, actually worked in practice.

Several grins greeted his remarks. Chris Reynolds asked innocently: 'What fucking war is that, sir?'

Clisby removed the straw from his mouth and pointed it at Reynolds.

'Careful, my love,' he said. 'Only senior officers have permission to swear, as frequently they suffer great provocation and cannot express their feelings in any other way. Unless of course they happen to be poetical, like me! Let me tell you that what you see in the other room is a *giant step forward* for the Brigade. Have you told them, Conoff Denbeigh, what an advance the system represents? Have you stressed its utmost importance – to us and to the public?'

'I hope so, sir,' said Denbeigh.

'Transmission of messages to stations has been speeded up by five hundred per cent!' said Clisby. 'What's the system called?' he demanded of Roger Davey.

'VDU, sir.'

'Fireman, you will go far – you know the magic words. VDU! With VDU nothing will ever be the same!'

'It's a commercial for a new detergent,' whispered Garner to Dave, who whispered back: 'Sounds like a good one to go sick with though.'

'We can now progress into the computer age,' continued Clisby, addressing his captive audience in the corridor. 'Do you know that twenty years after the telephone was invented the Brigade had its first one installed? Twenty years after radio was first used, the Brigade took it up. And here we are – quarter of a century after computers were invented – just about to install a computer-based mobilizing system. VDU is the first step towards this. Let me tell you about Tesco's.'

'Tesco's, sir?' asked Reynolds, looking puzzled. 'The supermarket?'

'Yes,' said Clisby. 'Tesco's at Cheshunt use computers to mobilize their butter, eggs and lard far quicker than we mobilize our appliances.'

This raised some laughs.

'Girls,' he continued. 'Girls sitting at VDUs at Cheshunt see from an altered order form sent in by the manager of one of their many branches, say at Barking, that he only wants fifty whole cheddar cheeses instead of the usual hundred. The girl simply types the address of the branch on the VDU screen and – bingo! – in 250 milliseconds, quick as a flash, the usual order for the branch of butter, eggs, cheese, what have you, appears on the screen straight from a computer bank of information. The girl alters the number of cheeses required, presses the "Go" button, and miles away in their main despatch centre a teleprinter clatters away and up pops the order for Barking. Warehousemen run in all directions, load a lorry, and away it goes, flat out, for the branch. Now, when I first saw the Tesco system in action I thought – what a dream of a mobilizing system!'

'He must have shares in Tesco's,' muttered Garner.

'The next thing we know,' Dave murmured, 'is that we'll all be riding around in red food-trolleys in Tesco overalls.'

'Now, what I did not tell you about Tesco's,' said Clisby dramatically, 'is that the VDU *talks* to her!'

'*Talks* to her?' Reynolds was amazed.

'Yes. It talks to her – but only when she makes a mistake.' Clisby paused, still with the straw in his hand, which he was using to emphasize his words.

'Imagine she types out – "Barking Branch, 101 High Street, Lewisham". The screen flashes – "Try 101 High Street, Barking!" In other words, it tells her she has made a *mistake* and offers her an alternative. Now can't you see how useful such a system would be to *us*? For instance, if a caller gives our conoff here a wrong address, a computer would then tell him the address was *wrong* and suggest alternatives. It could even specify a certain address was near a church or on which side of a canal bridge. Think of the possibilities! Not only that. Type out the *right* address and the computer can present the full attendance required and say which appliances are available. More. All the highly desirable gen about particular hazards in a particular building, the nearest water supply, and anything else you want to know can be added. Put in *fast* printers in stations – *and* on appliances – working at 110 bands, say, instead of 50 as at present, and you have a newspaper in your hand as you turn out. In seconds. Think of *that*!'

There was no denying Clisby's enthusiasm nor the significance of what he said. The ET crew, despite themselves, were impressed, and gazed with a new respect at the VDUs in the control room.

'I see,' said Clisby triumphantly, 'that you feel as I do, like

discoverers – like the miner who sees *gold* sparkle in his pan!'
'Who got the idea in the first place?' asked Jim Griffin.
'The Chief Officer, Joe Milner,' said Clisby. 'That man has bloody nigh *revolutionized* the Brigade. He and I went to Denmark last year to see the system the police use in Copenhagen. Miraculous! Before long we'll be working miracles here!'

'Well, I *am* impressed,' said Reynolds, seriously.

'Say no more!' said Clisby. 'Praise enough. Thank Joe and God and the GLC. In that order!'

The next moment he shot into the control room as the buzzer sounded, to listen in on earphones to the call coming through and to watch the switchboard operator at work.

Beside the revolving card-index a conoff two stood ready. In the corridor, Dave once again read out the typed-out message as it appeared on the monitor of the Officer of the Watch.

'Fire . . . Rubbish chute . . . Freeling House, Boundary Road near Finchley Road . . . G26 – That's Belsize's ground. There's nothing – Yes, there is! They've called out our TL!'

'It's a block of flats,' said Denbeigh.

The ET crew buzzed with excitement and comment, thinking of the scene at Paddington where the bells at that very moment would be clanging out their summons, bringing the pump, PE, and TL crews to the appliance-room, to find that only the TL was wanted.

'Must be back on the run' – 'Who's riding it?' – 'Pincher Martin, isn't it?' – 'He's the Number One' – 'Dunlop's with it' – 'Yeah. So is Keith Cheal' – 'It's only a chute' – 'Bet they get turned around before they get there.'

They waited impatiently for the Belsize station officer's radioed report from the fire-ground. But before it came, another telephone message was received.

'*Smell of burning,*' said the typescript on the monitor screen. '*Rand Services, 53 Oxford Street.*'

'Soho's ground that end,' said Reynolds. 'Yes. There it is – A24. And look, they've called out Euston's pump and TL. Shiner's having a busy morning.'

'Quiet!' said Griffin. 'Here comes the one at Boundary Road.'

'Go ahead. Over,' said the radio operator.

'M2FN from Golf 26/2, from Station Officer Newstead. . . . Stop. Freeling House, Boundary Road . . . Rubbish. . . .'

'Told you so!' said Reynolds.

'Pincher's bashed the bell for nothing,' Garner added.

'Nearly always the way, isn't it?' remarked Nice.

'Right, lads – let's get going!' Griffin said. 'It's after twelve-thirty. Let's get the mess manager back for dinner. I want a full afternoon's work out of you lot.'

They said good-bye to Conoff Denbeigh and waved at the control room staff through the windows. Dave gave a final smile and wink at the girls.

DACO Charles Clisby raised a hand in farewell – in blissful ignorance of the tragic circumstances in which he would before long come into contact again with the Red Watch, A21.

'Everything all right?' asked Neil, putting his head around the watchroom door.

Keith Cheal was writing up the log-book. It was nearly one o'clock.

'Yes, Guv,' said Cheal. 'Everything's under control.'

'Don't forget,' said Neil, 'when the ET crew get back, they've got a BA drill at 14.30.'

He went upstairs to the mess and was tucking into a plate of gammon, egg and chips, and discussing the events of the morning with Ernie Arthurs, when Reynolds' vociferous arrival announced the late return of the ET crew. Clamouring for food and attention, they got their lunches out of the hot-plate, settled down and launched into colourful descriptions of their morning's activities.

Dave Webber threw in a few insults about Orchard's cooking abilities, seized a cheese sandwich left over from stand-easy and with a cup of tea betook himself to the TV room. Jim Griffin joined Neil and Arthurs. At the other tables the outburst of repartee and banter continued during the meal – to the general delight of the Watch, especially the Wombles, and with the particular approval of their station officer. Neil viewed their high-spirited exchanges with a paternal and professional pleasure. Their morale was high, and as this was related to efficiency, it augured well for the Watch.

Frank Nice was airing what the others claimed were some very ancient riddles. 'What's a twack?' he asked. 'What *twains* run on,' came the answer. 'Where do you weigh whales?' – 'In a *wail*way station.' 'How do you circumcise a whale?' No one spoke. 'With four skin-divers!' said Nice triumphantly. Several jokes about Irishmen were also aired – the most approved being the answer to the question: 'How do you tell it's an Irishman who works on an oil-rig?' – 'He's the one that throws bread at the helicopters!' Chris Reynolds' perspiration problem was as usual a cause for some comment. It was suggested he could make himself useful by removing his shirt, swinging it around his head and so kill all the flies in the kitchen. 'I *know* I've got a problem,' said Reynolds sadly. 'I got some pills for it and put them under each arm and it didn't make *any* difference!' The jam tart that followed the main dish occasioned more jokey criticisms of Orchard's efforts in the kitchen. But it was Ray Wade who indirectly promoted the biggest laugh. On account of his wide and toothy grin Ernie Arthurs had been referring to Ray as 'Railings' and 'Tombstones'. Then Lewis, who had said very little, suddenly came out with a classic remark which widened Ray's grin further. 'When you see Ray's teeth,' Lewis mused, 'it's like you've found where the elephants go to die.'

The ringing of the teleprinter-bell cut across the laughter. It was followed by a tannoyed message from Cheal in the watchroom.

'Pump's crew,' he said. 'Immediate relief. Oxford Street. A24.'

They finished off their cups of tea and slid down the poles to the appliance-room, where Neil glanced through the details of the teleprinter message that Cheal gave to him.

'*A21 P Stn O. Required as relief at 53 Oxford Street. KD38. A24. Last message smell of smoke, search being made. KW 1328.*'

Their journey was made at normal speed and without horn or bell. So it was not until two o'clock that the pump managed to overcome all the obstructive delays of lights and lunchtime traffic in Marylebone Road, Great Portland Street and Oxford Street and reach its port of call.

Euston's pump was parked in the middle of the narrower end of Oxford Street against a traffic island. The thirty-four storeys of Centre Point towered beyond it. Cars and buses winding either side of it increased its isolation. Brian Riley, who was driving Paddington's pump, tucked it in facing its opposite number, in front of which stood Shiner Wright, his hands on his hips.

Neil, in full fire-gear, jumped out of the cab. Shiner, likewise equipped, moved forward to greet him, grinning under his ginger moustache.

'Hallo, Neil. And about bloody time! Where the fuck have you lot been?'

'Hallo, Shiner. Isn't it time you cleaned your bloody helmet?'

Being a station officer, Shiner's helmet was a white one with a single black band. Now its surface was smudged and smirched and nearly as black as a fireman's.

'Well, I *have* got a fire-fighting ground,' said Shiner grandly. 'Not like *some* I could mention. I've been out all sodding morning – been here since half-past twelve! But even Euston's supermen have got to eat.'

'Right then,' said Neil. 'We won't keep you from your canapés. What have you got here?'

Shiner told him that the call had been to investigate a smell of burning in the office of Rand Services on the first floor of Number 53 which, Neil saw, was a narrow four-storey redbrick building dated '*1900*' at the top. The ground floor was occupied by a suede and leather boutique called '*Sir Mark*'.

Soho's pump escape, said Shiner, had been part of the first attendance – it was their ground – but they had since returned to their station, leaving him in charge. Euston's pump crew had now been there for an hour and a half and had been unable to trace the source of the smell, which was still in evidence, although nothing in the building had been or was on fire. They had taken up all the skirting at the front of the office, exposed and examined most of the wiring, taken down part of the facia surrounding the neon-sign of the boutique, checked through the whole building, including the basement, and inspected the premises on either side. They had found nothing untoward.

'We'll leave you to get on with it,' said Shiner. 'Just don't go and make it *four* pumps! And don't panic just because Euston's leaving. It's all yours. I'm off!'

There was not much for Paddington's pump crew to do that the other crews had not already done. The people in the long open-plan office, mostly girls, continued with their work as *'secretarial and office staff consultants'*, as their sign said, while the pump crew – Leroy, Marven and Dyer – set about taking apart and examining what electric fittings and floorings were still untouched. Neil associated the pungent smell in the room with some electrical fault. But although he and the other three firemen checked and re-checked everything that might be its source, they failed to identify it. One of the girls said it had been with them since Monday – at first they had thought it had been caused by the carpet which had just been cleaned.

After three-quarters of an hour the smell of burning had faded. Neil came to the conclusion that they were hunting a ghost, a smell that had drifted in from a completely innocent and separate source. He could think of nothing else that could be done. So after getting Leroy and Dyer who had started chatting to the girls to clean up – to make everything good and operational again – he went outside to the pump to send the Stop to Wembley control. It was 2.45.

'M2FN from Alpha 21/2,' he said. 'From Station Officer Wallington. Detailed Stop for 53 Oxford Street. Alarm caused by smell of smoke.'

The smoke around Dave Webber was so thick that the light from his torch, refracting and reflecting off the ash-grey impenetrable mass surrounding him, hindered more than it helped. Its diffused glare seemed further confounded by the laminated glass of his goggles, which narrowed his vision and made him twist his head to focus on his immediate predicament. It was like being buried in masses of grubby, steaming cotton-wool. At best he could only see ten inches in front of him; and the sight of his pale hands rising up like ghosts from a foggy sea as they sought and seized on protruding edges added to his unease.

To see so little was to be too aware of his difficulties in the constricted space, made more awkward by the bulk of his helmet, the apparatus of the BA set, the spring-clips on his nose,

and the clumsy rubber bar of the mouth-piece lodged between
his teeth and his gums. It was better to grope his way forward
on his belly in total darkness without using his torch: to feel
that his hands were a part of him and that in conjunction with
his arms, shoulders, back and legs were making every effort
to feel and find a way out. He worked his way forward with his
eyes closed, pretending that when he opened them it would be
in daylight and that he would be out of the basement room.

He knew roughly where he was, also that Reynolds was
ahead of him and that behind him was Garner. But this knowledge was not a comfort, being unconfirmed by any sight or
sound of them. All he heard was the thudding of his limbs as
they collided with obstructions and the measured clicks of the
valves on the set through which he was able to breathe.

He was dragging himself along with his hands and heels
through a narrow box-like tunnel, when his hands made
contact with a boot.

It had to belong to Reynolds. He shook it and it vanished.
But from the muffled confusion of sounds ahead of him, which
he heard above the throbbing of his heart, he reasoned that
Reynolds had got stuck. Reynolds' size, encumbered by all the
accoutrements of his gear, made it difficult for him to cope as
easily as a smaller man with changes of angle and direction.

As Dave lay unmoving in the darkness, tensely inactive,
waiting for Reynolds to free himself and move on, his mind
pictured what might happen if at that moment his oxygen
supply ran out, if the set failed, if something happened to
Reynolds, if they were trapped in the dark and smoke with
only poisoned fumes to breathe; and in the panic of knowing
he was powerless and liable to die he wondered how he would
react. Would he struggle? Would he cry out? Would he lie
there patiently, hoping that they would find him in time –
before his staring eyes, that saw only darkness, and his mind
that longed for light and life were slowly blanked out by unconsciousness and the ultimate darkness of his death?

He felt a hand grasp his foot and he started. Then he
realized that Garner must have moved up behind him.

Spurred into convulsive action, Dave heaved himself forward with his feet and elbows, suddenly encountering the
drop in the flooring that had held up Reynolds. A very faint

glow in the blackness on his left told him that Reynolds, who could be no more than two feet away, was invisibly standing up and trying to find his way out of the cupboard-like space into which Dave now wriggled and rearranged his limbs until he too was on his feet.

This is bloody ridiculous, he thought, groping about in the blackness for the low cross-beam which he knew to be there, barring his way across the broken floor.

He had tried to get out of being sent in with the rest of the ET crew, pleading his great experience in smoke and the fact that as mess manager he should be in the mess. But Jim Griffin had been deaf to all entreaties. None of the crew, he pointed out, had been through the Rat-run for over a month, or in smoke, and they needed to renew their acquaintance with both. It was not as if, said Griffin, they also had to go through the Humidity chamber, as the pump crews had done. And finally, if they were put down for a BA drill, then a BA drill they all would do.

Five minutes later, having negotiated the rest of the obstacles in the Rat-run – the caged-in areas of broken flooring and fallen beams – Dave emerged through the exit door into the lighted basement corridor under the appliance-room. Smoke from the canisters that had been detonated in the Rat-run followed him out.

Griffin, Reynolds, Hughes, and Nice were already standing there in their BA sets. When Garner joined them, Griffin told the six of them: 'Report to control and knock off.'

In single file they walked to the end of the corridor, where Archie Waldron (the driver of the BA control van that day) had set up a control board on which were recorded the crew's whereabouts and the time when the whistle on their BA sets would sound, warning them they had only nine minutes of oxygen left. Also slotted into the board was each man's personal tally, showing the amount of oxygen he had in his cylinder and the time of his entry into the smoke. The tallies were handed in before the firemen entered the smoke and had to be collected on the crew's exit.

This was done on this particular occasion under the watchful eye of Station Officer Powell from A27 (Chelsea). His pump crew was one of the three who had already been through the Rat-run and the Humidity chamber. Other rooms in the basement representing domestic and industrial lay-outs had not been used on this drill.

Dave and the ET crew stumped upstairs and out into the appliance-room, where they thankfully removed their nose-clips, helmets, goggles and mouth-pieces and drank in the clean, cold air and the sweet smell of diesel fuel.

'Thank Christ that bastard's over!' Reynolds said hoarsely, blowing the clotted mucus from his nose.

'I second that,' said Dave, joining in the crew's chorus of nose-clearing and coughing. 'I'm fucking knackered!'

They plodded across the appliance-room, carrying their weighty sets, and up an iron staircase to the BA room. There each man dismantled his set, cleaned the breathing-bag and disinfected the mouth-piece. The cylinders were then exchanged in the charging room next door where Sid Simmonds, the BA maintenance man for the area, handed each fireman a fresh one, fully charged.

'Had a good sweat?' asked Sid with a grin.

'Of course we bleeding have!' said Dave. 'We don't normally go round dripping like this, now do we?'

'Chris does,' Garner remarked. 'Perpetually.'

'Give over, you poncey git!' said Reynolds. 'I took enough stick from you lot this morning.'

Next they reassembled their sets, tested them, and took them downstairs to the ET, where they hung them up beside their seats.

All this took some time, and it was nearly half-past three before they left the ET after brushing down and setting out their fire-gear.

They ambled more cheerfully now across the appliance-room to the stairs.

'Come on!' said Dave, brightening up. 'Must have a cup of tea! Last one up's a ginger beer!'

He scampered up the stairs to the mess, whooping and yelling, and gleefully shouted at Orchard: 'Come on, Tosser – where's the tea? Skyving bastard, you've done eff-all all day!'

The next moment he was sliding down the pole, as the fire-bells rang through the station.

'Those bloody sods at Wembley!' he wailed as he hit the

mat. 'I need my bleeding cuppa more than I need a shout!'

The blue and yellow lights went on above the folding doors.

'ET and TL!' called Griffin, coming out of the watchroom. 'Let's have you!' he snapped at the ET crew, who were dawdling by the poles. 'This isn't Cropper's End!'

They piled into their machine – Griffin and Garner up front; Dave, Reynolds, Nice, Davey and Hughes in the rear. As they worked themselves back into the fire-gear and BA sets which they had just taken off, Dave called out to Griffin.

'Where are we going? What is it?'

'AFA actuating,' Griffin shouted above the sudden blast of the horn as the emergency tender moved out of the appliance-room after the TL.

'Grosvenor House Hotel, Park Lane!'

'Jesus Christ!' yelled Dave 'Not *another!*'

He adjusted the shoulder-straps of his set and slumped back on his seat, cursing the demands made on a fireman's time and nervous energy by over-sensitive alarm systems and easily alarmed people. It was bound to be another futile outing, he felt. Yet, as he knew, there was always the chance he could be wrong.

With the ball in his hands Ray Wade froze, looking over his shoulder. On either side of the volley-ball net the other firemen in the floodlit yard halted, switching their eyes and ears away from the game to the appliance-room and the ringing of the teleprinter-bell. Nothing followed its warning. They relaxed.

It was twenty-two minutes to five. The wintry dusk had given place to night and the wind had died. But it was still as cold.

'Come on, Ray,' said Riley. 'Keep it going or we'll all freeze to bloody death.'

'I'm bloody frozen already,' said Waldron.

Ray punched the ball over to Leroy, who smashed it over the net. Waldron returned it, and so the game continued – the Wombles versus the Old'uns.

It had started ten minutes earlier at half-past four. Fifteen minutes before that the ET and TL crews had returned with blighted hopes and weary resignation from the shout at Park Lane.

They had had some difficulty getting there – heavy traffic and parked cars getting in their way – and coming back without the benefit of bell or horn both machines had been involved in a snarl-up of rush-hour traffic at Marble Arch. The shout itself, at the Grosvenor House Hotel, had been caused by another automatic fire-alarm accidentally going off. A26's station officer had sent them back as soon as they arrived. They were now upstairs in the mess, warming themselves with cups of tea and enjoying a very belated stand-easy.

In the yard the volley-ball game had hardly got going when the teleprinter-bell sang out again. Again the firemen stopped where they were and waited – the ball was in Wickenden's hands.

'It's just got to be *this* time,' said Leroy.

The fire-bells clanged out shockingly.

Ray moved with the others at a fast pace towards the machines. Wickenden dropped the ball. Falling at speed down the poles came the ET and TL crews. The Number Ones on each appliance who were not already in the watchroom ran towards it. The rest of the firemen hovered beside their machines, waiting for details and watching the lights.

Ray saw them flash into colour – red, green, yellow – for the pump escape, the pump, and the turntable ladders.

The ET crew gave an ironic cheer.

It was Ray's first shout that day. Automatically he stepped into his boots, pulled up his leggings and climbed into the cab. Nicholls and Wickenden followed him in, slamming the doors. Orchard started the engine. Ernie Arthurs pulled himself into the Number One seat, holding a route-card.

'Harrow Road, junction with Ladbroke Grove,' Ray heard him say to Orchard. 'North Kensington's ground. You know the way. Let's get going! All on?'

'All on,' said Ray.

'What have we got?' shouted Wickenden above the noise of horn and engine as the PE swung left into Harrow Road, its headlights full on.

'Fire!' Arthurs called out. 'At a pub. The King William. Could be a job!'

Ray refused to let his mind dwell on the possibility. It was not something at the end of the day that he viewed with pleasure or excitement. He hoped it was nothing serious – even a false alarm – like the hoax-call the PE had had the evening before at about the same time to Ladbroke Lower School. Harry had been with him on that occasion.

As the PE roared along the westbound carriageway of Harrow Road under Westway, Ray recalled that Arthurs had gone to Kensington in the morning as a temporary relief for the station officer there. He had only been there an hour and a half and on his return told Ray he had seen Harry playing volley-ball with some of the Kensington Red Watch. They had not had any shouts.

'He sent his love,' said Arthurs jokingly, and Ray had replied, smiling broadly – 'That's nice.'

He did not feel like smiling now. He had been looking forward to an early relief – to getting away early and picking up Harry at Kensington, then Mick at Knightsbridge and Alan at Westminster. Once Ray had set his mind on something he did not welcome any change or interference. Now he sat gloomily in the swaying cab of the PE, which led the clamorous cavalcade of A21's appliances through Kensal Town, with Ernie Arthurs repeatedly battering at the bell.

Four minutes after leaving the station they reached the junction named in the message. But the pub they found there was called The Plough.

A fireman stepped into the road and waved them on.

'Further up!' Ray heard him shout. 'On the right!'

The three machines moved on, and almost immediately the PE crew caught sight of North Kensington's PE, parked on the junction of Harrow Road and Warfield Road under a large red neon-sign – TAKE COURAGE – and beside an ample building called The William IV.

'Never get it right, do they?' grumbled Arthurs as the PE swerved across the road to halt behind the other PE.

He jumped out. Ray and the other three did likewise, as the pump drew up behind them. The TL halted in the side street. Their crews also dismounted, spreading out on the pavement. No sight or smell of a fire met their senses. The pub's doors were barred, its windows dark.

'Have a look around,' Neil told the crews.

They did so, as far as they could. Ray walked up the side

street. But A29's PE crew had already checked out the back of the building and had found nothing to report.

He returned to the front of the building to find that Neil had joined up with Sub Officer Gamble, who was acting up as A29's station officer in the absence of Tom Barrett on a course. They were standing by Gamble's pump escape and having already ascertained from the pub's occupants that there was no fire inside, Gamble was now having the address verified by Wembley control. The rest of the firemen gathered near their appliances, waiting patiently for developments, watched by a fat old woman, two skinny boys and three shabby-looking black men.

Ray went towards A21's PE and stood with Orchard near a telephone box in the middle of the pavement. The orange glow from the overhead street-lights gave every man's features and vaporous breath a jaundiced hue and threw sulphurous shadows on the high brick wall concealing Kensal Green cemetery across the road.

Wembley's reply came crackling over the RT – the address had been correctly transmitted.

'Ask them to check where the call came from,' said Gamble.

His driver repeated the request into the hand-mike.

'What do you think?' asked Neil.

'It's nothing,' said Gamble and shrugged.

'Pity it's not opening-time, Guv,' said Leroy, who had been dutifully following Neil around.

Neil glanced at him disparagingly and examined the tele-printer slip he was holding to check on the caller's telephone number.

'969 0995,' he said. 'What's the number of the box there?' he called out to Ray and Orchard. 'You go too, Leroy,' he added.

Ray peered through the glass at the dial.

'969 . . . 1647,' he called out. Orchard entered the box and lifted the receiver.

'It's working all right,' he said.

'That just about proves it,' remarked Ray to Leroy. 'If there *had* been a fire in this pub, they would have called us up from *here*. Would have been daft not to.'

The PE's RT transmitted Wembley's reply – the call reporting the fire had come from a telephone box at the junction of Kilburn Lane and Harrow Road.

'That's two hundred yards back the way we came,' Neil said.

'Yeah,' said Gamble. 'The Lane's the continuation of Ladbroke Grove. The bloody box must be up the road from The Plough.'

They looked at each other then looked away. The eighteen firemen who had raced to the scene had drawn another dud.

'That's it then,' said Neil disgustedly. 'Malicious. All right – you send the Stop. We're off.'

'We'll see you,' said Gamble and picked up his PE's hand-mike to call up Wembley control.

The Stop went out at 4.54 p.m., nine minutes after the bells had gone down in the two stations, to which the four appliances now returned, their crews reacting with anger or dull acceptance to their wasted journey.

Ray was silent. Normally he would have joined in the exchange of comments between Nicholls and Wickenden in the back of the cab and Ernie Arthurs up front. But what he had half hoped for had happened – it had been a false alarm, and now they were returning to base much sooner than they would have done from a fire. In the event this did not please him. Inevitably, as a fireman, he felt the frustration of having only two shouts in the two full days he had come to work – and both had been malicious. This and the actual gross misuse of the station's capabilities now served to revive his earlier feeling of gloom.

He stared unseeing at the dismally illumined premises along the Harrow Road, which was now crammed with cars at the start of the rush-hour and whose traffic-lights always seemed to be at red.

The bump as the PE swung into the yard through the rear gate and the single horn-note announcing their return aroused him.

It was always good to be home again, and Ray's depression lifted when he saw Harry standing outside the appliance-room, silhouetted against the empty bays.

Ray grinned and Harry raised a hand as the PE glided past him and came to a stop by the watchroom.

'Thank you, driver,' said Arthurs in the customary way.

'Thank you, Number One,' replied Orchard.

Ray jumped to the ground and Harry came towards him as the appliance-room filled with the sounds of the returning pump and TL and their crews.

'How was it?' asked Harry. He was wearing a pale blue V-necked sweater over a dark blue T-shirt.

'It was a bloody mickey.'

'No, I meant your day. I know about the shout.'

'A real let-down,' said Ray. 'How about you?'

'I had a good time. They're a lively lot.'

'Hold on,' said Ray. 'I'll see if I can get an early relief.'

He went into the now crowded watchroom, followed by Harry, and found a White Watch fireman, who had come in early, to act as his relief. He asked for Neil's permission and told the duty-man, who removed Ray's name from the nominal-roll board of riders on the pump escape.

Harry remained in the watchroom while Ray quickly got out of his fire-gear in the uniform room, leaving it hanging neatly on some pegs.

A few minutes later, after changing his overall trousers for a pair of slacks up in the dormitory and putting on the rest of his civvies, he was back in the watchroom and eager to leave. An acrid smell of smoke from the BA drill in the Rat-run still lingered in the hallways and on the stairs.

'Wait a minute, Harry!' he said, remembering something. 'I better see what I'm on tomorrow.'

'I've had a look at the board,' said Harry. 'You're on stand-by at Kensington.'

'Sod it!' Ray exclaimed. 'Where are *you*?'

'Here. On the PE. They've swopped us round.'

'That's all I bloody well need!'

'Never mind, partner,' Harry said. 'You'll be all right there. You'll see. Come on – I want to get home.'

From the window of the inner office Neil noted the departure of Ray Wade's white Cortina as it sped up the road to the roundabout. He secured the louvre section he had opened to let in some fresh air, thereby also increasing the noise of home-going traffic on Westway and in the Harrow Road.

Christmas trees decked with coloured lights blazed in the windows of the flats diagonally opposite the station. Seeing them, he remembered that two boxes of decorations belonging to Paddington had been lent to Euston and never returned – and that at lunchtime Chris Reynolds had asked if he and some of the other firemen could decorate the second floor and the mess for Christmas.

Picking up the internal phone Neil got through to Euston's watchroom and asked to speak to Station Officer Wright. But when Shiner Wright responded, Neil's next question was forestalled by an outburst of amiable abuse about a certain visit Euston had just made to Oxford Street. It appeared that A23 and A24 had been summoned back to the offices of Rand Services at quarter to five to re-investigate a smell of smoke.

'You can't rely on Paddington to do *anything* properly!' complained Shiner. 'That wasn't much of a detailed Stop, was it? Did you get bored – or not want to miss your afternoon tea? Frigging Paddington rub-outs!'

Despite Neil's amused protests, Shiner carried on to say that Soho and Euston had found the cause of the trouble within ten minutes of their second visit. The smell of burning had come from an overheated transformer below the ceiling of the suede and leather shop on the ground floor. He had only just got back, said Shiner, and was sweaty and horrible, and was going to hand over now to the White Watch.

'About these decorations!' interrupted Neil.

'What decorations?'

'Those you purloined from us many moons ago.'

'I don't know *what* you're bloody talking about!' Shiner exclaimed.

'Come off it, Shiner,' retorted Neil. 'They're *our* Christmas decorations and we want to put them up.'

'I would have thought there's enough bloody fairies and tinsel at Paddington to decorate the whole Division!'

Neil laughed. 'All right, Shiner,' he said, knowing he would get no further that evening. 'I'll ring you tomorrow night.'

'If you catch us in, that is,' said Shiner boastfully. 'Euston's a busy ship, laddie! Not like A21, Hollywood. Cheers!'

Smiling, Neil put down the phone, sat back and slackened the knot of his tie. Such badinage was typical of Shiner, and typical of most jocular exchanges between station officers, each of whom prided himself on his own station and thought it was the best in the Division.

Neil got to his feet. Now what did he have to do? . . . There was the drill-book to sign, the fuel-books as well as the outside visits book to check, the petty cash to count, the handing-over book to be written up, and a queue of firemen waiting for their reliefs to be sanctioned.

He was about to unlock the safe when the sound of a car stopping by the forecourt made itself heard above the general hubbub of traffic outside. His curiosity aroused, he crossed to the window and looked out.

Dave Webber's battered blue Consul had pulled in to the kerb, and he was offering a lift to a tall pedestrian in a sheep-skin coat, whom Neil identified in a moment as the newest recruit, Leroy Hough.

He watched the car drive away and wondered what the two firemen would have to say to each other.

'Where are you going?' Dave had asked.

'Charing Cross or Victoria,' Leroy had answered.

'Okay, jump in. I'll drop you off at Victoria.'

'Terrific. Thanks.'

Dave had spent the last half hour in the mess, making it tidy for the White Watch and washing up the cups of tea that the crews returning from the Harrow Road shout had made for themselves. Then at half-past five he had found himself an early relief and soon afterwards he left the station in his car.

Seeing Leroy walking up the road he had pulled up in front of him. Apart from Leroy's assertive cockney accent, Dave recognized in him a style of behaviour and a manner similar to his own at that age, and although he was only two years older than Leroy, he felt he might be able to offer him some advice.

For a minute or so he said nothing. Then, when they halted at an intersection with Praed Street, he said casually – 'What do you think of it so far?'

'Great!' said Leroy. 'It's better than bleeding training-school.'

'Yeah,' Dave nodded. 'Had any shouts?' he asked.

'Four,' said Leroy. 'Nothing special. No *flames*. In fact,' he admitted, 'I haven't done anything.'

'You will,' Dave assured him.

'Yeah. . . . Well. . . . What exactly should – I mean, what do you do when you pull up at a job?'

'Pick up something,' Dave replied. 'Like a line or an extinguisher. And stay with one of the older hands. . . . You'll soon learn how it goes.'

He swung the car left into the mainstream of traffic on Bayswater Road, heading for Marble Arch and out of A21's ground.

'It's been dead quiet since I been here,' said Leroy.

'What do you expect after two days?' Dave retorted. 'As it happens, just lately we've gone through a very quiet patch. Don't expect too much all at once,' he warned. 'You may not like it.'

Leroy sighed. 'Yeah. . . . Well. . . . It would be just my luck to pick up a big job tomorrow night,' he said.

*

That night the White Watch had five shouts, as many as those they had on the previous night.

As it happened, their first call at 7.20 p.m., on A21's ground, was to release a person shut in a lift at Randolph Road – not a hundred yards from the Worsley Hotel in Clifton Gardens, where a fire would be lit the following night that would bring injury and death to the Red Watch. It might have happened that Wednesday night when the White Watch were on duty – and it might then have happened differently, with different firemen involved. But it was the White Watch, not the Red, who went in the station's pump escape and pump to Randolph Road on the Wednesday night, and it was the White Watch who then took the TL to a nurses' home in Foley Street at 7.25 p.m. to investigate a smell of smoke. They found nothing. But what seemed like being a routine night was broken at 7.43 by a call for the ET to an explosion at the In and Out Club in Piccadilly.

It was on A26's ground, and the incident turned out to be less dramatic than had appeared at first from the message. A small explosive device had been thrown through a ground-floor window of the club, causing a small fire. Shots were fired at pursuing taxi-drivers by the escaping bombers. But no one was injured and the ET was not required. The Stop was sent out by ADO Tom Rowley an hour later – towards the end of a TV series called *The Streets of San Francisco*, which some of the Watch were viewing. The episode that night was about the suspicious death of a man in a hotel fire.

Immediately the programme ended, at 8.59 p.m., the bells went down in Paddington again. The call this time was for the pump – to a rubbish fire in Conlan Street on North Kensington's ground. After midnight the White Watch were roused once only, when the TL was called again to North Kensington, to Marks and Spencer's warehouse in Hythe Road. It was another false alarm.

At 9 a.m. on the morning of Thursday 12 December, the White Watch went home, and the Blue Watch took over.

Their nine-hour duty that day was a busy one: not a pleasant one either. It was bitterly cold and rained or sleeted most of the time. In their first half-hour they had three shouts – the ET, TL and PE being called respectively to the Grosvenor House Hotel, to Bourne and Hollingsworth, and to Whiteley's, a store in Queensway. All were false alarms, caused by fire-alarms accidentally actuating themselves. At 12.50, the pump and PE were called to a garage on North Kensington's ground to assist A29's PE right a car that had got into a precarious position on a ramp. At 2.40 p.m., the ET returned to the Grosvenor House Hotel yet again on another wildgoose chase caused by an AFA. At 3.03, the PE, the pump and the TL rushed to a fire in a block of flats in Kilburn Park Road. They found no fire, and after checking the call classified it as malicious. Finally, at 4.36, the pump was called to an explosion on A22's ground, at Harewood Avenue – a pillar-box had blown up. They stood by for over an hour in the wet and freezing darkness while police and bomb squad experts combed the area in case another device had been planted there. Nothing was found. A22's pump returned to Manchester Square. But Paddington's pump was detained at the request of the police until 6.20 p.m., when the acting station officer on the Blue Watch, Sub Officer Nobby Hall, sent out the Stop –

'*Street pillar letter-box damaged by fire and explosion. Hose-reel.*' The explosion had been caused by an electrical fault in a cable under the pavement.

By this time the Red Watch were already on duty. They had left their homes and families at various times after sunset, and as they came into London to start the first of their two night-duties, most of the city's populace were heading out, escaping from their offices and businesses, factories and places of work. Twenty-two men of the Red Watch, Paddington, reported for duty that night, as did about 1500 of their colleagues on the other Red Watches at every one of the London Fire Brigade's 114 stations.

At 6.0 p.m., at all these stations in the metropolis, a roll-call and a parade were held, and the firemen settled down to watch and wait, ready to deal with the unknown dangers that accident, malice and error could bring to others, and to themselves.

Before the night's end, more than a hundred of them would meet – brought together on Paddington's ground to fight the worst and most fatal fire in the Division that year.

Thursday 12 December

That afternoon Malcolm Jackson went to a funeral. It was the second one he had attended that day. At noon he had driven the hearse carrying the floral tributes from the deceased's house to Kensington cemetery in Gunnersbury Park where, after helping to arrange the many wreaths at the graveside during a fall of sleet, he had been one of the four who solemnly lowered the coffin into the grave. The service over, he had taken the hearse back to the funeral parlour and loaded it with another coffin for a cremation, which was to take place at the West London crematorium at 2.15 p.m. He then returned with the hearse to its base at the funeral parlour, where after donning a water-proof motor-cycle suit, a crash-helmet, black gloves and a visor, he mounted his Honda 90 and drove off to a squash club in North Kensington.

Unable to get a game there, he watched some other games being played, passing the time pleasantly until he was due to report to Paddington fire-station for the first of his two night-duties that week. The two previous days he had been away on leave. Very occasionally, to help a friend, he worked in his spare time as an undertaker's assistant, in which he was assisted not only by his strength, but also by his saturnine dark good looks and his trim and sombre Spanish imperial beard, the only one that was tolerated in the Division.

Jacko, as he was known by his colleagues at Paddington, was probably the most respected fireman on the Watch – very professional and conscientious about his job, forthright in character, devastatingly frank in speech, and very fit. He was thirty-five, and since the retirement of Jack Hallifax at the age of fifty-one in November, Jacko was now regarded as the senior hand, with a special responsibility for the well-being and guidance of the younger firemen. For a brief period he had been a leading fireman, but at his own request he had reverted to the rank of fireman, valuing more the close comradeship of the mess than the complications of leadership and office-work. Yet in the mess he guarded his independence, not showing a preference for anyone's company and being as blunt about his closest friend, Martin Walker, as he was about himself.

Martin was a year younger. Both men were married – Jacko for the second time – and lived in North London. Jacko and his wife had a flat in a disused fire-station at Tottenham. He and Martin had been firemen together for nine years – initially at A22 (Manchester Square) – being posted to Paddington when the new station was opened. Martin had none of Jacko's extrovert qualities; he was reserved, sensitive and quiet, although the calm exterior was sometimes broken by flashes of dry wit and a sharp temper. What he and Jacko most obviously had in common was a near-fanatical interest in keeping fit, which had recently concentrated on playing squash. They did so two or three times a week, and Martin, who in his youth had played football for Winchester City and had signed for Southampton FC as an amateur when a cartilage injury ruined his chances, usually won.

On that Thursday afternoon Martin, also back on duty that night, was in his capacity as mess manager out buying the necessary stores for the Watch's next two suppers and breakfasts. So it was that Jacko, on his own at the squash club and not finding another partner for a game, left early and drove through North Kensington to Paddington, where he arrived at about 4.45 – the first of the Red Watch to report for duty that night.

He found that he would be riding the turntable ladders, as their driver and operator, and after officially relieving the Blue Watch TL driver at 5.00 p.m., he put his fire-gear on the machine, changed into his overalls and began a lengthy check on the TL to ensure that it was in full working order. Twenty minutes later, undisturbed by any shouts – the pump was away, he had learned, on a shout at Harewood Avenue – he left the neon-lit appliance-room and went upstairs to wash.

As he passed the watchroom, the Blue Watch duty-man called out to him – a teleprinter message had just come through from the Ops room at Lambeth with a warning that strong north-west winds would exceed thirty knots that night.

This was of particular concern to the driver of the turntable ladders whose stability in extension would be threatened by high winds.

A loud banging and some violent language greeted Jacko when he entered the dormitory bed-section he inhabited. On investigation he discovered a tall youth he had never seen before thumping a tin locker at the far end of the section.

'You having some trouble?' asked Jacko in a strong south London accent.

The youth calmed himself. 'I left me sodding locker-key at home,' he said despondently. 'And I don't want to have to tell the Governor as it makes me look like a bleeding amateur. Have you got a knife?'

'I got something better,' said Jacko. 'Leave it to me.'

He went to his own locker, opened it and took out a fireman's axe, a spare one he kept in case of need. With the help of its blade and his biceps he soon forced open the other locker's door.

'All right?' asked Jacko.

'Yes. Thanks,' said the youth and smiled.

'You're new, aren't you?' Jacko demanded. 'What's your name?'

'Yeah. It's my first night. I'm – er – Lee.'

'I'm Jacko. Welcome on board!'

They shook hands.

'Did you say "Lee"?' queried Jacko, sensing a certain awkwardness about the announcement. 'Is that your proper name?' He stared at the boy, who was several inches taller, with a fixed and demanding gaze.

'No,' confessed the youth, becoming abashed. 'It's not. It's – um – Leroy. . . .'

Jacko's eyes brightened. '*Leroy!*' he exclaimed. 'Christ, the Brigade *is* getting desperate – getting Wombles from America! Well, anyway,' he added more restrainedly, 'we all forget our keys sometimes. They keep spares in the office safe. The Governor won't eat you – not in the first week anyway. Still, don't make a habit of it.'

'No,' said Leroy. 'Thanks.'

Jacko returned his axe to his locker, on whose inner door was a photo of his wife, Margaret, and a list of various things he had to remember to do. He then walked around to the kitchen, hoping to see Martin there. His expectation was gratified, for Martin was unloading various stores from a cardboard box onto the hatch. He had just walked up the stairs after parking his car in the yard and was still in his civvy clothes. A tall, athletic man, he had brush-like hair without a parting, which was flecked with grey. But his hands were his most notable feature. He had very long, large fingers which Jacko was wont to say were like marlin-spikes.

'Evening, Mart!' said Jacko.

'Hallo, Jacko. Did you get a game in today?'

'No. I couldn't get a match. But I'll wop you tomorrow.'

'Will you give me a hand with the rest of the heavy stuff?' asked Martin. 'I've got some more to bring up from below.'

'Okay,' said Jacko. 'We might as well wear the Old'uns out first. Come on.'

The Red Watch went on duty at 6.0 p.m.

Roll-call was as usual held in the appliance-room and the parade was taken by Neil Wallington. His sub officer, Paul Taylor, gave the orders and detailed the riders, including the pump crew, although they were temporarily without a machine.

Taylor's return to duty, together with that of Jacko, Martin, and Joe Forrest, heightened the pitch of experience in the Watch and meant that a substantive officer would be in charge of each appliance. Tony Stewart was back on duty from Chelsea, and Harry Pettit from Kensington, whither Ray Wade had already gone on standby.

Ten firemen happened not to be on duty that night. It was the turn of five of them for rota leave – Norman Wooldridge, Frank Nice, Roger Davey, Winger Hughes, and Martin Nicholls who would be twenty-one the next day, 13 December. Pete Morris was still away on a driving-course. Ted Cheer and Phil House were now on annual leave, and off on PH (public holiday) leave were Brian Riley and Chris Reynolds.

Twenty-two remained; and depending on their qualifications and seniority and on Griffin's selection when he roughed out the roll-call board the day before, they had been detailed to ride particular appliances and to take on certain duties for the next fifteen hours, until 9.0 a.m.

On the pump escape were Jim Griffin, Keith Orchard, Harry Pettit, Kevin Cheal and Leroy Hough. On the pump were Neil Wallington, Roger Lewis, Paul Marven, Tony Stewart and Kevin Wickenden. Ernie Arthurs, Malcolm Jackson and Dave Dyer were on the turntable ladders; and in the emergency tender were Paul Taylor, Malcolm Garner, Martin Walker, Archie Waldron, Pincher Martin, Bob Dunlop and Dave Webber. Dave was also mess assistant. Driving the BA control van was Mick Haskard. The driver of the Divisional van was Joe Forrest. Dave Dyer was the duty-man in the watchroom.

Neil, with Paul Taylor at his side, stood in front of the crews and drivers, looking them over as they answered their names and then heard to which appliance and duties they had been detailed.

Joe Forrest made a face when he was named as the Divisional van driver – it meant he would be ferrying equipment, packages and reports about the Division that night as required, and would not be riding to any fire. But no one else gave any sign of displeasure or aversion and in Neil's eyes they looked especially alert. All of them were not only glad to be back on duty, but glad because it was a *night* duty. Nights were special.

After an hour and a half of drills between 6.30 and 8.0 p.m., the firemen's time was their own, to be spent in whatever way they pleased – playing billiards, darts or table-tennis, watching television, studying, overhauling their cars, swopping stories, jokes and points of view over cups of tea or coffee or halves of beer, in the mess or in the bar. They had supper at 8 o'clock and breakfast at 8.0 a.m. the following morning. They went to bed when they pleased after 11.0 p.m. It was like being at a club.

Wives would complain, half-jokingly, about this aspect of the job, saying their men just couldn't wait to get out of the house and off to work. More seriously they viewed the absence of their men for two long lonely nights – which could turn into three complete days if the wives worked during the day and the home was a long way out of London – with silent worry and dislike. At night, the dangers of the job seemed to the women more real, and their husbands' return the day after the second night-duty, which was followed by two days off work, was greeted by the women with sometimes ill-concealed relief. The men were also glad to be home again with their families, and this division of their lives into home and away, into clearly defined and separate areas of responsibility, interest and loyalty, fulfilled a basic masculine need. The result was that firemen as a breed were remarkably well-balanced and content, as were their marriages – if and when the wives, as most of them did, came to terms with the demands of the job.

These demands were exaggerated at night. Because of the darkness, any difficulties and dangers at a shout would be increased. This put the firemen more on their mettle and was also more of a welcome trial of their skills and resolve. Apart from this, the drama of their occupation intensified at night. People depended more on them when the rest of the city slept; and from the moment the bells went down, summoning the firemen from whatever they were doing and from their slumbers, their task took on an added significance and its external aspects were enhanced – the flashing lights, the red machines, the sound of horn and bell, the roaring ride to the rescue through deserted city streets, the noisy pumps at work, the wet and the cold and the lurid light of flames. At night the firemen lived an augmented existence, and experienced then, as they put it, what the job was really all about.

'Red Watch – Shun! Red Watch for duty – Fall out!'

Neil Wallington went upstairs to the office after telling the duty-man, young Dave Dyer, to let him know when the Stop came through from Harewood Avenue. The last message from Nobby Hall at 5.50 p.m., had been that A21's pump had been detained there at the request of the police. Wembley control had added that Euston's pump would be relieving the Paddington crew after six o'clock.

Neil settled down in his office to tackle the backlog of routine paperwork and to draft a probationary report on Fireman Nicholls upon the conclusion of his first six months at Paddington.

In the meantime Griffin started working out the availability and duties of the Watch on Friday night, while Taylor glanced through the handing-over book to see what had happened during his two days off duty. He then had a look at the station diary and saw that the Watch would have no extra visits, duties, drills or visitors to disturb their routine.

Being a sub officer and Neil's second-in-command, Paul Taylor shared much of the station officer's responsibilities and deputized for Neil in his absence. He was the same age as Neil – thirty-two – and his bright and cheerful disposition offset some of the more deadpan characters and comments in the mess. In fact he had an almost boyish enthusiasm for his job, not unlike Neil's, and his intelligent interest in it had led to him being a senior officer with the Fire Brigade's Union. At 6 feet 2 inches and 14½ stone he was one of the largest men in the Watch. He had been a fireman for twelve years, and lived with his wife and two children in a village near High Wycombe.

He put the diary back on Neil's desk.

'Looks like a nice quiet Thursday night,' he said happily. 'Just what I need to get back into the routine!'

At 6.25, Harry Pettit, in undress uniform and cap, reported to the office before going down to the Divisional offices to be interviewed by DO Bob Keable, who was the senior officer in charge of 'A' Division that night. Harry's probationary report, which had been written up by Neil some weeks earlier, together with ADO Rowley's report on the probationers' drills Harry had done the previous week, would be fully discussed at the interview, after which all the reports and recommendations on him would be forwarded to Lambeth. In Neil's opinion, with which Keable and Rowley both agreed, Harry Pettit had the most promise of all the recruits.

'I'm going down to Staff now, Jim,' said Harry.

'Right-ho,' Griffin said. 'Good luck. Away you go. And see the Staff sub officer first.'

As Harry left, Dyer came into the office carrying a tele-printer slip and brought it through to Neil. It was the Stop for Harewood Avenue.

'Good,' said Neil. 'That means the pump will be back soon and we can get *our* gear on board.'

Dyer returned to the watchroom and depressed the switch that rang six bells at 6.30 p.m. 'All working hands to the appliance-room,' said Taylor over the tannoy.

He and Neil had decided earlier that the drill period would be taken up with a session in firemanship about knots and lines. Taylor had thought that the Wombles in particular would benefit from some practical revision of the knots that might be used to secure lines to objects in different emergencies. From his office desk Neil could now see Taylor organizing the drill squad, getting them to fetch a scaling ladder and lines from the PE, after which he took them, thus equipped, out of the chill appliance-room into the warmer, more comfortable uniform room for the session.

Ernie Arthurs, who had started work on the necessary documentation relating to Leroy Hough's posting to Paddington, suddenly appeared at the door.

'Excuse me, Guv – why's Fireman Hough on the PE tonight?'

'I wanted to have Stewart under my eye on the pump – both nights,' said Neil. 'His probation drills are coming up shortly.'

'Oh. Right-ho, Governor. I'll leave you. I see you're snowed under with paperwork. I'll get on with me knitting.'

He grinned and went away and Neil once more set his mind to drafting Nicholls' report. But hardly had he picked up his pen when the pump returned. It slid into position in the second bay of the appliance-room.

'The pump is now on the run,' announced Dyer over the tannoy. 'Check your riding positions.'

Neil threw his biro on the desk, leapt to his feet, and went downstairs to the uniform room, where he collected his white station officer's helmet, belt and axe, boots, leggings and tunic. The session on knots and lines in the main part of the room was temporarily disrupted as Tony Stewart, Lewis, Marven, and Wickenden also gathered up their gear.

'Great heavens!' Taylor exclaimed. 'We *have* done well. We had at least ten minutes before the first interruption. Hurry back, lads.'

The Blue Watch crew were already wearily climbing the stairs when Neil and the pump crew entered the appliance-room to place their gear on and beside the pump.

'Check all your levels, Roger,' said Neil. 'The pump's been fairly busy today.'

Marven, Stewart and Wickenden returned to the uniform room while Lewis set about checking the pump's fuel tank and working equipment.

Neil ran upstairs to the office where, after deputizing Pincher Martin to fetch a cup of tea for Nobby Hall, he and the other Red Watch officers heard details of the Blue Watch crew's experiences at Harewood Avenue.

'I hope we don't have any bleeding bangs to attend to tonight,' said Neil.

In common with the other firemen in 'A' Division, which covered central London, they were anxious about any repetition of the bomb-blast in the In and Out Club the previous night. The morning papers had been full of it, coinciding as it did with the Commons vote in the hanging debate – a majority of 152 MPs had voted against the restoration of a death sentence – and the evening papers and radio news were now reporting that the two men who'd been charged with murder after the Guildford pub explosions had also been charged that day with murder as a result of the Woolwich pub explosion. Moreover, in Birmingham, seventeen people had been remanded for another week on charges of murder and of causing explosions there. It was disquieting, particularly as firemen did not relish being involved in any kind of anti-social political action. If, for instance, the situation arose in which they were requested by the police to turn their jets on a rioting crowd, many would be most reluctant to do so. The firemen's view was that they were primarily a priority rescue and emergency service, ready to assist in any humanitarian need, and not an aid to law enforcement.

It was not until 7.0 p.m. that Nobby Hall left the office and the discussion about bomb incidents. He had had one hell of a day, he said – five false alarms, a cock-eyed car, and an exploding pillar-box. 'We'll be losing our touch as *fire*men soon,' he said. 'Anyway, Guv, I'll love you and leave you. Have a quiet night. I'll see you in the morning.'

Neil returned to the inner office, closed the door and sat himself down once again at his desk. He picked up his biro, and gazed out into the appliance-room, wondering what the night would bring.

A fireman came swiftly down one of the poles – Harry

Pettit. He was in his overalls, and Neil surmised that after the interview with DO Keable Harry had gone straight upstairs to change before joining the rest of the Watch doing knots and lines.

Someone in the main office knocked three times on the glass wall and must have mimed a question about the interview, for Harry looked up, smiled and gave a thumbs-up sign.

'How did you get on?' Taylor inquired as Harry came into the uniform room.

'Pretty fair.'

'Jolly good,' said Taylor. 'Come in and join the throng. Jacko's showing us how to tie a cat's-paw.'

'The cat's not enjoying it,' Stewart said. 'And that makes two of us. Otherwise, we're having a thrill a minute.'

Harry went and stood between Orchard and Dyer, who had also joined the drill squad. There were now twelve of them standing against a background of the other Watch's fire-gear, and besides Jacko and Stewart they included Lewis, Cheal, Wickenden and Leroy. Marven and Dunlop were sitting on the cleaning-table and Archie Waldron lounged against it. The session was a relaxed one, and Taylor had given them permission to smoke.

He had asked each of the squad in turn to choose one of the twenty knots in the drill-book, then demonstrate how it was tied and untied, and explain its particular use. The first six firemen had naturally chosen the easier knots. Jacko's choice – he was next – had been a knot he considered to be un-complicated but interesting, although as he said – 'It's hardly ever used on a job. Anyway, *I've* never seen it used in anger, or at all.'

With the rope stretched between finger and thumb he made a loop with both hands, twisted each length into a spiral and then brought the two loops together.

'Its function,' he explained, 'is to assist in the pulling apart of irregular-shaped beams and baulks, as at a rubbish fire.'

'Fair enough,' said Taylor. 'But what are its other uses?'

'I was just about to expatiate on them,' remarked Jacko coolly, 'when I was interrupted.'

'He's so bloody cultured,' muttered Waldron.

'Let's hear them then!' said Taylor.

Speaking slowly, almost ponderously, Jacko outlined the other uses of the knot. He always chose his words with some care, relishing the sound and strangeness of some and the shock value of others.

When he had finished his discourse, Taylor beamed and said – 'Okay, Jacko. Not bad. Ninety-seven per cent. . . . All right, Stewart. Now let's see what *you* can do.'

'Great!' said Stewart. 'Watch this. Rolling hitch in the middle of the line.'

Tony Stewart had been at Paddington for nine months, and at twenty-nine was the oldest of the recruits. Previously he had been with the RAF at Medmenham as a records and documents clerk. He was a broad and stocky man, with a keenly assertive and self-confident manner which had not endeared him to some of the Watch. However, he was well able, both verbally and physically, to stand up for himself. All the male members of his family had been in the armed Services, and the prospect of a similar life – he knew several firemen in Bedford, where he lived with his wife, Jennifer, and their three little girls – had prompted him to abandon his thoughts of emigration and to join the Brigade instead. He was already having some reservations about the job, and would very soon have cause for much regret.

'There you are!' Stewart said, holding out his arm with the rope knotted around it. 'Task completed! How's that?'

Eventually all the knots in the drill-book were demonstrated and explained, and as there was still some time left Taylor gave the squad a few unusual examples of knot-tying in tricky situations. He showed them how to tie a bowline knot behind the back, without being able to see what the hands were doing. He also showed them a self-rescue knot for use in extreme situations in a burning building. The knot was to be tied to an axe embedded in a window-sill, from which a fireman could suspend himself with the line going under his arms – a dangerous prospect in itself.

'My arse would have to be well alight before I used that one,' remarked Jacko.

At 7.45 the session concluded, and the squad doubled upstairs, eager for supper, for a chat, for the social activity and interchange of the games-room and the mess.

Unusually, the fire-bell had been silent for two hours – since their duty began – and their pent-up energies, unreleased by any shout, gave an edge to their behaviour and a loudness to their voices, which was underlined by a certain tense expectation of the first shout of the night, especially among the firemen who had newly returned to the Watch.

In the kitchen Martin was dishing fried cod in batter onto twenty-four plates. He was wearing a bright yellow football jersey, which his wife had bought for him the day before. He had put it on while the Watch were at roll-call and when they came upstairs there had been cries of – 'Who's a pretty boy then?' – 'Where's your perch?' – and – 'Sing us a song, Mart!' This resumed with variations when the Watch came into the kitchen just before eight o'clock to pick up their suppers. Jacko helped Martin by spooning out peas and tomatoes. He assured the odd anxious fireman that the green peas *were* peas and not the result of the parrot disease, psittacosis, which he carefully mispronounced. He also indicated that with reference to the cod in batter Martin would soon be arrested for GBH, and that the tomatoes were really the product of a motorway accident involving several tom-cats. Ernie said they reminded him of his Farmers.

Neil came in, commented on Jacko's fitness and suggested some cross-country running the next day.

'I'm playing squash with Martin, Guv,' said Jacko. 'Otherwise I'd be delighted. But honestly, I don't know why you bother. If you just had a couple of games of table-tennis with *me* you'd cover at least ten miles.'

'By the way,' said Neil. 'Jack's here. He's in the bar.'

'Oh, yeah? Can't the old bugger keep away from the station?' demanded Jacko.

'He's come back *specially* to see you.'

'Oh, really? Great. I'll try and squeeze a pint out of him before he goes.' Jacko grinned. 'Anyone with him?'

'Joe's looking after him.'

'Fine. I'll see him after I've had my cuppa.'

Six bells sounded. It was eight o'clock. All the suppers had now been dished out. Jacko started to make himself a cup of tea at the hatch and listened to the conversation of Neil, Taylor, Griffin and Ernie Arthurs, who sat apart from the firemen with the two Staff sub officers, Alan Stanley and Paddy Prendergast. They were talking about the state of Brigade appliances. Behind him, Dave was noisily piling pans and utensils into a sink. Martin sat down on a high stool beside Jacko and lit a cigarette.

'Cup of tea, Mart?'

'Yeah. Thanks.'

In the mess Stewart's voice loudly rose above the general swell of talk and laughter.

'Hear that?' he called. 'Harry's failed his driving test! That weren't so clever, Harry.'

Neil and the junior officers looked up from their table. Harry looked down at his plate, and said nothing. There was an appreciable break in the social chatter of the mess.

The warning-bell rang. The fire-bell rang.

The immediate clatter of cutlery and the scraping of chairs drowned the firemen's comments as they made for the pole-house doors in the corridor, leaving the two Staff sub officers alone in the mess. It was a minute after 8.0 p.m.

Jacko and Martin were among the first to reach the appliance-room floor and to make for their machines, while Neil, Dyer, and the Number Ones on the PE, TL and ET hastened towards the watchroom.

In a moment the yellow light flashed on, and Griffin's voice announced on the tannoy – 'Launderette. Smell of burning. Boundary Road. TL called.'

There were cheers from the other crews, and Ernie Arthurs retorted – 'It's only the *real* fire-fighters who have to leave their suppers! Another bleeding run-out,' he muttered to Jacko as they climbed into the front of the cab. Dyer ran up with the route-card, which he gave to Arthurs, and clambered in behind them.

'Thanks, me old son.'

Jacko flicked up the master switch and started the engine.

'Must be doing the laundry on the fifth floor now,' he said. 'Bloody launderette. I wonder how many other wasted shouts we'll have tonight . . .'

'TL away, mate!'

Acting Station Officer Newstead stepped into the road between Belsize's pump and pump escape and waved the TL on as it drew up outside the launderette.

'Thanks, mate,' Ernie Arthurs replied.

They had a glimpse of a fireman on a scaling ladder beside the launderette's neon-lit sign, an extinguisher in his hands, then Jacko switched off the flashing blue lights and the headlamps, changed gear and drove the TL on up Boundary Road. Arthurs picked up the hand-mike and told control the TL was 'mobile and available'.

As Jacko had imagined, they were not required. A smell of burning in a launderette had not seemed likely to result in the TL's ladders being employed. The appliance had only been called as a safeguard, as Boundary Road contained several blocks of flats.

Jacko turned the TL into Loudoun Road and headed it southwards, back to the station. Beside him Ernie Arthurs, who was a family man with two young teenage daughters, commented on the amount of colourfully lit Christmas trees in the windows of people's homes and mentioned that he would be putting the decorations up in his own home that weekend. Jacko answered briefly, concentrating on the road ahead. But when the TL had to stop at intersections he glanced about at the festive, brightly lit windows in houses and shops and idly assessed how they might add to the risk of fire, while the taller houses he contemplated with an eye for the pitching problems the TL would have in reaching people on the upper floors.

It was really surprising, he thought, when the risks were so many, how few fires there were – and how few they had had in the last four weeks.

The TL drove on down Grove End Road, along St John's Wood Road, across Maida Vale and into Clifton Gardens.

It was passing the Worsley Hotel when a voice on the RT said – 'Return emergency tender.'

'Hallo,' said Arthurs. 'The ET's had a shout as well. That's two lots of suppers spoiled.'

'Serve them right!' said Jacko as he turned the TL left into Warwick Avenue. 'If they can't take it, they shouldn't have joined.'

Arthurs' supposition about the ET was confirmed almost at once when Wembley control told the ET crew over the RT to return to base.

'Alpha 21/6,' said Taylor's voice. 'Received. Over.'

'I wonder where they've been?' asked Arthurs.

Another voice on the RT answered him – that of Sub Officer Diamond of D23 (Hammersmith) who informed control that he was at Hammersmith Broadway where a motor lorry had overturned and that no persons were trapped.

'Now you know,' said Jacko.

The TL entered the rear gate of the fire-station – nine minutes after leaving it.

'Thanks for the nice ride, Jacko!' Arthurs said as the turntable ladders came to halt in the third bay beside the pump.

'My pleasure!' Jacko replied.

They jumped down from the cab, leaving the doors wide open, and Jacko removed his fire-gear with a sense of satisfaction and a slight feeling of relief. The first and second shouts of the night had come and gone, bringing no dramas nor dilemmas, and it seemed as if the unexceptional pattern of the month was going to be repeated.

In the office he filled in the necessary details about the shout in the vehicle log-book. The teleprinter-bell rang and was cut off by Dyer in the watchroom. It was the Stop for Hammersmith Broadway, now being transmitted by Wembley control to the stations concerned. The Stop for Boundary Road came through as Jacko sprinted upstairs to the mess. Paul Taylor and the ET crew who had just returned were collecting their meals from the hot-plate, where they had been temporarily stored and kept warm, with their owners' names in black chinagraph on each plate's rim.

'Did you get there?' Jacko asked Martin.

'No. Usual bloody thing.'

'I been robbed!' yelled Dave Webber, looking at his plate. 'Someone's pinched a chip!'

Jacko decided against pouring himself another cup of tea and resolved to call on Jack Hallifax in the bar. He passed through the mess, and then went downstairs to the bar.

'Hallo, you old bastard!' he said, grinning broadly and gripping Jack's hand. 'How are you going on?'

'Jacko! – You bugger!' Jack replied. 'Great! How are you?'

'Not so bad. How's it going?'

'All right. I'm all right. Miss you a lot – all of you, I do,' said Jack.

Jacko slapped him on the back. 'Well, you shouldn't have bleeding well retired, you old sod,' he said. 'Should you? But as you're here, you can buy us a pint. No. Make it a shandy – a half. I'm driving.'

Behind the bar, Joe Forrest got out a glass. A cassette tape was playing Shirley Bassey songs.

Jack gazed happily at Jacko who said, with a grin: 'Got your gear with you? I bet you have. You can ride the ET if you like – we're short of qualified men.'

'Not bloody likely!' said Jack. 'I've finished with you lot. But how's the Watch? Everything going all right on the ship, is it?'

'Yeah,' said Jacko. 'Everything's fine.'

Jack Hallifax had retired from the Red Watch, Paddington, nine weeks earlier. He had chosen that night to return to the station for his first visit for several weeks.

He was fifty-one, and looked ten years younger. His glossy black hair, as bushy as his eyebrows, was unmarked by any grey. His dark eyes were as bright, his strength was as great, his voice was as steady as any of those who were thirty years his junior, against whom he would willingly test himself, on drills, at volley-ball, and in the horseplay and buffoonery of the mess. Yet as the senior hand he was always ready with advice and encouragment, and brought to his responsibilities in the station and on the fire-ground a deep and zealous concern. He had been a fireman for over twenty-five years.

He joined the Brigade in 1949, after two dismal years as a stoker in the retort house of a gas-works. As a fireman serving in London, he had seen many changes as the Brigade expanded, as Divisions and stations were reorganized, as National Service ended and reduced the intake of ex-servicemen, and when the cleaning of fire-stations passed into the hands of civilians. Most notably he had seen working hours decrease and wages rise. In 1949 he was working a ninety-eight hour week and earning £5 5s. od., plus a thirty-five shilling rent allowance for a married man. In those days firemen worked for a week on day-duties, and a week on nights, and on Sunday for twenty-three hours. Now a recruit was earning on average £48 for a forty-eight hour week, and the union were pressing again for the week to be still shorter and the wages higher. Of this he approved. What was not to his liking was the relaxation of discipline, and the loosening of the bonds that had made firemen one of the country's closest social groups, in the best working-class traditions. He was also wary of the bright but casual youngsters who had joined the Red Watch in his last year. Their self-possession he had to admire, and he saw for himself that on the fire-ground their courage was never in doubt. But their coming served to emphasize the break-up of the old order and the growing, isolating age-gap between himself and the rest. In addition, despite his boundless enthusiasm for the job, his age was imposing its own limitations. Always realistic, Jack realized it was time to go.

In the end, it was the ill-health of his wife, Louise, and his concern for her that overrode his concern for the men and the job. For years she had patiently endured the demands the job made on them both. She had borne his absences night and day without complaint, and concealed her anxieties about the dangers of his job. Five times her fears had been realized. He had been gassed, injured, burned and his bones had been broken in five different shouts. Once, in 1960, he was almost killed when the glass roof of a blazing ballroom collapsed on top of him, trapping him, unnoticed, in the burning debris for some time. But she had never questioned his choice of being a fireman and his continuance as one. Their sons grew up and went away. Then suddenly for the first time in her life she became ill. It was not too serious, but Jack realized that she alone really depended on him and needed him, and he knew how he should spend his next twenty-five years.

His spare time had previously been spent in helping her run an old people's home in north London – an occupation also taken up by Martin Walker, Joe Forrest, Sid Simmonds, and their wives; for borough councils considered that the good character and capabilities of firemen and their wives made them excellent wardens. Jack decided that this would now be his full-time occupation.

However, for months after he left the Watch he still talked about 'my job'. As his wife said – 'He missed all the jokes, all the fun, and his comrades, and he seemed a bit bewildered at first. . . . He was still a fireman when he was talking. . . .'

'You're always a fireman, Louise,' said Sid Simmonds. 'Even though he's retired, he's still a fireman. He'll be a fireman until the day they screw him in his box – God forbid! – but he'll still be a fireman!'

'How are you going on?' asked Jack.

He had just left the noisy company of the crowd in the bar, where it seemed that the whole Watch had now turned up to have a drink with him, and was heading upstairs to the toilets when he all but collided on the landing with Harry Pettit who was on his way down.

'Very well,' replied Harry as they passed each other.

'Enjoying your time?' Jack demanded as he continued up the stairs.

'Yes.'

'Good! Are you coming in for a drink?' Jack paused, looking down onto the flight of stairs below.

'No,' said Harry, looking up. 'I don't think so. I'm working – studying. How are you?'

'Not so bad. Can't complain. I'll see you.'

Harry raised a hand and went on his way as Jack bounded on up to the second floor, pleased that he had met the young man, who had impressed him ever since Harry's arrival at Paddington, back in June. He was not only a very diligent fireman, he was intelligent, pleasant, forceful yet quiet, and so self-opinionated that inevitably he often offended Jack's particular sense of what was right and wrong. Harry took nothing for granted and would question the established view on most matters. 'You'll learn,' Jack would say.

He wondered where Harry was going – he had seemed quite cheerful. Rightly so, Jack thought. According to the others in the bar Harry had had an apparently satisfying interview with DO Keable – as expected. Then Jack remembered a reference to 'Harry the failure' by someone in the bar. Apparently he had failed a civilian driving-test that afternoon. This was most unexpected, and Jack wondered what had gone wrong.

It was the only discordant note and soon died away in what for Jack had been a very happy evening, during which Jacko kept him company at the bar, entertaining him with stories about the Watch and his home life while puffing away at his Sherlock Holmes pipe. One by one nearly all the Watch, in assorted T-shirts and denim trousers, had gathered after supper in the bar, where Jack bought each of them a drink.

The two Staff sub officers, who were in charge of the BA control van that night, were joined by Archie Waldron who wasn't, as Jack had thought, on standby but – as Jacko informed him – had been posted to Paddington from Kensington. Tony Stewart was the next to enter. He told them he had just been visited in the TV room by an insurance man who for a £5 premium offered to give him full twenty-four hour cover for six months against any accident. The man would return the next day to collect his cheque. Stewart was followed by Ernie Arthurs, who had been playing snooker with some of the Wombles after losing to Harry at table-tennis. Then Dave Webber breezed in. He had been helping Martin Walker clean up the kitchen and the mess and prepare the Watch's breakfast. As Griffin only ate cornflakes – 'You can't bugger them about,' he said – they had calculated the portions on the basis that twenty-four men would have breakfast in the mess at 8.0 a.m. the following morning. When Martin himself came in, still wearing his yellow jersey, he put his arm around Jack in an uncharacteristic display of affection and said: 'You old bastard, how are you? Come on, I'll buy you a drink.' 'No, I'll get you one,' said Jack. 'What are you having?' Martin only drank on rare occasions and seldom entered the bar. He had a shandy; the others were drinking lagers, light ales, and halves of draught beer. Jack himself was drinking pints of draught with chasers of Scotch. He was enjoying himself hugely. When asked if he had sold his presentation watch, he took it out of his safari-jacket pocket and proudly showed it to them. 'This isn't Sotheby's, Jack,' said Neil, coming into the bar with Paul Taylor. 'None of us here can afford what you want for it.' 'No one below station officer that is, Guv,' added Taylor. By ten o'clock Orchard and Pincher Martin had made brief appearances, along with Mick Haskard who was driving the BA control van that night. The last to arrive, diplomatically late, were four of the Wombles. Dyer was known to Jack, but new to him were Wickenden, Cheal and Leroy Hough. He went over to talk with them, bought them drinks, and wished them well. 'Any time you're in a bother, always go and see the Guv,' he advised them. 'If you've got any troubles at home go and see the welfare officer. And don't forget to join the union.' The youngsters smiled and nodded, and after a few more exhortations he backed away from them with a boisterous – 'That's enough of me then! Mind how you go!' – all of a sudden sharply aware of the distance between them, and envying the happy prospect they had ahead of them of twenty-five years as firemen. 'I'm going for a slash,' he told Jacko, who said: 'Do you want a hand? – Up the stairs, I mean?' 'Don't forget to put on your glasses!' called out Dave. 'You'll need them, me old son!'

When he came down the stairs a few minutes later – after meeting Harry Pettit – Jack made a swift detour into the deserted office to see his last entry in Form 181, the BA record sheet. Then he stood for some seconds staring down into the darkened appliance-room, at the great red machines couched behind closed doors. He felt himself becoming emotional, and in case someone coming out of the bar should catch him at a disadvantage he tore himself away, and advanced along the landing, straightening his tie, putting himself in a party mood again.

'I hope you bastards have all done your 181's tonight!' he said as he entered the bar. 'Since *you* left,' said Jacko, emptying his pipe in an ash-tray, 'nobody *ever* forgets them!'

The warning-bell cut across all conversation. Then the fire-bell rang.

Immediately, and impassively, the Watch put down their drinks and cigarettes and made for the door.

'Won't be long, Jack,' Martin said.

'What about getting on board?' added Jacko as he moved away.

'No, no!' responded Jack. 'I want to live long enough to enjoy my retirement!'

Within seconds he was alone with the two Staff sub officers, and Joe Forrest behind the bar.

Suddenly the clamour of the fire-bell ceased.

Jack sat down on a bar stool, his heart thumping, his hands trembling.

'That made my pooper pout!' he confessed. 'I was nearly on my way there, Joe. I was nearly with them.'

This is it, thought Neil, as the pump in full cry stormed through the night up Abbey Road in the wake of the pump escape.

The message in his hand read: *'Rear 23 Ryder's Terrace NW8. Explosion. Called by police.'*

It was the very last thing he had wanted – to have to deal with an explosion, especially one on his own ground. Ironically it was the first incident on A21's ground that they had had that week. Visions of bomb-blast and ruin spun through his mind. The exploding pillar-box earlier that evening seemed now like a prelude of worse to come.

As if in confirmation of his fears, the sirens of two police cars and a police van added their notes of discord to the horns and bells of the fire-engines, and converged on them as the PE and pump turned into Blenheim Terrace.

Oh, my God, thought Neil, comparing the route-card with his forward view of the street – Ryder's Terrace must be a mews. . . . Some Irish bomb-factory, he thought, has gone and blown itself up – or perhaps they've booby-trapped some politician's home.

Lewis brought the pump to a halt behind the pump escape, which had double-parked outside a pub called The Drum and Monkey as both sides of the street were packed with cars.

'Stay where you are!' Neil told the pump crew as he jumped out. It was the standard practice when there was a bomb scare for officers to investigate an incident before allowing their crews to join them. The PE crew, who included Leroy, also remained in their machine. Harry Pettit leaned out of the cab window to see what was going on.

Neil and Jim Griffin met up between the appliances, opposite an alleyway leading down the side of the pub that intersected with Ryder's Terrace, which proved to be a mews road behind a row of shops.

They swiftly sized up the immediate and negative aspects

of the situation. There were no signs of devastation, no windows had been blown out, nothing was damaged, and there was no smell of explosive or burning. Apart from some inquisitive onlookers and a few people peering down at them from windows, there was nothing to indicate anything untoward had happened. Most significantly, the pub was still filled with revellers. Evidently the so-called explosion had not been a big one.

'Leave your crew here, Jim,' said Neil. 'I'll just take the pump crew.'

'What's going on?' asked a policeman, who had arrived in the police transit van.

'Come and have a look,' Neil suggested as he set off down the alleyway with Griffin.

At the intersection an agitated woman's voice hailed them from the dark confines of the mews road on their right.

'Here!' she called. 'I'm over here! Quickly!'

She was hovering under a single lamp on a wall that made the surrounding darkness more black, while a blank wall opposite shadowed by wind-shaken branches of trees heightened the likeness of the cobbled mews to a set for a mystery movie. It was also very cold.

The woman was slim and in her forties. She was dressed in brown slacks and a jersey. Her dark hair blew about as if in sympathy with her alarm.

'Oh, I'm so glad you've come!' she said, shivering with both cold and shock. 'There was this explosion! In the bedroom. I don't know what it is but I heard this terrible crash and a bang! I thought it was a bomb . . .'

Although the front door was open, Neil's senses could not detect any trace of fire or explosion. Something had happened in the small house to cause the woman such distress – but what?

'All right, madam,' he said soothingly. 'You stay here with the constable and we'll go in and investigate.'

'The back room – on the left!' she warned them. 'Be careful!'

Neil grimaced at Griffin. There were no precautions they could take. They switched on their torches.

'Wait here,' Neil told the pump crew – Lewis, Marven,

Stewart and Wickenden. 'And stand back. We'll just take a look inside.'

He and Griffin edged their way into the little hall, already invaded by chilling draughts of the wind, which had set the pendant overhead light swaying to and fro. Neil assured himself that the bang could have been caused by a fault in some domestic appliance – there was still no smell of burning. Other more dangerous possibilities sprang to his mind. There might be a second blast – or some intruder might suddenly rush out waving a gun.

The bedroom door was ajar. Neil shone his torch through the gap and saw nothing but a line of tufted carpet. He glanced at Griffin who, like him, was listening for any sound within the room. Griffin shrugged his shoulders.

With the toe of his left boot Neil pushed open the door and they shone their torches over the room.

To their right the carpet was covered with gleaming sections and splinters of broken glass, and in their midst were several pieces of rotten timber and some dirt.

Neil switched on the bedroom light.

'Look!' said Griffin, pointing his torch at the sloping panels of frosted glass that roofed one side of the room. One of them had been shattered, revealing the night sky above. The timbers had clearly crashed through the glass roof into the room, but whether by accident or design had still to be resolved – also what they were from.

'See if you can get above it, Jim, and see where this lot came from,' said Neil.

'Right-ho!' Griffin found a hall light, switched it on and shot up the narrow stairs while Neil examined the bedroom to see if there was any other damage. None was apparent. Only the unsightly mess of weathered boards, dirt and shards of glass marred the tufted yellow carpet and the comfortably furnished room.

Griffin returned a few moments later, having found no disturbance upstairs nor any origin for the mishap, and said he would examine the rear of the mews house from the back of one of the buildings in Blenheim Terrace. He hurried out to do so while Neil, who had followed him out of the house, informed the woman and the pump crew of what had happened in the bedroom.

'You're *sure* it's not a bomb?' she insisted. 'It could be, couldn't it? They could have thrown it over the roof. You're sure it's safe?'

The constable had been joined by two of his colleagues, and after also reassuring the woman he asked her to repeat her story. In the background the pump crew waited patiently for further instructions.

Before long Griffin returned, breathless with haste.

'It's all right,' he told Neil. 'It was a window-box. Must have been empty. It must have been blown off a ledge on an extension of one of the other houses. The wind did it!'

'There you are,' Neil exclaimed. 'Your bomb's a window-box! There's a bit of a mess inside, I'm afraid. But come in and have a look.'

'Are you *sure?*' repeated the woman.

Briskly he ordered Lewis to back the pump down the alley-way into the mews, and told the other three firemen to fetch brooms and start cleaning up the bedroom. 'Get the escape away,' he said to Griffin. 'We'll see you later.'

At exactly 11.0 p.m., Neil sent the Stop for 23 Ryder's Terrace to Wembley control.

'Ground floor glazing of private house damaged by falling timber,' he said, speaking with precision and some satisfaction. 'No persons injured. . . . No explosion situation. . . .'

Jacko looked up at the red light in the appliance-room signalling that only the pump escape had been called. The bells stopped ringing.

Seconds ago the firemen who were still in the bar had come leaping downstairs; others had slid down the poles from the dormitory and the mess. Dyer had tannoyed the details of the shout as the teleprinter clattered them out – 'Kennet House. Church Street. . . . Persons shut in lift. . . .'

Jim Griffin and the PE crew were piling once again into their machine, ten minutes after their return from Ryder's Terrace. The pump was still out. As Jacko passed behind the PE on his way back to the stairs he noted that the three getting into the back of the cab were all recruits – Pettit, Cheal and Hough. Their eagerness to be going out, even on such a routine call, was evident.

'We'll earn your money for you tonight!' shouted Harry Pettit as he pulled himself up into the machine.

The door slammed behind him and the PE moved out of the station. It was just after 11.15.

'Coming back to the bar?' Jacko asked Martin, who with the rest of the ET crew was also heading for the stairs.

'No. I just made myself a cuppa in the mess. Maybe later.'

Jacko nodded and sprinted back up the stairs to the bar. Ernie Arthurs and Dave Webber followed him. The others went on up to the second floor, to resume their interrupted pursuits.

'What they got?' Jack demanded, as Jacko re-entered the bar.

'Persons shut in lift,' he answered nonchalantly.

He sat on a bar stool beside Jack and started refilling his pipe. The cassette was playing orchestral arrangements of popular music.

Before the bells had gone down – for the fourth time so far that night – the group around Jack had been having a serious discussion about several aspects of their job, prompted by a snide letter from a 'K' Division fireman in the *London Fireman* which had criticized A21 for posing for a fire protection advertisement wearing BA sets and incorrectly, due to an oversight, their tallies. The letter implied that A21 were so busy adding up their fire-calls or the miles they had rowed or the TV documentaries in which they had appeared that they had little time for proper fire-fighting procedure. 'We set ourselves up,' Paul Taylor had complained. 'Every time we make a mistake, someone will pick it up and try to shoot us down. But you don't expect to be criticized by other firemen who don't know the circumstances!' In fact, few issues of the magazine did not have some reference to or contribution by A21 and in particular by the Red Watch, whose feelings of grievance over the letter soon expanded to take in other topics of dissatisfaction – the Press, the police, and awards to firemen.

In common with many firemen the Watch felt that the Fire Brigade were seldom given their due by the newspapers, whose reports on fires, besides sensationalizing some details and misrepresenting others, gave the role of the police too much prominence. It was always, they felt – 'Police assisted by firemen . . .' As Jack said: 'All I see in the papers after a job is that the police got out two people from a fire, and ambulances stood by, and we did bugger-all. What we did is hardly ever mentioned!' Stories were told how some policemen had been commended for heroic rescues which they had never in fact made. Jack said – 'If they get a chance to get an award and some publicity for the force they'll take it!' 'You can't blame them,' Jacko said. 'Actually I think I would blame the Brigade. They've always put their foot down on any kind of publicity. They don't actually *encourage* it as much as they might.' 'It's better now,' said Ernie Arthurs. 'Well, it's getting better,' Jacko conceded. 'But it's also the reason why the public haven't a notion what the Brigade really does. They don't realize what being a fireman involves. Ninety-nine per cent of the population don't even know, I'm sure, where their fire-station is. It's not the public's fault. It's the Brigade's.' 'People only think of us when they need us,' Taylor concluded. 'Right!' said Jack. 'The rest of the time they need us like Custer needed Indians!'

They went on to discuss the way in which the Brigade were now imitating the police by issuing an increasing amount of commendations and awards – a process which in Jack's opinion had now gone berserk.

'When you read about the jobs for which blokes get commendations you think – Jesus Christ! Everybody's been doing that *all the time*! And then you think – Where's the rest of the crew? Where the hell are the rest of them?'

'Well,' said Jacko, 'I think you get a pretty good idea what's gone on from the Press releases. You go through them and you think – Well, that one's for the Fire Brigade committee who are trying to keep the batting averages up. And there's another one for the averages. And you see a third and think – Blimey! That bloke probably did well. . . . That's the way it goes.'

The discussion was eventually summed up by a story Jack told.

'We was on a hotel job some years ago,' he said. 'I was on the ET. It was a nothing job. Don't get the wrong idea that I should have got something, because it really was nothing. *But* – I assisted five people down a builder's ladder. You know. . . . When it was all over, Arthur Nicholls – he was the DO then – when he heard what had happened he called me over and said: "What did you do?" So I told him. And Fred Alcock was there. He was in charge of A22's pump. He had gone in with me on a branch and on that particular part we got the fire out. Fair enough. Now just before we went away on the ET Fred come in and said: "Look, Jack – they got an idea that you and I are going to be bunged up for some award. I don't want nothing. What do you want?" I said: "Buy me a pint." He said: "That's it!" And that was the end of that. I was just doing my job. He never did buy me that pint,' Jack added and laughed.

The debate about these matters had almost ended when the bells went down at 11.15 p.m. for the shout to Church Street involving the pump escape. When Jacko, Dave and Ernie Arthurs rejoined Jack Hallifax in the bar, the discussion broadened into a consideration of how the Brigade had changed over the years. Even in the past month, since Jack's departure, the working week had been cut from fifty-six hours to forty-eight. But, despite the changes, there was a feeling that not much had improved.

Jack regretted the fact that most firemen at the present time had never been in the Services. 'They come into the job,' he said, 'without a Service discipline behind them – no self-discipline, if you wish. No one knows how to *give* orders, and no one knows how to *take* them. They learn – they *have* to learn. But there is a lack of leadership. There are these re-cruits all waiting to go, to be told what to do, and nobody tells them what to do. This is the trouble today.'

'Well, I agree with you in some of that,' said Jacko, drawing on his pipe.

'Not all of it,' said Arthurs.

'But on the fire-ground,' added Jacko, 'these blokes, by and large, do an admirable job.'

'I never said they didn't,' said Jack. 'I was talking about them on the station.'.

'They're good blokes, these young lads,' remarked Arthurs. 'Like Dave here.'

'Cheers, Ernie,' said Dave. 'What do you want for Christmas?'

'No, I mean it,' Arthurs continued. 'We had a job the other

week. There was myself and another leading fireman. We went to the job and there were ten other blokes with us and *nine* of them were recruits. The other was the driver, who had to be with the pump. So what did we do? We got on with it. They went in like it was a drill. They didn't need to be told, not all of them anyway. A lot of them was using their initiative. And that's a good thing. Because you can only learn this job by *doing* it, don't you think?'

'Yes, but you still need *leadership!*' said Jack.

Jacko cleared his throat and furrowed his brows. 'I'm not sure you can treat every job like a drill, Ernie. There's some things on a job you can't *ever* anticipate!'

'That's right,' Arthurs answered. 'But you got to go by the book to start with – and have confidence in the back-up while you get on with it.'

'You're never aware of a back-up,' said Dave. 'I'm not.'

Jacko grinned. 'You are if you've got someone behind you who you don't trust!'

'I don't think of that,' said Dave. 'I just think of getting on with it.'

Jack leaned forward. 'You must agree though, Dave,' he said, 'there are times when, for instance, you've got a jet going at a job and all of a sudden you think – Fuck me, old what's-his-name is the pump-operator! And you *know* he's a wanker. So don't tell me you don't get a little bit frightened. And invariably it all works out when you lose your water. But there comes another time when you pick up more or less the same type of job and you think – Who's the pump-operator? And it's so-and-so. No bother. No trouble at all. You're never going to lose your water.'

'I can give you an incidence of this, Jack,' Arthurs remarked. 'I'd just passed my ET course and I'm doing an ET job down at Clerkenwell. First job I had with the ET. I'm in charge of it. We got to this job and I thought – Christ! What do I do now? I've got to tell these ET men what to do. And I looked round and I saw Jacko and Martin and my fears went. I wasn't worried any more, because I'd served with them – I'd worked with them, and that was it.'

'You were lucky,' said Jack. 'You had a good team, and this is a team job. I understand *that*. The point I was trying to make is that – these days – not every bloke in your team is a Jacko or Martin. You have to admit that. Not every bloke has their experience, not these days. It's not possible.'

Jacko tucked in his chin and fixed Dave and Arthurs with a big-eyed stare. *'I* think one of the biggest reasons for apathy in the Brigade, at station level, is station work – or rather the *lack* of station work. I know Jack fought for years as a union man to get station work abolished, because the men didn't like being called janitors and station cleaners and they thought it was belittling. In actual fact, I think we've now learned, since station work was abolished, that there was a certain station *pride* instilled in keeping a station clean.'

'There's not so much pride in your station now,' Jack observed. 'No *pride*. Not in the station itself.'

'I'll go along with you there,' said Dave. 'When I first joined, I was one of the laziest sods on the station. I still am really –'

'No, you're not,' interrupted Arthurs. 'You're *the* laziest.'

'Oh, that's nice. Thanks,' said Dave imperturbably and continued. 'Well, I came into the job just before station work was abolished and I *hated* cleaning up the station and polishing and all that. But the one thing I liked about it really was the fact that it made us just one unit. We fended for ourselves in every single way – except for actually building the place in the first place. We cleaned our own windows. We polished our own floors. But now we've got contractors who come in and do it for us. And the station's a mess really because they can't cope with the amount of work.'

'And they haven't got the interest,' said Arthurs. 'Naturally.'

'There was a time,' said Jack, 'when no one would *dream* of stamping out a fag-end on the appliance-room floor. Blokes would actually go around picking up feathers and bits of fluff!'

Ernie Arthurs grunted. He turned to Dave Dyer who, after coming up from the watchroom, had been sitting at the end of the bar listening to them. 'What do you think?'

'Well, I haven't *done* any station work,' he answered, speaking cautiously. 'When I applied I thought you *did*. I don't know whether that's for a good thing or a bad thing.'

'How long you been in, David?' asked Jack.

'Two months. But –' He hesitated. 'Can I say? – I mean, when I go home at nights – well, you do feel a *sort* of pride, especially if you've been to a job and you know you've done well, or you've gone out and done drills and you know you've done well at them. You get a good feeling inside.'

'Hear, hear!' exclaimed Jack. 'That's what it's all about!'

'I'm sure we would all agree with that,' said Jacko. 'But if you ask me, we'll be disagreeing about everything else till kingdom come.'

'It shows we care,' murmured Arthurs. 'Don't it?'

'Hallo! You still here?' demanded Martin coming into the bar. 'Still giving them a bit of earhole drill? You never give up, do you?'

'What'll you have?' demanded Jack. 'Blimey! This is a bleeding *honour*! *Two* visits in one night! Come on. What's yours?'

Martin was prevailed upon to have a ginger ale, and as Joe Forrest poured it out for him he informed the others that both the PE and the pump had now returned from their shouts. As if in confirmation of this Leroy entered the bar to finish his twice-interrupted half of lager and smoke the cigarette he had rolled for himself an hour ago. He was followed by Neil, who came in for a quick Guinness and to ensure that the bar would not stay open for too long. At the same time the two Staff sub officers decided to retire to their sleeping quarters on the ground floor, and their departure, after a jovial exchange with Jack, was followed by Archie Waldron's.

By then it was 11.40. The firemen who remained in the bar were now all firmly grouped around Jack Hallifax.

'Last orders!' said Joe. 'Come on, I want to get to bed!'

The only takers were Jacko, who had another ginger ale, and Jack who asked for his pint to be topped up. In the meantime Neil had been challenging Jacko to a game of squash the following afternoon.

'I'm very, very sorry, Guv,' said Jacko, puffing out clouds of smoke from his pipe. 'But I'm playing Martin tomorrow.'

'Excuses!' Neil said. 'But you'll never be ready to take me on until you've given up smoking. Will you?'

'When I die – aged fifty,' Jacko remarked blandly, emitting more fumes – 'I'll be the fittest man in the cemetery.'

The others laughed. Jacko gave a modest smile.

'I know one thing,' said Arthurs. 'With that hooter of yours, you'll be the only one there with an L-shaped coffin.'

'It's like a shark's fin,' said Jack.

'You know,' said Martin, contemplating Jacko's nose. 'If you had another one of those on the *back* of your head, you'd look just like a pick-axe.'

Even Jacko had to laugh, once he had worked out the image Martin had presented. He nodded approvingly. 'All right,' he said. 'Go on. Anybody who comes out with an *original* joke about my nose, I'll give him a fiver.'

He sat on a bar stool beside Jack for a minute or so savouring his pipe and the comfortable comradeship of his mates. Idly he gazed at their open faces and bare-armed gestures without concentrating on what was being said, wondering how such men, all highly individual, had come to be firemen.

'Why aren't you a policeman?' asked Neil. 'For instance.'

Jacko blinked and realized the others must have been airing what had been on his mind. Neil had addressed his question to Ernie Arthurs, but before he could answer, Jacko spoke.

'I *was* a policeman,' he said. The others looked at him.

'That's right,' Jack said. 'He was.'

'When was that?' Neil inquired.

Jacko took a breath, wanting now to contribute something worthwhile to the discussion.

'Just before I joined the Brigade,' he replied. 'I did three years in the Army, as some of you may know – and I didn't like it very much. But once I'd come out and went into Civvy Street I missed the Army, particularly the comradeship, and also the very things I rebelled against – calling people "Sir" and obeying orders. I actually found I missed them. Afterwards – over two years – I had in the region of twelve jobs, which was a bit of a problem when I had to fill in my application for the Brigade because there wasn't enough room to list my previous occupations. Anyway, I came to a point in my life – I was married, had a young baby – when I decided I needed security, and I weighed up the jobs which gave security. The two I came down to were the police and the Fire Brigade. I didn't in fact know anything about either of them, especially the Fire Brigade. I was one of the few kids in

London, I suppose, who'd never seen a fire. So I joined the police, the Brighton police; got a warrant, a nice uniform, and I was sent off to the training centre. I did six weeks, six weeks with blokes that were *really* policemen. Everything I disliked in the police *before* I joined the police these blokes in training high-lighted. The first night-out we had in town I went to the pictures, had some fish and chips, had a pint, and came back – had a good evening. Well, I was the *only* one that hadn't moved somebody on for parking or arrested somebody for loitering!'

The others laughed at Jacko's exaggerated claims.

'This is *true*,' he assured them. 'You can laugh. But they were all *tuned in* to being policemen. I had six weeks of this and I thought – I can't do thirty years of this. So I resigned without any more ado.'

'All right,' said Neil. 'But what made you join the Brigade?'

'Money.'

'You're joking,' Arthurs said. 'In *those* days?'

'No, it wasn't the money,' Jacko agreed. 'Otherwise I would have signed on straight away. That come later. But when I found out after leaving the police that by becoming a bus-driver I could earn about £16 a week – which was quite good in 1962/63 – I became a bus-driver. But I found it most soul-destroying, being in my little cab, in charge of my bus, and the only respect I got from anyone was by stamping on the brakes and making them all *bow* to me. I had two months in the cab of a bus and I thought – I wasn't very intelligent; I hadn't been trained for anything; I could fire a rifle and drive a bulldozer. That was all. Then I saw an advert, in the *Daily Mirror* I think it was, when they had just started advertising for the Fire Brigade, and I thought – Well . . . So I applied to the Brigade, as a last measure, to find some sort of security. I didn't know *anything* about the job. I was scared of heights. But in actual fact – directly I got to training-school, I liked it. I am a fairly lazy person, and the more people do for me and organize my life, the less worry *I've* got. I've never looked back on the Fire Brigade.'

He had been speaking strongly, fixing his gaze on each of them in turn. Now he lowered his eyes to concentrate on re-lighting his pipe. The others who had listened to Jacko's declaration with respect and interest, were silent for a moment. Most of them had never heard him talk at such length about himself before, and all of them felt that he had in places sold himself short.

'I would never have said you was lazy,' said Jack. 'Not in the station.'

'Nor on the fire-ground,' added Arthurs, turning to Jack. 'He's always one of the first blokes at the front.'

'Cheers, Ernie,' said Jacko.

'This is your life!' Dave commented wryly.

'Oh, stop . . . you're making me cry,' said Martin.

Neil hunched his shoulders. He was standing with his hands in his pockets. 'I'd never have thought you were scared of heights,' he said.

'I'm scared of *most* things,' Jacko responded. 'The very idea of living makes me uneasy. Maybe that's why I am a fireman. . . . No, in actual fact I'd never been up a ladder before. The highest I'd ever been was upstairs in my bus to sort out a couple of drunks on a Saturday night. I'd never been up a ladder. I quite enjoyed it at training-school, and going up the extension-ladder was quite okay. It seemed a fairly stable ladder. But *hook-ladders*! Going up to the first floor, getting off and getting on and coming down – that was all right. Going up to the second floor seemed okay. But the *third* floor! I hooked the ladder onto the sill from the second floor and climbed up all right and into the balcony. But then I had to come down. I got onto the sill, stood on it and put my foot on the ladder, before transferring my full weight onto it, and I froze! I couldn't move . . . ! My instructor was a typical instructor – very understanding. He called me a woman's dicky.'

'A *what?*' exclaimed Dave.

'Or something. He shouted up at me and asked in effect what the hell I thought I was doing and whether I'd stay up there all day and whether I liked the view. It worked for me. It annoyed me that this pompous little man down below who probably couldn't do hook-ladders anyway was shouting at *me*! And in the end I finally cocked my leg over and came down. My knees were all trembling, you know, and my nose was bumping the rounds as I went down.' The others laughed. 'The instructor came over and he wasn't such a bad bloke. He said: "You all right? What went wrong?" I said I was just scared, and he immediately said – "Well, fuck off up again!"...'

Again the others laughed, excepting Jack, who raised his head and his voice and said: 'There's not one bloke in the Fire Service who *hasn't* got a fear. Most blokes are frightened to say what their fear is, but we've all got them. Right? – Heights, darkness, smoke, poisonous gases – basements, falling, being trapped. And fire itself!'

'Fire is the enemy,' Neil agreed. 'But it's all right if you can *see* it. Then you can deal with it, and you always know that water, *enough* water, will put it out.'

'That's true,' said Jacko. 'Actually, we're really more scared of our peers – aren't we? – of the fireman behind us, than of the actual job. Rather than lose face you keep going. And it's only when you have two or three blokes working together who know each other well that they'll look at each other, or if they're in smoke somebody's hand will touch, and you'll realize that you're thinking the same thing – the old pants are in danger. And then you'll come out. You won't get *one* come out. You'll *all* come out or you'll *all* go on. The rest of the time you just keep going – because *they* do. Even though you're scared.'

'I agree!' Jack said.

'Although it is a team effort,' Jacko continued, 'it's the fact that *you* can stay with the rest that is most important. And the most satisfying thing – as far as I'm concerned – is a two hose-reel job, when you shoot up the stairs with a hose-reel and prevent it becoming a make-up. So they don't need to send for more machines, more jets, more water, more men. Just a *few* of you blokes, the pump or the pump escape crew, have fought a blaze and *won*.'

Jacko paused, gazing now at the smoke curling out of his pipe. He realized he had been monopolizing the conversation and speaking at some length – unusually for him, and in an unusually serious vein. The others expressed their agreement with his views while Joe Forrest switched off the cassette-player, which had been silent for some minutes. Jack said nothing, but very deliberately drained his beer-glass and then banged it down on the bar to attract everyone's attention.

'Basically,' said Jack Hallifax, speaking slowly and glancing at each man. 'Basically, the whole thing comes down to self-proving and achievement. Right? It's a team effort, a team job, but what matters most is self-respect. I mean *everybody*, every child, every boy, likes to prove himself. And when you are in this station, and on the fire-ground, you *do* that – with men you *value*. You are one of them. Do you follow me? They are you. We are all one person.'

The others looked at him gravely, unsure of what Jack was trying to say, but in sympathy with the evident depth of his feelings. Then he spoke again, and left them in no doubt.

'The fact remains,' said Jack. 'This is it – that this is the best job in London. I am certain of that! The best job in the world . . . !'

No one presumed to depreciate or add to what he had said. It was left to Neil to bring things back to normal.

'Well, gentlemen,' he said. 'I think it's time for one and all to turn in. . . . Christ! Look at the bloody time! It's midnight. And we've still got nine hours to go!'

'Mind how you go!' called Jack. 'Keep safe!'

A taxi waited in Harrow Road to take him home. Jack clambered into it and sank heavily onto the seat. As the taxi pulled away from the kerb he looked out and up at the station which was all in darkness, except for a dim light in the watch-room and a blaze of lights in the office.

Jack felt very tired. For no definable reason his party mood had gone and had been displaced by a feeling of desolate sorrow.

*

In the office, Neil drafted reports on the last two shouts on A21's ground. He had already changed into his usual night attire – an old pair of trousers, a white T-shirt with '*A21 Rescue Company*' on it in red, a navy pullover and an old pair of running-shoes. Some forty minutes later, having finished the drafts and tidied his desk, he switched the lights out and retired to his bedroom, where he lay down on the bed, propped up by a pillow, and by the light of his bedside lamp began to read one of the many books in his locker on the history of the railways. Now and then he dipped into a tin of home-made rock-cakes.

At 1.0 a.m. he turned on his radio to listen to the news and then left the radio on. It formed a musical background to his reading, softening the sporadic roar of traffic on the Harrow Road and Westway and the clangour of shunting trains in Paddington goods-yard.

By this time nearly all the Watch were in their beds, still wearing for the most part their socks, denim trousers and T-shirts, and most of them had fallen asleep – though their slumbers were inevitably fitful and their bodies unrelaxed. Martin Walker never slept well in the station, and lay awake on his bed smoking a cigarette, listening to the muted night-sounds of the city. Leroy heard them also, and the traffic and the trains kept him awake for a long time, as did the strangeness of the dormitory and his unremitting apprehension of a fire-call. In the mess, Dave and three other firemen who had resolved the difficulty of getting to sleep by staying up talking until they felt tired, sat around a table reviewing the events of the day.

Eventually, about 1.45 a.m., the group broke up. No one said 'Good night' – they might soon be seeing each other again when the bells went down. By the glow of the ever-burning light above the pole-house door Dave went to bed. He was a heavy sleeper once he fell asleep, and in order not to miss a shout he always pulled his bed out a foot into the passage between the lockers and slept the other way around – so that the others in his section would collide with his bed and make sure he was awake. Opposite him was Keith Orchard. Tony Stewart slept opposite Harry Pettit in the beds nearest the pole-house door. Dave was vaguely aware of their shapes and their breathing. But it was Harry's feet under his blankets that Dave in his reversed position last saw before he shut his eyes.

In the station officer's bedroom a light still burned. The radio was silent, and Neil was asleep, having dozed off over his book.

Only Leroy was still awake.

At 2.21 the fire-bells rang, summoning the Red Watch

from their beds and down to the appliance-room.

The warning lights went on – red, green, yellow – and the PE, pump and TL crews climbed into their machines. They set out into the dark, cold night for the North Kensington end of the Harrow Road. In a pavement excavation a minor build-up of gas had somehow ignited and was burning like a squib. But when A21's machines arrived, A29's pump crew had already dealt with the emergency, using a hand-extinguisher.

They returned home about 2.40. The three crews went straight back to their beds, trying not to wake up those of the ET crew who had already gone back to sleep. The others were soon asleep again – except for Leroy, who was now even more keyed-up, and Neil, who picked up his book again to finish a chapter.

At 2.57 the bells rang out again, automatically turning the lights on and dragging the weary Watch again from their beds and sending them tumbling down the poles. This time it was only the blue light that flicked on, for the ET, and the other crews raised a ragged cheer. The call was to an accident on Cromwell Road, involving two cars in collision by a roadworks. But the ET's assistance was not required.

By 3.15, the ET had returned to Paddington, where the other crews were now back in their beds, trying to mend the shattered peace of their slumbers. Exhausted by the harsh awakenings, the build-up and collapse of tension caused by the fire-bells, they lay hunched and curled-up under their blankets uneasily sleeping. The Stop for the RTA at Cromwell Road came through and the lights went out.

Leroy turned over, in tired anticipation that the six shouts there had been on his first night would not now be followed by a seventh, at least not until morning. Soon he slept. In the station officer's little room Neil wearily switched off his bed-side lamp, pulled the blankets over his shoulders and despite his tenseness drifted into unconsciousness.

Minutes after the ET's return only five firemen were awake. In the kitchen, Garner and Pincher Martin, feeling restless and unsleepy, were making themselves a cup of coffee. In the junior officers' quarters, Paul Taylor was still trying to relax, as was Archie Waldron in the dormitory, in whose far section

Martin Walker was lying in his bed smoking, dreamily watching the cigarette-end glowing in the dark.

A quarter of a mile away a fire had already been lit in Clifton Gardens.

It was noticed first by a resident who woke up feeling thirsty and smelt smoke. He left his third-floor bedroom and came downstairs to the ground floor, where in a connecting passage he discovered flames shooting up from the carpet near an armchair against the wall. Shouting – '*Fire!*' – he ran about looking for extinguishers, but those he found he operated wrongly and so failed to get them to work. The fire spread. Seizing a hand-bell next, he raised the alarm, ringing the bell until it broke. Then he ran upstairs, shouting and beating on doors as he went. He woke his room-mate and together they descended by another staircase to tell the manager, still raising the alarm as best they could, trying to rouse the many occupants of the hotel. Over 150 people, mostly foreign, were asleep in the eight, interlinked terraced houses in Clifton Gardens called the Worsley Hotel, used as a hostel for hotel employees. One of them dialled 999, making the first of three telephone calls received within minutes by Wembley control.

At 3.32 a.m. the bells went down in A21, Paddington – for a shout at Clifton Gardens, Maida Vale.

The Shout at Maida Vale

FIRE

WORSLEY HOTEL

CLIFTON GARDENS W9

289 0082

JE37 A21

A21 PE P TL ET

A22 PE

TOO 0332

Red – green – yellow – blue. The little rows of warning lights in the ceiling of the appliance-room flicked on together. Four at once, calling out all four machines, meant that the emergency was a high risk one, and at that time of night it was unlikely to be a false alarm.

'I can *smell* it!' said Neil amazedly to Jacko, with a jerk of his head, his nostrils flaring.

Back to back, beside their respective machines, they were pulling on their fire-gear, their boots, leggings and tunics. For an instant they paused, incredulous and agog, sensing the faint stench of smoke invisibly invading the station.

'Yeah!' said Jacko, his eyes widening. 'You can smell it all right!'

The crews were climbing into their cabs, some only half-awake, and the Number Ones were hastening towards their machines, teleprinter slip in hand – there were no tannoy announcements after midnight – when Neil and Jacko pressed the buttons opening the exit-doors and saw the smoke.

A hundred yards away black wraiths wafted silently past the street-lamps at the roundabout, muffling and dimming their lights.

'*Christ!*' said Jacko, astonished at the prospect but with his fire-fighting spirit aroused. 'We've got a job here! – We got a job!' he called to Ernie Arthurs, on the other side of the turn-table ladders. 'Clifton Gardens!' shouted Dyer, running with the teleprinter slip for the TL. Marven brought the pump's copy to Neil. He knew where Clifton Gardens was – they all did. He pulled himself into his seat in the pump. His cab-door slammed – other doors slammed. 'Clifton Gardens!' he said to Lewis, putting his white station officer's helmet on his head. Headlights flashed out into the forecourt. 'Clifton Gardens!' repeated Orchard, starting the pump escape's engine. 'The Worsley Hotel,' said Jim Griffin grimly, adjust-ing his belt. He reached up for the bell-strap. 'Crew! – All sets!' shouted Paul Taylor into the back of the ET, knowing from the sight of smoke across the roundabout that firemen wearing breathing apparatus must be required. It was the first time he had given that command before the ET left the station. 'We got a job!'

One by one and in their customary order the four red machines turned out of the appliance-room, their headlights on, their blue lights flashing, their horns and bells cumulatively adding an eightfold discord to the night. The pump escape, the pump, the turntable ladders and the emergency tender surged out onto the forecourt in turn, swung left and powered up Harrow Road to the roundabout.

Behind them the appliance-room, empty but for Divisional cars and vans, gaped through the open exit-doors, ablaze with lights like the rest of the station, deserted but for Mick Haskard, who waited in the watchroom for the follow-up call. Alone in the dormitory, Joe Forrest went back to sleep.

In Warwick Avenue, the pump escape had to slow down momentarily as thick dark smoke descended on the canal bridge. For a moment its density made Griffin in the PE and Neil in the pump think that they had been given the wrong address, that the fire must be in Warwick Avenue itself and not in Clifton Gardens. But it was evident that the smoke was being blown by the gusting northerly wind from somewhere else. 'Keep going!' Griffin commanded, and the PE at the head of the cavalcade forged on through the smoke and on down the road. In the cab behind him Leroy, who had only fallen asleep half an hour before, sat in a daze, as confused by what was happening as if it were a dream. On either side of him Cheal and Harry Pettit hung expectantly out of the cab windows – as Tony Stewart did in the pump. 'Can you see it?' asked Ernie Arthurs of Jacko – '*I* can't see it,' he added, anxiously peering through the windscreen of the TL. 'You will!' Jacko said. In the confines of the ET the crew were labouring to get into their boots, pull up their leggings, and put on their tunics and belts. Only half-awake, Dave was oblivious of everything but the practicalities of getting rigged. No one spoke. Garner drove the ET at a steady pace – to give the crew a chance, after getting their fire-gear on, to don their breathing apparatus. It was better to arrive fully rigged rather than half-rigged. In the front, Taylor, tightening his body-belt, said – 'It's going a bit! There was no smoke when we got back from Cromwell Road, was there? Look at it now!' In the pump, Marven, a qualified BA wearer, leaned over to Neil and said – 'I better get my set on, Guv.' 'You do that,' said Neil, gearing his mind and body to face whatever the emergency might demand.

Ahead of them the PE turned right and into Clifton Gardens.

A mêlée of over a hundred people filled the road, half naked and hardly dressed, some in pyjamas, shouting, pointing, looking up. Partly obscured by the tall bare arms of trees and clouds of black smoke that mingled darkly with the night was the high white façade of a building looming above them. The orange street-lights made the upturned faces and the scene more ghastly and dimmed the fire-glow within the building. In the street the blue flashing lights on police cars added their urgent counterpoint, while uniformed policemen tried to control the crowds, directing them away from the densely smoking hotel. As the pump escape and the pump lurched to a halt beside the trees, the sound of people screaming rose above all other noise.

Neil leapt out into the road.

'Make pumps – ! No. Forget it!' he said to Lewis, unable because of the thick smoke and the trees to make an immediate and proper appreciation of the situation. 'Get your pump set in!' he shouted and made for the pavement and the building.

He jumped over a low stone wall, on whose other side stood tall barren beech-trees, lining the wall to left and right, and found himself on a slip-road, parallel to Clifton Gardens. It served as an access road to ten high terraced houses along its length, out of which half-dressed people still fled in panic. Parked cars lay on both sides of the slip-road, some half up on the pavements.

In that first instant he realized that because of the obstructive wall and the trees and the cars, the only way of getting machines and escapes up to the building was via the ends of the access road where, opposite numbers 19 and 1, it entered the main thoroughfare of Clifton Gardens.

Later he would find out that the Worsley Hotel, whose name was on each pillared, balustraded porch jutting over basement areas, consisted of eight inter-connecting terrace houses, formerly numbers 17 to 3, and that three of them were five floors high with attic rooms in the roof.

For a second he stood motionless opposite the front door porch of one of those houses – number 13. A man hung perilously from the fourteen-foot high porch above it, nerving himself to jump. But Neil's eye was caught by the flicker of flame in the smoke pouring out of the front door, which was ajar, cracked open by the heat. For the first time he saw the reflection within of flames through the smoke and a red glow in the rooms on either side. Obviously a serious fire on the ground floor was spreading upwards internally through the building.

At that moment the wind parted the shroud of smoke masking the front and he saw to his horror that across the face of four houses – on the first-floor balustrade, on the second and third floors – people hung out of windows and clung onto ledges, screaming for help. Then a tongue of flame flicked out of a window on the third floor above him.

He turned and found he was now near the PE. He looked for his driver, Lewis, to pass a priority message back to Wembley. But Lewis, having parked the pump beyond the PE, had by then doubled on up the road with Wickenden to find a hydrant, carrying the necessary stand-pipe, key and gear and two rolled-up lengths of hose between them. Beside the PE Orchard was opening up the valves on the PE's pump.

Neil ran to the wall and called over to him – 'Keith! Make pumps eight! Persons reported!'

Orchard repeated the message and made for the cab.

'I'll go inside!' shouted Griffin, having made his own assessment of the fire.

'Right! Get inside and see what you can do!' Neil replied. 'I'll stay at the front!'

He ran on down the slip-road to establish what difficulties of access the follow-up machines and crews would have and how they could get to the rear of the building. Distraught civilians in all states of undress clutched at him, in broken English entreating his help for the people in the building, who shrieked and cried at him from the windows. An anxious police constable asked him what help he required.

'Get the people *out* of here!' he snapped. 'Get the cars out of the slip-road! Do what you can!'

Broken glass plummeting from upper windows shattered in the basement area. Neil glanced back and up and saw a man sitting on a third-floor window-sill, enveloped in smoke. The room behind him burned. More glass shivered and fell as flames broke out of another third-floor window. For a moment the magnitude of the task on their hands appalled him – the amount of people involved, the speed at which the fire had spread, the impossibility of getting machines into the slip-road and near the building and around the back. A civilian confronted him, gesticulating wildly at the hotel.

'You help! My friend! He up *there!* Please – *help* him!'

'Don't worry!' said Neil. 'We will!'

He raced back up the road, determined to effect in full the firemen's first priority – rescue. It was now 3.35 – three minutes since the bells went down in Paddington.

The first rescue had already been made, by Harry Pettit and Jim Griffin.

The instant the pump escape arrived Griffin had seen that a man unsteadily poised on a porch was about to jump or fall. He ordered Cheal to get a first-floor ladder off the roof of the machine, and while this was done he sized up the general situation and briefly spoke with Neil. With Harry's assistance Cheal took the ladder across the wall and over the slip-road and placed it against the porch of number 13, where Harry footed it as Griffin climbed up a few rounds to assist the man down to the pavement. There they left him and the ladder for others to use, and as they ran back over the wall to the PE, Griffin gave the order for the wheeled escape to be slipped.

In the meantime Leroy had started emptying the lockers of rolled-up hose, and Orchard, having transmitted Neil's message to Wembley control – which they received at 3.35 – had moved the pump escape back a few feet at Jacko's shouted request from the TL.

Initially unsighted by the clouds of smoke and the trees, Jacko had drawn up the turntable ladders beside the PE. Then he glimpsed a man on the third-floor window-sill of a burning room. Unable to get the TL into the slip-road, the nearest he could get to the hotel was to drive up onto the pavement. His first impulse was to crash the machine through the wall. But it might have stuck there. So once Orchard had backed the PE he drove the TL onto the pavement and stopped it head-on against the wall.

'We're not going to reach him from here!' shouted Jacko as he and Ernie Arthurs jumped out.

'We got to!' said Ernie. 'Come on!'

Far above them the man climbed out of his window onto a six-inch ledge as the curtains beside him burst into flames.

Orchard's message to Wembley came over the RT in the emergency tender as Garner parked it in the middle of the road, to the rear of the other machines. The crew piled out, still hurriedly completing the securing of their BA sets and head-harnesses, leaving to the last their goggles and helmets and the fitting of their nose-clips and mouth-pieces.

As Paul Taylor, Martin Walker, Waldron, Dunlop and Dave assembled at the front of the ET, Garner ran to the back and went inside to pick up his set and the stage one board. Pincher Martin, whose goggles had fallen apart as he put them on, was still there, desperately trying to mend the defect, as without the goggles he could not enter thick smoke – the role of ET men wearing BA.

As the others waited momentarily for him and Garner, civilians approached them, clamouring for immediate action. The firemen, gazing at what they could see of the smoke-logged building, said nothing. Then with Garner carrying his set and Pincher still trying to repair his goggles, Taylor led them up the road in irregular file at a smart pace towards the other machines, towards the crescendo of sound and fire.

It was Garner, running up the road after the others, who saw the two youngest and newest members of the Watch – Cheal and Leroy – and Harry, struggling to slip the escape and finding out it was not the same as doing the slip and pitch drill they had done together the day before. Bedevilled by the dreadful immediacy of the fire, they had also been betrayed by their haste and their eagerness to do well.

Garner shouted at Dunlop, who was nearest him, to lend a hand. In a moment the five of them slipped the three-quarter ton wheeled escape off the trunion-bar and it crashed to the ground. As they pushed it out into the road, Dyer joined them on Neil's orders, and Cheal and Harry were called away by Orchard and Griffin to render other assistance.

The re-formed foursome then trundled the wheeled escape up the street towards the slip-road and swung down inside it towards Neil.

It was nearly 3.36.

By then Griffin and Harry, with Orchard's assistance, had taken two lengths of 1¾-inch hose into number 13.

Griffin kicked open the door and a blast of hot and acrid fumes rolled over them. The blazing hall ahead of them was alive with fiery light and darkness. Everything burned. The back of the front door and the dummy ceiling rippled with fire; blackened wallpaper flared up and flaked off; the carpet, spattered with burning spars and embers, smouldered. Further on, double doors on their left – one was open – wore masks of flame, as did the face of a single shut door opposite. Beyond, the false plasterboard ceiling was a billowing mass of flames which roared out of sight up the stairwell, wherein the stairs, with banisters ablaze, were being buried by ever-falling fiery debris from an inferno above, unseen but heard by the firemen.

They knelt, crouching in the hallway. Harry held the branch. Griffin, close behind him, supported the hose already charged with water.

Harry opened the control valve, and with both hands clasping the branch, directed the jet of water first at the ceiling, then at the walls, then at the floor, whirling it round and round.

Scorching steam swirled down around them. Water flew off the walls. Pieces of burnt-out, blown-out plasterboard were cast to the floor. Shards of broken glass from a fan-light shot through the smoke amidst a shower of flying ash.

Secure behind the hissing, swivelling beam of water, Harry and Griffin advanced down the blazing hallway to the stairs.

Outside, Paul Taylor had crossed over the wall into the slip-road and was making his own assessment of the scene. He saw Harry and Griffin enter a door and decided to follow them in.

The ET crew's task was to penetrate a building, reach the top floors and find and rescue people overcome by smoke. With Taylor went Walker, followed soon by Pincher Martin.

Archie Waldron and Dave had delayed by the wall for some seconds, having been told to wait there by Neil who, as Taylor was hidden from him by the trees, had thought the two firemen were the first of the ET crew to arrive. For a while they hovered by the wall, using their time to make final adjustments to their sets, to the hooks on their harness, with their eyes on the seeming chaos about them.

Nearby, Dave saw the TL mounting the pavement beyond the PE; he saw its ladders extending and Ernie at the top of them disappearing in the smoke; he saw the wheeled escape coming towards him down the slip-road, pushed by Garner and Leroy, with Dunlop and Dyer urging on the wheels.

Wide-awake now, and ready for action, Dave waited no longer and crossed the wall.

Neil had run back up the road after meeting with the PC and the civilian. Seeing only Waldron and Dave of the ET crew he told them to wait where they were for the others to arrive. Seeing Dyer by the TL he shouted at him to help with the wheeled escape. Marven had joined the ET crew. Tony Stewart he saw laying out hose from the pump and ordered him to join the escape crew.

Getting water on the fire was secondary to the prime task of rescue, in which all available hands must assist. He knew people were crying out for help at second-floor windows, but not much smoke came from their rooms. It was different higher up.

He saw that the TL crew were dealing with a man spread-eagled on a third-floor ledge fifty feet above the street. At the same level, immediately above Neil were two other men, one astride a window-sill.

'In here!' he yelled at the crew on the escape. 'Head left! – Extend! – Well! – Out in the carriage! – Well! – Into the building! – Down blocks!'

As Garner furiously wound the handle extending the upper half of the escape's ladders, the turntable ladders were being retracted. Ernie Arthurs had been forced to come down without reaching the man on the ledge.

What Jacko had feared had been realized. At the operator's console on the rear of the TL's platform he had simultaneously extended and elevated the ladders between the trees to their maximum and trained to his right. But the distance, the angle, and the limits of projection which if exceeded would cause the whole machine to topple over, meant that although Ernie, hooked on at the top, was level with the man, they were still ten feet apart. Clouds of smoke billowed up between them and out of the windows to left and right. It seemed that the whole of the third floor across three houses was ablaze, and no room more so than the one the man had vacated. He was an elderly man, in a dressing-gown down to his ankles. With his hands clutching a cornice above his head and his bare toes clinging to the ledge, he looked over his shoulder at Ernie Arthurs in unspeakable disbelief.

Ernie's despair was almost as great, for if the man fell or jumped he would plunge into the basement area or be impaled on the railings between it and the pavement.

'*Don't you jump!*' yelled Ernie. '*Don't you dare!* If you do – I'll bloody *kill* you!'

Jacko heard him over the intercom that connected whoever was at the top of the ladders with the operator at the console.

'Come *down*, Ernie!' said Jacko. 'I'll try to reach him without your weight at the top!'

Ernie unhooked himself and speedily descended, swearing profusely and worriedly glancing upwards. The man on the ledge waited unmoving. But although Jacko was now able to add an extra round to the ladders, they were still too far away from the wall. He spoke into the intercom and his voice reached the man from the top of the ladder.

'Hang on, mate!' he said. 'We'll get to you. Just *hang on!*'

'We can't do a fucking thing from here!' groaned Ernie.

'You stay here, Jacko. If you get a chance, re-site the ladders. I'm going to help the other crews.'

'Okay,' said Jacko, jumping down from the machine. 'The escape will get that bloke off the ledge. They're almost up to him. . . . Isn't that Dave?'

The sight of the wheeled escape's ladders being extended had spurred Dave into immediate and automatic action. It was now some seconds after 3.36.

He ran diagonally across the slip-road and started climbing up the ladders as the final section was extended. The tensed-up, panting crew on the wheels and levers, prepared for any eventuality, viewed his sudden appearance and subsequent disappearance in the smoke with equanimity. Encumbered by his BA set as he was – he had inserted the mouth-piece, turned on the oxygen and fitted the nose-clips – he swiftly reached the top. His goggles were on his forehead.

Near him on his left he found a foreign-looking young man in trousers and a jumper sitting astride a window-sill. He stared at Dave wide-eyed, and for a moment seemed impervious to the smoke winding around him, and disinclined to move. Holding onto the escape with his right hand Dave reached out with his left, grabbed the man's arm and pulled him onto the ladder. He came across quite easily, but then froze on the ladder behind Dave, saying not a word.

'Get down!' ordered Dave, unclipping half his mouth-piece – 'Get *down!*'

He yelled down to the escape crew for someone to come up and assist the man, but in the hubbub of shouting and engines running, no one below heard him. To his right another man at a window that was belching volumes of dark smoke was yelling even louder. He was half-standing on the window-sill, trying to reach a drain-pipe and screaming in a foreign accent for help.

'For Christ's sake!' he was saying. 'Get me out of here!'

Suddenly the first man started moving down the ladder, swiftly and comparatively smoothly. Dave debated with himself about entering the room on his left, then finding a corridor and leading the other man back to the escape. But for all he knew, the rooms might not be connected by a corridor, and if they were it might be blazing and impassable. The best thing was for him to descend and for the ladders to be re-pitched.

'Hang on!' he called across the gap. The other man's imprecations became hysterically abusive as the fireman climbed rapidly down.

Dave jumped off the escape and helped Garner, Dunlop, Dyer, Stewart and Leroy to re-pitch the ladders six or seven feet to the right. Garner had already half-retracted them to make the escape more manageable. But its weight, the sharp and short angle, the kerb and the slope of the road, made the pitch less than perfect.

Dave was half-way up the ladders, whose top had still to be rested against the building, when the man at the second window flung himself wildly across the gap. The escape yawed and tilted as he landed clumsily on the extension. At its base the crew bore desperately down on the levers and wheels to prevent the ladders keeling over or throwing the man back against the wall.

When the escape steadied, still at an angle, Dave continued his ascent, containing his anger at the man's recklessness. He contented himself by giving the jumper's trousered backside a hard slap when he got to the top.

'Come on! Get going! Move your feet!'

Relinquishing his prostrate position on the ladders, the now silent man began to back down them, his bare feet being guided to the rounds by Dave, who went down first.

While the first man was being rescued, the pump escape from A22 (Manchester Square) – which had been called to the fire as part of the first attendance – arrived at Clifton Gardens. A22's station officer, Fred Alcock, one of the most senior and experienced in the Division, ordered his crew to slip their escape. He then ran on ahead of them down the access road to Neil, who told him to use the escape to rescue people hanging out of two windows on the left.

The Worsley Hotel approximately 3.50 am.

Facade of the hotel approximately 3.55 am.

Fire-fighting outside the second floor, shortly before the collapse – room 213 on the left. Dave Dyer with the jet.

Only five minutes before the collapse. Wickenden and Cheal ascending the right-hand escape ladder. On the left Harry Pettit is about to enter room 213.

Soon after the collapse. In the window of 213, looking down, is Roger Stewart; Neil Wallington is on the balcony and A.C.O. Watkins on the ladder.

Here Keith Orchard, on A21's TL, joins the attempt to rescue Stewart and Searle.

Above Awaiting rescue –
the young man who
jumped into the tree from
the roof of No. 19.

Left Tony Stewart
(arrowed) about to be
lifted out of room 213.
Webber and Griffin are on
the balcony below.

Facing page

Top left Tony Stewart
being lifted out 70
minutes after the collapse.
Roger Stewart is holding
the beam.

Top right Colin Searle,
moments after his rescue
from the building.

Right Martin Walker is
lowered onto a stretcher
by Malcolm Garner. The
Sub Officer (left) is Paul
Taylor.

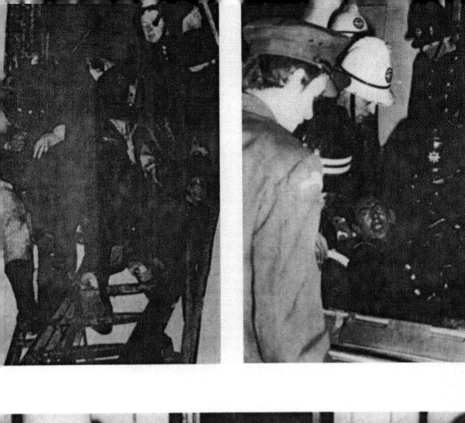

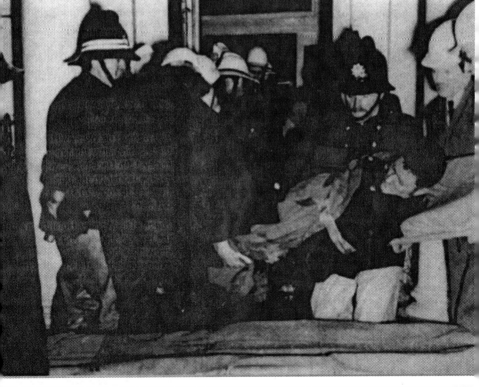

Above Ground floor passage in No. 15. The left foreground is where the first fire was started. On the right, the door to room 007.

Left The collapsed stone staircase of No. 15.

Top right The Worsley Hotel the morning after the fire – Friday 13th December – with the escape ladder on the right (leading to room 213) still in position.

Right The Worsley Hotel from the rear on the morning after, showing a hook ladder and an extension ladder still in position at the back of No. 15.

(Back row left to right and inset) Eric Hall, Ray Chilton and Neil Wallington: recipients of The Queen's Commendation for Brave Conduct. (Front row left to right) Roger Stewart, Ron Morris, Peter Lidbetter and David Blair who received Queen's Gallantry Medals.

Gordon Honeycombe with the Red Watch, A21 (Paddington) on the station forecourt, July 1975.

Among several civilians who had approached Neil demanding and pleading for the firemen's assistance had been one who spoke agitatedly of the fire at the back and of other people requiring to be rescued there. Another man, half-clothed, now stumbled up to him repeating the same information. But every single fireman he had was committed to the immediate task facing them of rescue and fire-fighting at the front. This could not go unco-ordinated, nor could he leave his command. He saw that Alcock's escape was already being put to use on his left. It would be up to the crews of the three appliances making up the 8 pump call to go round the back. He hoped they would soon arrive.

In the meantime, after telling the civilian – 'We're doing all we can!' – and urging him to inform Alcock and also put him in the picture, Neil directed the re-pitching of A21's escape to the right for its second rescue, and then, seizing the opportunity to find out if the pumps were being well supplied with hose and water, he told Garner to take charge of the escape, and ran over to the wall and the pump escape.

He learned that Lewis had connected the PE's pump to a hydrant, via three lengths of hose, and was in the process of twinning it, assisted by Wickenden and Cheal. They had already taken a length from the PE to the pump, and two jets were now operating from the PE on the side nearest the building. Orchard told Neil that water pressure was low in the area, with the result that insufficient water was coming into the PE. It was yet another problem. He told Orchard to get the pump connected up to another hydrant as soon as possible and to put every length of hose in both machines to work.

At that moment a policeman came up to him, asking if he wanted any help, and then a confused bellow of shouting and cursing came from the crew on A21's escape as the second man leapt onto it from his third-floor perch.

'Give us a hand!' Neil said and plunged towards the escape as it swayed and tottered. The policeman followed.

'Hold it down!'

The PC assisted the firemen, and when the ladders steadied enabling Dave to continue his ascent, Neil told the PC to stay where he was, grabbed hold of Leroy and took him at a run back to the PE where they started to strip the machine of all hose and lay it over the wall. Telling Leroy to carry on and help Orchard, Neil looked around to see who else might need him.

He saw that Ernie Arthurs and Harry were engaged in hook-ladder rescues on his right, that Dave was about to descend the escape with the second man, and that on his left A22's escape, which was outside number 17, had only a fireman and a civilian at its base.

He ran over to them.

'Where's your crew?' he demanded. 'Where's your Governor?'

Fireman Morgan told Neil that Alcock had gone around the back with O'Dwyer carrying a hook-ladder, and that his colleagues Norris and Beattie were making a quick search of the third-floor room from which three persons, including a woman, had just been rescued. The civilian, a young man in shirt and trousers, had volunteered to assist on the levers. Norris and Beattie reappeared at the top of the ladders, came down, and Neil directed the three firemen and the civilian to re-pitch the escape to their right to a second-floor window where a woman and a man were calling for help.

At the same time the clanging of a fire-bell heralded the arrival of the pump from G26 (Belsize), which had been called out by Wembley control as an additional appliance in the first attendance. It arrived at about 3.37.

Being involved in the re-pitching and extension of A22's escape, Neil was unable to meet the Belsize firemen, but he noted that after running into the slip-road they were met by Alcock, who had emerged from number 19, and were then engaged in fetching hook-ladders and lines to take around the back. He also noticed with some anxiety that his own men were having some difficulty manoeuvring Paddington's escape under the still extended ladders of the TL, endeavouring to reach a man on a third-floor ledge.

Exhaustedly, Garner, Dunlop, Dyer and Stewart manhandled the escape, its ladders part extended, to the right, and awkwardly under the TL. The PC helped them.

For the third time Dave ran up the ladders, not waiting till they touched the wall, still wearing his BA set. So intense had been his concentration on the first two rescues that he had not noticed the grey-haired man in the dressing-gown, whose rescue the TL had been unable to effect, hanging below the parapet like a spider on the third-floor wall. The window beside him was now like the open door of a furnace.

Without waiting for Dave to get to him, the elderly man reached out and lurched into space. He clutched at the ladder and fell on it and lay prone upon it, gasping.

Dave seized the man's waist with one hand. He could feel him shaking.

'I've got you,' he called. 'You'll be okay. Come on now. Come on, me old mate. . . . Let's get going!'

But the descent this time was a slow one. The old man's strength had almost gone, and Dave had to stay close behind him, alternately placing his feet on every round as they descended.

'Come on, come on!' exhorted Dave. 'Keep your feet going. Bit faster. . . . Keep going! Come on!'

Eventually they reached the ground. The old man, his eyes agape, was put in the care of a policeman and some civilians and led away. He said nothing to the firemen and never looked back. Nor did Dave watch him go. The moment he had jumped off the escape he had turned to scan the hotel front to see if he would be needed for any more rescues. But the windows of the burning hotel were now empty of people, and he saw that other firemen, escapes and ladders were in action.

As A21's escape was re-positioned by Neil to act as a means of ingress for fire-fighters armed with hose, Dave re-attached his mouthpiece, re-fitted his nose-clips, pulled down his goggles and at about 3.45 entered the door of number 13.

Minutes earlier Neil, after A22's escape had crunched against the building, had left the crew on it to make their second rescue and stood back to check that all was being done that could be done.

It seemed that all the rescues at the front would now be successfully completed. But the fire had greatly extended. From his new position and despite the dense smoke he could see that flames were now not only surging out of third-floor windows but also out of windows in the attic roof. Again he was dismayed by the acceleration and seriousness of the fire and he feared that for some people in the upper rooms they were already too late.

Knowing that more machines would be needed to fight the blaze, he ran over to the nearest available fireman and told him to send a priority message to Wembley control – 'Make pumps 15!' he said. 'BA required!'

The fireman ran to A21's pump, the nearest appliance, and passed on the message to Wembley control. It was heard by the three pump escapes and the pump that on receipt of the 8 pump call were clamorously approaching from Belsize, North Kensington and West Hampstead. It was by then 3.41.

Neil turned, and noticed a man sitting in a tall tree on his left, by number 19. A spectator, he thought, and looking up himself, saw through a sudden break in the billowing smoke the pale figures of several people on the roof, huddled between the parapet and a chimney-stack. They were also seen by people in the road, who renewed their calls of alarm.

Knowing the escape ladders were not long enough to reach the roof, he sprinted back down the slip-road, looking for Jacko.

He found him standing on a first-floor ladder that leaned against the porch of number 11. On top of the porch were Harry and Ernie Arthurs.

Neil called to Jacko, telling him to re-site the TL. 'There's people on the roof at the end!' he shouted. 'See if you can get the TL into the slip-road! Do what you can!'

At this point ADO Tom Rowley, who had driven over in his car from Paddington on the heels of the BA control van – they had received the 8 pump fire-call from Wembley at 3.38 – met up with Neil and said – 'How is it?' His arrival, which immediately followed the transmission of the 15 pump call from Clifton Gardens meant that he, as the senior officer, would now assume responsibility for the fighting of the fire.

'A hell of a job!' Neil answered, panting. 'About thirty rescues involved. Alcock's here. He's checking the back. No chance myself.'

'All right,' said Rowley. 'You stay at the front. I'll go and see how they're doing.'

They separated. Neil ran back to reposition the escape for fire-fighting. Rowley, after making his own assessment of the fire, went to the BA control van.

Near it, on the pavement, Mick Haskard was setting up a stage two board while Sub Officer Stanley unloaded a resuscitator and spare oxygen cylinders for an emergency crew. Sub Officer Prendergast had already gone on up the road to direct the crews of the appliances arriving at the Maida Vale end of Clifton Gardens to go to the rear of the hotel; Stanley would direct the make-up appliances arriving at the Warwick Avenue end.

Rowley told him to send three messages back to Wembley via the van's RT. Stanley jotted them down.

'Make it TLs three,' said Rowley. 'Follow that with thirty persons involved on upper floors – TL, escapes, first-floor ladders in use. . . . Then give them an informative – hotel, five floors and basement. Give them the size, and tell them that half the second, third, fourth and fifth floors are alight. Right?'

'Right!'

The messages, each of which had to be noted and double-checked by Wembley control, were received there at 3.46, 3.47 and 3.49. The two additional TLs – A21's being the other – were ordered out from B22 (Lambeth) and A28 (Kensington) at 3.49.

On the latter was Ray Wade.

By then the fire originally attended by Paddington's PE and pump, Manchester Square's PE and Belsize's pump (A21's TL and ET were not *pumps* but extra and specialized appliances), had been joined after the 8 pump call sent out by Wembley at 3.38 by A29's PE, G26's PE and G25's PE and pump. The hose-laying machine from G24 (Hendon) and the ET from C27 (Clerkenwell) were also sent.

Neil's 15 pump message at 3.41, transmitted by Wembley at 3.44, brought seven other appliances to Clifton Gardens – the PE from A28 (Kensington) and both PE and pump from A24 (Soho), from A25 (Westminster) and from C27 (Clerkenwell).

At 3.46, Wembley began the process of sending appliances from other stations and Divisions to stand by in case of local need in the mainly deserted stations of 'A' Division.

One station in the Division was never called to Clifton Gardens. It was left undisturbed by Wembley control to deal with any other emergencies that might arise in the area. For hours Shiner Wright and the firemen of A23 (Euston), Paddington's neighbour, heard and saw other appliances racing along Euston Road. With real frustration they read the story of the fire as it unrolled from the teleprinter machine, and they swore as the blaze turned into the biggest in the Division that year. But they were never called to the scene of the fire – not until 7.46 a.m. that morning, when their TL was ordered out as a relief. By then it was all over, and the Worsley Hotel was a blackened, smoking ruin.

At the beginning, the fire was fought from the hall of number 13, and fierce though it was no one dreamed what disasters it would bring. Harry Pettit and Jim Griffin, who had been the first firemen involved in rescuing a man – from the porch of number 13 – were also the first firemen to enter the building and attack the fire.

After extinguishing most of the flames in the hallway as far as the stairs and enveloping themselves in dark masses of steam and smoke, they were replaced by some of the ET crew wearing BA. Paul Taylor and Martin Walker, their sets turned on and their goggles pulled down, took the jet off the other two firemen, who then went out again into the cold night and the orange glare from the street-lamps.

Within, Taylor and Martin Walker, backed up initially by Pincher, Waldron and Marven, started to ascend the rubble-choked stairs. Progress was very slow. At that time they had no idea of the true extent and fury of the fire, nor indeed of the extent of the hotel. Seeing a blazing hall and stairway in front of them when they entered the building they assumed that this, if not the only stair, was the main one, and that persons might well be trapped above. They were not to know that the hotel covered *eight* houses, which were connected by a warren of corridors, and that even then the fire was spreading, through doors left open by residents in their panic, to *four* of the houses and had already engulfed not one staircase but two.

They toiled up the first flight of stairs in number 13 largely working in the dark, apart from the flicker of unextinguished flame here and there and a fiery glow above them penetrating the stairwell. Vapours of steam and smoke washed over them. Their goggles began to mist up and constrict their vision even more, and their feet were impeded by the debris on every step. Through the regular clicking of the valves on their sets they dimly heard crashing sounds and a dull roar and glimpsed the vague fall of flaming objects from above.

At last, on reaching a landing where the darkness was less, Taylor, Martin and Pincher turned and found that the next flight of stone stairs, leading up to the first floor, had vanished, having cracked and collapsed after being subjected to fierce heat and then the sudden cold torrent of water from the jet. Jagged ends sticking out of the wall showed where the steps had been. Their collapse in the general darkness and confusion of sound had gone unnoticed by the firemen. Ten feet away, beyond and above, a raging bloom of flame illumined a pulsing skin of smoke and steam. It came from a partition across the first-floor landing and from the false ceiling above, and streamed out of sight to the second floor, joining the torrent of fire that was funnelling all the way up the stairwell to the roof, fanned by the swiftly rising currents of hot air. The higher it went, the fiercer and hotter and the more indestructible and destructive it grew, finding new impetus and fuel at every open door.

Meanwhile Archie Waldron, fifth in the line of firemen taking the jet up the stairs – Marven was in front of him – and with nothing to do other than straighten and pull in the hose, had looked round for some more positive action as soon as he entered the building.

At the foot of the stairs, he saw that what he thought was a room was ablaze. One of its double swing-doors was ajar, and both were on fire within. He told Marven he was going to get another jet, went outside, found Orchard at the pump of the PE, and in a few seconds, with Wickenden's assistance, carried a fully charged 2¾-inch hose back with him into the building – the second jet to attack the fire.

They kicked in one of the swing-doors and knelt, and Archie turned on the jet. With Marven backing him up, he directed the powerful column of water at the obscure seats of fire in the ceiling and around the walls, overwhelming them both in a fog of smoke and steam, while bits of false ceiling broke off and crashed down in a rain of cinders and water. The goggles of their BA sets began to cloud.

For some moments the fire-glow persisted, cloaked in dark confusion, seeming to resist and even annul the force of the jet.

Archie, peering wide-eyed through his goggles, felt a pang of fear – the fire seemed so deep-seated it could not be put out. Then suddenly the water failed.

They dodged backwards out into the hall, swearing and alarmed at losing their safeguard. Archie dropped the branch and sprang to the front door, angrily shouting at the firemen at the pump.

'The pressure dropped!' someone shouted back. 'It's all right now! Coming on again!'

He and Marven picked up the jet and returned to the attack, advancing slowly through what was now evidently not a room but a passageway – their purpose being, as BA wearers, to blast a way through the fire and to reach the upper rooms.

Marven kicked in a door in a badly burned partition wall on their left, whose fan-light windows of meshed glass had melted in the heat. The room beyond was a bedroom, smoke-blackened but largely unburnt, whose high window opened onto the basement and the street.

It was empty – the occupants had fled.

The hotel's chef and his wife had been asleep in this room when they were woken by shouts of '*Fire!*' The man opened his door to find a circle of fire on the floor immediately outside. As he stared at it in stupefaction, it exploded into much stronger life with a 'whoof' like a gas-jet being lit. Slamming shut the door, he and his wife clothed themselves as best they could, seized some personal belongings, and struggled out of the window. Before he left the man momentarily opened the bedroom door to verify the extent of the fire, and found the whole passageway now ablaze.

Some ten minutes later, Archie and Marven made their way through the passage, hardly aware through the gloom and the mist on their goggles of the charred wrecks of an armchair, a small cupboard and two upright chairs on their right – unaware that the blackened carpet beneath their boots, now sodden with water, had earlier been soaked with meths.

They emerged through the burnt, black swing-door at the other end – it was also open – following the main exit of the smoke, and found themselves surrounded by fire at the foot of another stair.

To their left was the blocked-off and unused front door of number 15, its entrance hall forming an office space. The door to it, shut, flamed on the side facing the stairs, as did a fire-door opposite them, also shut, and all the false ceilings, door-frames, banisters, and other doorways around the staircase.

The fire here was brighter and newer, and fierce though it was, it was soon damped down and extinguished by the swishing stream of the jet.

Wiping the mist off the interior of their goggles with their fingers, Archie and Marven moved on, still crouching, to the foot of the stairs – their uniforms and bodies soaked with sweat and drenched in the throwback of water from the jet, their faces and hands scorched by the heat: it was as if an electric fire were burning only six inches away. The dark smoke burgeoning upwards hid the conflagration above them. But they sensed its magnitude in the fire-damage around the stairway and the convulsing fire-glow seen up the stairwell.

It had to be arson, thought Archie, and again felt fear.

Then suddenly Dave Webber was with them – he had followed the line of their hose from number 13 – and Archie indicated with a nod of his head that he and Marven intended to go up the stairs.

Dave took over the branch, and moved up three steps with Archie behind him, directing the jet ahead of them.

Then Archie grasped his arm in warning. Dave turned. Archie mimed that a large chunk of stone had crashed down onto his helmet. It now lay, red-hot, on the bottom step between them.

Distantly, Dave heard Archie shout through his BA set – 'It's a *stone* staircase!' – meaning it was liable to collapse.

Dave nodded and descended. It would be foolishly danger-ous to ascend the stairs. He looked about, saw the charred, smouldering face of a fire-door that must, he thought, connect with another passage. He pointed it out to Archie, who nodded. They would go that way. To seek out people was still their paramount task.

Dave handed the branch to Marven and unlatching his mouthpiece said – 'We'll see if we can get up through there, Paul. Hold on!'

Leaving Marven to extinguish completely all fires adjacent to the stairs from the safety of a doorway, Dave pushed open the fire-door – which had served its purpose well – and followed by Archie found himself in a passage unmarked by fire and practically free from smoke.

On the landing leading to the first floor of number 13, Taylor, Martin and Pincher faced the dilemma of whether they should try to bridge the gap caused by the collapsed stair or descend and try to reach the upper floors another way. They had just been joined by Garner and Dunlop, who at the conclusion of the escape's three rescues, had completed the putting-on of their BA sets and followed Dave into the building. The ET crew were thus temporarily re-united – with the exception of Dave and Archie Waldron: these two were about to make their abortive attempt to ascend number 17's staircase.

'We need a first-floor ladder,' Taylor said.

At this point Station Officer Alcock appeared in the hallway of number 13, where Jim Griffin was pulling in and straightening a length of hose that had been added to the one the ET crew were taking up the stairs.

Alcock had returned to the front after taking one of his own men and Belsize's pump crew, armed with ladders and lines, to the rear of the building to make any necessary rescues there before entering the hotel. Having done this, he had rushed back through number 19 to the front, to see what jets had been put to work inside. He found two lines of hose from Paddington's PE going in at the door of number 13.

He mounted the first flight of stairs, and sizing up the situation roared at the ET crew on the landing to get across the gap and fight the fire on the first floor.

'Get some scaling-ladders!' he bellowed. 'Get *moving*! Don't just stand there!'

The firemen split up, their dilemma resolved. Griffin went

out into the road to fetch the first-floor ladder he had used to bring a man down from the porch of number 13. Martin, who had already told Taylor he would try to find another way up – 'to beat the stairwell', he said – made his way back down the stairs and out of the front door. Meanwhile Garner and Dunlop took over the jet from Taylor and Pincher while they seized hold of the ladder that Alcock and Griffin now passed up to them. They hauled it up to the landing. As they did so Alcock returned to the street, met Neil and told him what was being organized at the rear of the hotel, which he now re-visited, taking with him some other firemen who had newly arrived, as well as additional ladders.

Griffin also left the building, his aim being now to assist Lewis, Cheal and Leroy at the pump in laying out more lengths of hose and connecting other jets for use from the escape. But as he trotted up the slip-road he was confronted by a dishevelled civilian, wearing only trousers, who told him someone was calling for help at the back.

'Come with me! Quickly!' said the man.

Griffin glanced about. The nearest fireman was the newest one, Leroy Hough. There would have to be a first time to test his mettle and resolve – so why not, thought Griffin, on his very first night-duty?

'Leroy! Get a hook-ladder!' Griffin shouted. 'Come with me!'

It was a bad moment for Leroy. Scared and awe-struck from the beginning by the dreadful reality of the fire, by the noise, by the crowds, by the many needing rescue, he had blindly obeyed orders, trying to remember what his training had taught him and to think of nothing else. There was so much apparent confusion around him that he had had to concentrate very hard on slipping the escape, running with it into the access road and then pitching it to the third floor. In the aching, breathless pauses between the rescues his admiration for Dave, and for the men toiling beside him on the wheels and levers, greatly increased, and he found himself exulting in all the drama and excitement. But when Neil ordered him away to unload more hose he found his hands were shaking badly – all at once he felt dog-tired and in need of a quiet sit-down and a smoke. Yet his mind still raced. Keenly aware once more of his role as a fireman he hardly dared look at the building, which was now terrifyingly ablaze.

He was head-down laying out a length of hose to the pump when Griffin called to him.

Dutifully, but with his heart in his boots, Leroy unlashed a hook-ladder from the top of the pump while Griffin shouted at him, telling him to get a move on. He could see no one at a window requiring rescue – a fact which alarmed him even more, implying as it did that the person to be rescued was hidden by the smoke on the upper floors.

Despite his fears he moved quite fast, in approved training-school style, and was soon running up the slip-road after Griffin with the long thin ladder under his arm.

'In here!' shouted Griffin, vanishing into a porch.

Wonderingly, Leroy followed, confused by the need for a hook-ladder *inside* the building.

He found himself in a dark hallway, surprisingly free from smoke. The light from a torch in a room on his right showed him where Griffin must be. With the ends of the ladder colliding against walls and doors he manoeuvred himself into the room, a large room at the rear of the building, and was met by Griffin coming towards him.

'All right,' Griffin said. 'Take it out again! We don't need it. He's been brought down.'

Leroy gazed at Griffin in all kinds of disbelief.

'Move!' ordered Griffin – the youngster was blocking the doorway of the room.

Leroy moved. He turned and found his way out into the street, sweet relief and fearful frustration compounding the adrenalin flowing through his veins. Full of new energy now and excitement, he plonked the hook-ladder on the pavement by the railings and ran back to the pump.

There he flung himself almost joyously into the task of re-pitching escapes and feeding hose to the firemen on escapes and ladders – Dyer, Garner, Cheal and Wickenden were among them – as they directed jets through windows onto the flames.

Still apprehensive about doing well, Leroy could now none-theless hardly believe his luck – that on his first night there should be such a fire, a classic, and that he would be there. What tales would he have to tell his mates about what being a fireman was really like!

Unknown to Leroy, the house he had entered, number 9, had already been invaded by Ernie Arthurs and Harry Pettit, who were then searching the upper rooms. Also intent on rescue at the same time as Leroy, and similarly armed with hook-ladders, had been Martin and Orchard.

The former, on leaving the ET crew in number 13, had called to a fireman from another crew to bring him a first-floor ladder – his intention being to break into the hotel through a window and look for another way of combating the fire. While he waited, trying to get his bearings and assess the extent of the blaze, Jim Griffin saw him and shouted at him to grab a hook-ladder – for Griffin had concluded that as Leroy was an untried novice, Martin's experience would be more useful in any hazardous hook-ladder rescue. Such a ladder Martin obtained from the PE, and in doing so told Orchard that hook-ladders were needed. The latter, anxious for some more direct action than the albeit very necessary operation of the pumps, told Wickenden to take over, ran to the pump – both the PE's hook-ladders and the one on the TL had by now been taken – unlashed a ladder from the pump and ran after Martin, who had by then vanished into the front door of number 11.

By the time Orchard made his way in at the dark front door of number 9 and up to a half-landing overlooking the rear, Griffin had turned back both Martin and Leroy – neither of whom met, having entered by different doors. Nor did they see Orchard.

He descended the stair, his view from the landing window having been constricted, and bumped into Griffin in the hall.

'I'll go round the back!' said Orchard. 'There was someone shouting out there. . . .' He darted outside.

He reached the rear of the building by running with the hook-ladder along the full length of the hotel, past number 19 and around the end of the terrace, down flights of steps to a broad green and several gardens at basement level, where he climbed over garden walls, ploughed through bushes, and encountered knots of other firemen variously engaged in fire-fighting, including a group who were involved in a perilous hook-ladder rescue from a third-floor window. As the sunken garden was level with the basement, this meant that the third floor was seen from the front as the second floor.

Realizing that the firemen at the rear were coping and could cope with any rescues, and that he had nothing to con-tribute, Orchard left his ladder in a conspicuous position for others to use, and returned to the slip-road by the same route and went back to the pump escape.

Jim Griffin in the meantime, thinking that Orchard might have noticed something he had missed – his own view from the rear ground-floor room had been of a man coming down a builder's ladder footed by a civilian – had returned to the room, climbed out of the window and dropped into the base-ment garden. Here he came across the civilian in trousers who had originally sought his help. The man had reached the back – unknown to Griffin – by going down the interior basement stairs and then out through a rear door into the garden. With him was his newly rescued friend. Both were talking excitedly in Spanish about their adventures. Neither of them heeded Griffin.

He walked past them, looking up at the building, from whose upper floors and roof showers of sparks were being blown down by the wind into the gardens. Suddenly a man popped his head out of an inset second-floor window next to the lift-shaft. Before he began calling out for help, Jim Griffin had fetched the heavy builder's ladder from the garden next door and propped it against the back wall. Then he climbed up, and without much trouble was able to assist the man, a Frenchman, to the ground.

As the crews of firemen on his right seemed sufficient to deal with the fire bursting out of the windows at the back, he returned to the front of the hotel – by way of the basement stairs to the ground floor and so out into the street – with the intention of rejoining his colleagues and taking part again in fighting the fire.

He was about to enter number 13 to see how Taylor and the ET crew were progressing, when a voice hailed him from a first-floor balustrade.

'Hey! Jim! Give us a hand! We got a jet in here. Could you add on another length?'

Despite the masking mouth-piece, goggles and nose-clips of the BA set, Griffin recognized Martin.

'Right-ho!' Griffin answered. 'Will do!'

After his foray inside the building with the hook-ladder, Martin had dumped it and gone outside, where he discovered the first-floor ladder he had called for earlier parked against the railings. He re-positioned it against the porch of number 13, climbed up and entered a first-floor window on his left. Crossing the narrow room by the light of his torch, which revealed a fireplace, a bed and a cupboard, he opened the door and found himself in a smoky corridor. Proceeding along it to his left, he passed several closed doors – one of which concealed the now collapsed staircase of number 15 – and at the corridor's end he stumbled through an open door on his right, onto the landing of number 17. There was very little smoke here. But after running quickly up the stairs to the second floor, he came face to face with another serious fire situation.

Flames poured out of an opening, a corridor, on his left, reaching along a false plasterboard ceiling and up the stair-well. The rooms at the front of the building were blazing fiercely, as was the partition enclosing a smaller wooden stair-way on his right leading to the third floor. He could not understand how the fire could have advanced so rapidly and spread so far – through *two* houses. He was not to know that the first fire, which had been lit on the ground floor and had extended up the stairwells of numbers 15 and 13 had been augmented by a *second*, deliberately lit in the second-floor passage of number 17 on his left.

Hesitating only to check that the stair he was on and the landing were safe, while flaming debris cascaded around him from above, he turned and hurried back to the first floor. Retracing his route, he emerged on the balustrade, where he shouted down for a jet to be laid out and passed up to him. This was done by a mixed crew from other stations, including the driver of Belsize's pump. As Walker checked how many lengths would be needed to reach the second floor, he met up with Dave and Archie.

They had made their way up to the second floor of number 17 after searching the ground- and first-floor rooms and had been confronted, like Martin, with the unexpectedly ferocious fire raging in the upper half of the house. Keeping close to the wall on the second-floor landing, Dave had crawled as far as the corridor, under a ceiling of flame, and peering to his left through his goggles had glimpsed an unbroken corridor of fire tunnelling through three houses.

Astounded by the sight, and driven back by the almost unbearable heat, he had blundered back down the stairs to Archie Waldron.

With the same idea as Martin of getting a jet, the two of them had then withdrawn to the first floor of number 15 where they then teamed up with him.

Together the three of them began dragging the hose into the building from the balustrade, along the corridor of number 15 and up number 17's stairs – an awkward business, as the hose was heavily charged with water and bent with difficulty around the corners. They discovered that another length would be needed to give them more free-play on the second floor and Martin went back to the balustrade, where he saw Jim Griffin and asked for his help.

On returning to the second floor, Martin, Dave and Archie began attacking the blaze. They were joined before long by Garner and Bill Gocher, a friend of Archie from A29 (North Kensington). There was so much flame about and falling debris that they had to shelter in the doorway of a large room off the landing whose window overlooked the back gardens – while the belt of whoever had the branch was held onto by the others backing him up, keeping an eye on any signs of collapse. The heat was intense. Burning embers continually fell around them – some entered Dave's sleeve, making him yell and swear. It was not until Archie noticed that the partition dividing the room from the corridor had been almost eaten away by the flames on the other side that they devised another plan of action. They kicked a hole in the partition – and by poking the jet through it were able then to attack the heart of the fire.

By this time they had been joined on the landing by Sub Officer Ron Morris of A25 (Westminster) and Jim Griffin.

Also armed with a jet and backed up by another crew, they tried without success to get up the enclosed wooden stairs. Forced back by the heat, the danger of collapse below and above, they concentrated instead on extinguishing the fires in the two front rooms.

Earlier the embattled men in the rear room, alternately attacking the fiercely burning corridor from the doorway and through the hole in the wall, had been joined by Paul Taylor.

In the centre of the building, Taylor and Pincher had been for a time on their own. It had not been possible for more than two firemen, and then only one at a time, to cross the collapsed stair via the ladder. Dunlop, looking for more action, had gone back down the stairs, and after following the other length of hose had teamed up with Marven at the foot of number 15's staircase. Garner, unable to assist Taylor and Pincher once the crossing had begun, went outside and briefly joined a crew fire-fighting from an escape.

On the landing Pincher held the jet, spraying it all around, as Paul Taylor crawled up the ladder on his hands and knees across a seven-foot gap. Half-way across he asked for the jet. Pincher passed it over to him, and so he continued onwards, largely unsighted, balancing the heavy hose and himself on the narrow ladder. It was like crossing a volcanic rift, with dark vapours being swept by an up-draught all about him and a wall of fire ahead, while ashes, fiery fragments and chunks of stone spun past him down the stairwell. Many sounds assailed his ears, louder than the clicking of the valves on his BA set. But loudest of all was the many-tongued malevolent bonfire sound of the burning hotel.

Having reached the confined space of the first-floor landing, with walls and doors on three sides of him well alight like the stairway above, Taylor knelt and opened up the jet.

Pincher was about to follow him when a voice bellowed from below.

'You there!' shouted Station Officer Alcock. 'Get the hell *out* of there quick! Do you hear? – *Withdraw!*'

He had come back to them, knowing that other crews were penetrating the building from the rear with jets which might cause the collapse of the stairs above the two firemen. Several flights of number 15's staircase had, he knew, already fallen.

'They're putting jets in at the back!' he shouted up at Pincher. 'Get yourself *out!*'

Doing as he ordered, and gladly, as their situation was patently dangerous, Taylor retreated with difficulty back across the ladder, taking the jet with him. He and Pincher then staggered back down the first flight of stairs, which by then had also partly collapsed.

They emerged from the steaming hallway with the jet – smoke-stained, sweating, their uniforms soaking wet – to be taken unawares by the shocking cold night air and the spread of the fire above them. They stared upwards. Gouts of flame were bursting out of several upper windows, and the whole roof seemed ablaze.

'Good grief!' said Taylor. 'Just look at *that!*'

As they walked away, a hot blast of air swept out after them into the street through the front door of number 13.

The second-floor stairs had just collapsed.

Outside the hotel, all the people on the first-floor porches and at second- and third-floor windows and ledges had by that time (fifteen minutes after the Brigade arrived) been rescued – at the front and at the back, where the difficult rescue of a man at a third-floor window had been effected by Acting Leading Fireman Trotman of G26 (Belsize) and Fireman O'Dwyer of A22 (Manchester Square). Another very hazardous rescue took place at the front. West Hampstead's wheeled escape – their PE and pump had arrived from G25 at 3.42 – had been pitched to the roof above number 19. By using a first-floor ladder from the head of the escape to reach the parapet, T/Sub Officer Roger Stewart and Fireman David Blair had managed to bring seven people safely to the ground.

Inside the hotel, in a rear room of number 19, Fireman Harrison of G25 (West Hampstead) found an elderly woman still fast asleep after smashing open her bedroom door. It turned out later that the old lady was deaf. Astonishingly, another person was also discovered asleep in bed – half an hour after the Brigade arrived. Acting Sub Officer Allera, leading a mainly Belsize crew, had been told to double-check that the building was empty of civilians, and when they did so

Fireman Pat Neary (G25) and Fireman Stanley (G24) found a young man in a small ground-floor room at the back of number 17. They escorted him, still half-asleep, out into the street.

Some fifteen minutes earlier, a similar rescue, the last made by Paddington's firemen, involved Harry Pettit – as the first had done.

Out in the slip-road Harry had been adding another length to the hose that he and Griffin had taken into number 13 – they had just been replaced in the hallway by Taylor and some of the ET crew – when Ernie Arthurs ran past him, shouting – 'Grab a hook-ladder, Harry!'

Moments before, Ernie had told Jacko to stay with the TL after they had failed to rescue the elderly man standing on the third-floor ledge. He was now determined to succeed in rescuing three other people whom he had noticed on the right of the building. Fetching a first-floor ladder from A29's PE, which had just arrived, he ran over to the porch of number 11, where a fully-dressed man was leaning over the balustrade, clamouring to be brought down. He leaned the ladder against the porch and clambered up.

In the meantime Harry had unlashed a thirteen-foot hook-ladder from Paddington's PE. He carried it over to the porch, laid it on the pavement and footed the first-floor ladder, while Ernie on the porch above handed the man down. Harry guided his steps.

The man, aged about forty, was short and stout and de-scended slowly. As soon as he had reached the pavement Harry slung the hook-ladder up to Ernie, who extended the long white hook, heaved the ladder aloft and hooked it onto the second-floor window-sill immediately above him. As he did so, Harry quickly mounted the other ladder to the porch and without a pause continued his ascent up the hook-ladder to the window.

He climbed into the smoke-filled room and helped the civilian, a young man dressed in a suit, to get onto the ladder and make his uncertain descent. Leaning out, Harry held the man's arms. His legs were grasped by Ernie when they came within his reach.

They talked him down, reasuring him, telling him to take it steady and use alternate hand and foot.

'You're all right. Watch what you're doing. . . . Easy now. We've got you.'

Ernie also called encouragingly up to Harry. 'That's it. Talk to him, Harry. . . . You're doing all right.'

He wanted the younger man to do well, to prove himself at hook-ladder rescues – the first Harry had made – and he thought it lucky that Harry had chanced to be by the PE and been able to join him.

The civilian stepped unsteadily onto the porch. Ernie Arthurs turned around and shouted down at a policeman standing near the next porch.

'Oy – mate! Hold the ladder for this bloke, will you?'

As the PC footed the first-floor ladder, and as Ernie passed the civilian down to him, Harry descended the hook-ladder. He jumped off it onto the porch, and then Ernie, in trying to dislodge the ladder from the window, discovered that the hook had become jammed between the sill and an ornate iron bar a few inches above it.

He swore vehemently. Harry tried to help.

'It's no bloody use!' wailed Ernie. He cast about for some assistance.

The PC called up to them – 'What's the matter?'

Ernie sighted Jacko on his left running up the slip-road. He had been down to the Warwick Avenue end to see if the TL could squeeze into the road through the parked cars and concluded it could not.

'*Jacko!*' yelled Ernie. 'Can you get us another hook-ladder?'

Jacko gave a thumbs-up sign, and while he ran on up the road to fetch a hook-ladder from the TL, the two firemen on the porch continued to struggle unavailingly with the ladder above them.

'Don't you go away!' shouted Ernie at a man apprehensively gazing down at them from another second-floor window. 'We'll get to you – I promise you!'

Jacko returned with a hook-ladder and climbed up a few rounds of the ladder against the porch.

'Can you manage okay?' he asked as Ernie and Harry took the hook-ladder off him.

'Yes,' said Ernie. 'We'll manage. Thanks!'

At that moment Neil ran up to Jacko and asked him to re-site the TL and try to reach some people on the roof above number 19, at the end of the block.

Harry and Ernie moved further along the balustrade to their right.

Following the same procedure with the hook-ladder as before, they rescued the man at the other second-floor window. He had also managed to find time to put some clothes on and insisted on bringing a brief-case with him down the ladder. This made a difficult descent no easier and much slower. To hasten his descent, Ernie reached up, lifted him bodily off the ladder and planted him safely on the narrow balustrade. He was then led along it to the porch and passed down to the policeman, who had now been joined at the foot of the ladder by Tony Stewart.

'What's it like in there?' shouted Ernie up to Harry, who was astride the window-sill. The ladder's hook, caught on top of an iron bar, was all that held it in place.

'Very smoky!' called out Harry. 'The bedroom door's on fire!'

'Come down!' said Ernie. 'We'll go in here.'

Harry quickly rejoined him on the balustrade.

'We better check all the rooms on this floor,' said Ernie. 'Then we'll go up to the second. Leave the hook-ladder. Someone might need it.'

They entered the building through the open first-floor window in front of them. Using their torches they crossed the room, a bedroom, to the door and found themselves in a corridor, clouded with a pungent smoke that made them cough.

Ernie went left into a hall. To his right was a lift – there were no stairs in number 11. Opposite him was a fire-door, lined by black streamers of smoke, through whose small glass window at the top he could see that the corridor beyond was on fire. His eyes stinging, his nostrils smarting and clogging up with the fumes, he rapidly checked that both bedrooms opening off the hall were unoccupied. Harry, who had stayed with him, now went ahead of him back up the corridor, through another fire-door, to the first-floor landing of number 9.

In a small room hard on their right and facing the street, they found a young man heavily asleep in bed.

Amazingly he had slept through all the noise and confusion within and outside the hotel, and had not even been disturbed by the two firemen kicking in his locked bedroom door. The gas-fire in the room was on. Harry went around the foot of the bed to turn it off, while Ernie knelt on the bed and roughly shook the sleeper. The man murmured feebly in protest and remained fast asleep. Harry lent a hand, slapping the man's face several times while Ernie shone his torch on him.

'Come on! Come on!' said Harry. 'Wake up! The hotel's on fire! Come on – wake up. . . . *Wake up* – for Christ's sake!'

Ernie Arthurs was less gentle in word and deed. Between them they succeeded in making the man half open his eyes and regain some degree of consciousness, though he still remained half-asleep. It was as if he had been drugged. Calling the man all manner of names, Ernie dragged back the bedclothes. Harry pulled the unwilling civilian from his bed and onto his feet. He stood on the floor in a singlet and pale blue underpants, swaying and semi-conscious.

'Get a move on now!' said Harry. 'Come on – get dressed! You've got a fire here. . . . Here's your shoes. . . . Dash about now! The place is on fire!'

'Sorry,' mumbled the young man. 'Sorry . . .'

'Give him his trousers, for *fuck's* sake, and let's get him out of here!' said Ernie disgustedly. 'Fuck me! Some people will sleep through *anything*!'

Harry thrust the rest of the man's clothes into his arms and led him around the bed to the door.

'You take him down, Harry,' said Ernie. 'Can you manage? I'll check the other rooms.'

He turned and attacked a locked door near him with the heel of his boot.

Harry bundled the civilian down the stairs and left him under the porch struggling to dress himself properly, now thoroughly shocked awake by the freezing night and the nightmare scene outside.

The man was the very last civilian to emerge alive from that part of the building. As yet unknown by anyone, six others were already dead. Three more rescues would be made – but of firemen by other firemen. And the death of a fireman would bring the final toll to seven.

Harry Pettit ran back up the stairs, with only thirty minutes left of his life to live.

*

Divisional Officer Bob Keable, a tall thin man with an unblinking gaze and a benign and courteous manner, lived in one of the penthouse flats above Paddington fire-station with his wife and four pretty young daughters. He was forty-three, and had been a DO for over three years, since his posting to 'A' Division headquarters in 1971.

On Thursday 12 December, 1974 – at 6.30 p.m. – he had interviewed Fireman Harry Pettit in his office. It was Pettit's first probationary interview and followed the probationary tests and drills that had been set and marked by ADO Tom Rowley in November. Both men had been very impressed by the young man.

DO Keable, who wrote after the interview that it was 'very satisfactory' and that Fireman Pettit 'showed good potential for the future', was the senior office in 'A' Division on duty that night.*

DO Keable: *At about 0342 hours on Friday 13 December, I was informed by telephone by Wembley control that a 15 pump fire was in progress at the Worsley Hotel, Clifton Gardens, and I responded immediately. On arrival at that address, which was a row of eight terraced houses of four and five floors and basement, about 200 feet by 60 feet, converted for use as a hostel for hotel staff, I saw that a very serious fire involved two or three of these houses on all floor levels and was spreading to the roof and horizontally to the houses on each side. I instructed that my Brigade car and the 'A' Division control unit should be sited clear of the frontage, to enable oncoming appliances to get to work. I saw that three wheeled escape ladders were pitched to the front of the building from the service roadway, as was the turntable ladders from A21, Paddington; also first-floor ladders and hookladders were pitched at first- and second-floor levels respectively. Several*

---

*All the following passages in italics are taken from statements presented in December 1974 to the London Fire Brigade Honours and Awards Committee.

jets were already at work tackling the fire, and rescues were still being effected down one of the escapes at the Randolph Road end of the building.

Station Officer Wallington reported to me that multiple rescues had been carried out at all floor levels at the front by ladders of all types, and that a similar situation prevailed at the rear, except that only extension ladders and hook-ladders could be used, as the only access was via the garden or through the premises involved or adjacent thereto. He also told me that some internal staircases had already collapsed.

The crews in attendance on my arrival were fully committed, and I remained at the front for a few minutes to direct crews of the re-inforcing appliances, which were still responding to earlier requests for assistance from both Station Officer Wallington and Assistant Divisional Officer Rowley.

ADO Rowley then reported to me and confirmed the information given by Stn O Wallington, and I asked him to remain in charge at the front of the premises while I surveyed the rear.

On reaching the rear of the premises I saw several extension ladders and hook-ladders pitched into various windows, and it was reported to me that all persons known to require rescue had in fact been rescued. Several jets were already at work, and the spread of the fire appeared to me to be more extensive than it was at the front. I instructed that more extension ladders and hook-ladders should be provided to enable a more rapid search of the back rooms, and that jets should be got to work internally where possible and also from the heads of the extension ladders where they would be more quickly effective.

As I returned to the front I met ADO Baldwin and asked him to take charge of fire-fighting and searching at the rear of the premises.

ADO Baldwin: *On arrival at the rear of the premises, I saw that fire had involved most of the two upper floors and roof and was spreading laterally and downwards. I was informed by members of the crews in attendance at the rear that G26 pump's crew had carried out a rescue from one of the upper floors using hook-ladders, and that one other man had been taken off a drain-pipe at second-floor level. I at once ordered lines of hose and jets to be got to work at the rear of the premises, with the main idea of preventing further lateral spread of fire. Two jets were used to cover the roof and the outside of the premises, and three jets were taken into the first- and third-floor levels via extension ladders and hook-ladders. During the course of fire-fighting, two of the three stone staircases, which crews were using to gain internal access to the upper floors and roof, collapsed. Crews were withdrawn and fire-fighting at the rear of the building was then confined to jets working from the outside, and those that could be worked into the upper floors via the windows, using numerous hook-ladders to gain entry.*

DO Keable: *Thε number of jets was being adversely affected by a resultant water shortage, and when the hose-laying lorry arrived, I asked ADO Rowley to expedite a water relay from the Edgware Road to improve water supplies generally.*

T/Stn O Brooks, G24 (Hendon): *I have to report that the HLL (hose-laying lorry) attached to G24 – Acting Leading Fireman Roberts in command – was ordered by Wembley control at 0338 hours to the Worsley Hotel, Clifton Gardens, and on arrival reported to the control unit and was ordered by ADO Rowley to set into a 21-inch main in Edgware Road at the junction with Clifton Road, and an intermediate pump to be positioned half-way between the hydrant and the fire. Twelve lengths of HLL hose, twinned – twenty-four lengths in all – were laid, and A25's (Westminster's) pump was set in midway as the intermediate pump.*

T/Stn O Randall, G25 (West Hampstead): *T/Sub Officer Stewart approached me to say that he had seen the HLL, which was setting in to a hydrant in the Edgware Road and that an intermediate pump was being positioned. The majority of West Hampstead's crew, with the exception of myself and another fireman, were involved in this action. The twin lines were fed into G26's pump, which eventually supplied the ladders.*

DO Keable: *As the crews of all reinforcing appliances were now committed, I requested the attendance of an additional five pumping appliances.*

FROM DO KEABLE
AT CLIFTON GARDENS
MAKE PUMPS 20
TOO 0406

DO Keable: *I then detailed A28's (Kensington's) pump crew and C27's (Clerkenwell's) emergency tender crew to tackle the fire internally on all floor levels from the nearest intact staircase at the Warwick Avenue end of the premises, while other crews did the same from the Randolph Road end. At this stage the three escapes at the front were continually being re-sited from window to window, so that crews could tackle the fire from the ladders by directing jets through the windows. Three turntable ladders were now at work – A21's TL and A28's TL at either end of the premises in the service roadway – and B22's TL in the road in Clifton Gardens, opposite the section of the building most heavily involved in fire.*

Deputy Assistant Chief Officer Pearce then arrived and assumed control of the fire after I gave him a situation report.

DACO Pearce: *I informed him that I would take over, requesting him to continue with detailed fire-fighting operations at the front of the building, with his junior officers remaining as they were. This enabled me to survey the extent of the fire. . . . Fire was affecting the central part of the premises, at first-floor level, with considerable increase occurring progressively at the second, third and fourth floors. About thirty feet of the roof was enveloped in flames, and smoke frequently obscured the whole length of the upper floors and roof. . . . Several crews were at work at the rear of the premises. I observed hook-ladders at various windows. Jets were at work, and crews were still searching the central part of the building. . . . Fire was spreading at third- and fourth-floor levels and along the roof. Water supplies were over-stretched and all the crews fully occupied. I therefore returned to the control unit and ordered an assistance message, making pumps 30, to be sent, followed by an appropriate informative message, these being timed at 0415 and 0417 hours respectively.*

FROM DACO PEARCE
AT CLIFTON GARDENS
MAKE PUMPS 30
TOO 0415

FROM DACO PEARCE AT CLIFTON GARDENS
HOTEL 5 FLOORS AND BASEMENT 160 X 80 FEET
ONE FIFTH SECOND FLOOR   QUARTER 3RD
HALF 4TH FLOORS AND ROOF ALIGHT
UNKNOWN NUMBER OF PERSONS INVOLVED
SEVERAL RESCUES EFFECTED   WATER SHORTAGE
TOO 0417

So it was that the shout at Maida Vale that night became the biggest blaze dealt with in 'A' Division that year – a 30 pump fire.

When the 8 pump call, sent out by Neil Wallington, was transmitted to the stations concerned and to Lambeth HQ by Wembley control, the Operations room at Lambeth began telephoning the information to the Brigade's senior officers who were on duty that night.

The Chief Officer, Joe Milner, was asleep in bed at his home in Blackheath when the telephone rang. He was not on duty, but he was always informed of every 10 pump fire and above – wherever he was and whatever the time. A junior officer in the Ops room at Lambeth informed him that there was a 15 pump fire at the Worsley Hotel in Maida Vale. He asked for his official car to be sent from Lambeth to pick him up. Then he dressed, told his wife to go back to sleep and waited downstairs in the cold unlit hall. Filled with a vague foreboding, for such a fire involving a hotel at that hour augured only ill, he walked up and down in the dark, smoking his pipe. While he waited, the 20 pump call was transmitted by Wembley control, minutes before the car arrived. The 30 pump call he heard for himself on the car's RT as he was driven out of the windy, deserted streets of south London and across the Thames at Lambeth Bridge.

The Deputy Chief Officer, Don Burrell, was already on his way – as were several senior officers from Lambeth, some of whom had already arrived at Clifton Gardens. DACO Charles Clisby, on being telephoned at his flat in Lambeth HQ, drove out to Wembley, eager to see how his new VDU mobilizing system was coping with its first major emergency.

Already, in response to DACO Pearce's and DO Keable's requests for further assistance, appliances from all over London had been mobilized by Wembley control – from Acton, Hammersmith, Fulham, Chelsea, Cannon Street, Islington, Holloway, and Willesden.

Some were sent on by radio as they went to stand by at other stations. Some were called from their own stations and others from stations where they were already standing by. Thirty-eight appliances and machines came to Clifton Gardens that night, and with them came one hundred and ninety officers and men.

The fire was now at its height. But by now it had been contained on its flanks in the corridors of numbers 17 and 11, and was being fought from first- and second-floor windows at the front and rear. Any assault on it up the stairs of numbers 15 and 13 had been prevented by the total collapse of the stone staircases in these two houses. From above, the three turntable ladders poured jets of water into the blazing roofs of the three central houses – numbers 17, 15 and 13. Flames were also breaking through the roof of number 11, by the lift-house.

DACO Pearce asked the police to close all the roads nearest the fire and to endeavour to check that all the occupants of the hotel had been accounted for. They made lists, but it was an impossible task. More than 150 people were involved – many of whom, after fleeing from the fire, had been taken off the streets into neighbouring houses and given warmth, hot drinks and clothing. There was also a language problem – many of the hostel's residents were foreign – and not a few were confused and distressed. Despite all this, it appeared that several persons *were* missing.

Some of them it later transpired had elected to spend the night in other places and in other beds. Some, in the panic of their escape, had literally run away. In the circumstances it was astonishing that no one was injured and that only six bodies were found in the smoking ruin.

The six who died did so before the Fire Brigade arrived. The incinerated bodies of five of them could not be identified for several days. These five had been sleeping in attic bedrooms. Two of them, Wilfredo Lacap and Basdeobora Loakanadah, were in room 402 at the rear of number 13, next door to the third victim, John Lloyd, who slept alone in 401. Lacap, a luggage porter, was thirty-six and came from the Philippines; Loakanadah, from Mauritius, was twenty-three and a trainee hotel manager. John Lloyd was twenty-two and studying hotel management: he came from Sway in Hampshire. The fourth and fifth victims, who slept in room 407, at the front and top of number 15, were two young waiters – Ettore Vincon, who was twenty-two, and Patrick Dermitte, aged seventeen. Although the staircases in both their houses were a mass of flames they could, if they had been warned or wakened in time, have got out onto the roof through the attic windows. But they died within their rooms, overcome and suffocated, like most people trapped in fires, by fumes and smoke – not burnt to death. Their remains were discovered in the wreckage of the bedrooms immediately below their own, their bodies having fallen and been doubly cremated when the roof and attic rooms of the central houses collapsed one after the other onto the third floor.

The sixth body, that of Albert Simpson, aged sixty-four, a hotel porter, was found on the third floor of number 11, in room 306. His bedroom was at the front on that floor, in 308. He was recovering from a series of operations and walked with the aid of crutches. Perhaps in his efforts to escape from the fire and choking smoke he fell and dropped his crutches. Perhaps he threw them away. What is known is that another hotel employee found him and tried to drag him along the hall towards the lift – there being no stairs in number 11. The man had already pressed the button summoning the lift, seeing it as the only way down, not thinking in his panic of escaping along the corridor to the stairs of number 9 which were untouched by the fire.

He was tugging Mr Simpson along the hall towards the lift when suddenly it arrived. The lift doors opened. The other man fled towards them and safety, abandoning Mr Simpson in the hall. The doors closed – the lift descended.

Alone, the old man crawled into a bedroom on his right, an interior one, which had no window. He closed the door and very soon, suffocating in the thickening smoke, he died.

*

Unaware of Mr Simpson's stiffening body, squatting on the floor immediately above their heads, Harry Pettit and Tony Stewart, backed up by Ernie Arthurs, fought their way along the blazing second-floor passage of number 11.

Tony Stewart, given the chance to prove himself at the fire and win his colleagues' esteem, had, after seeing the bold hook-ladder rescues Harry and Ernie had made, determined to follow their lead. Using the first-floor ladder leaning against the porch, he climbed up it and on to the balustrade and went in through the window they had entered a few minutes before. He turned right, guided by the crashing blows

of Ernie's boot, and found him on the first-floor landing of
number 9 breaking open a locked bedroom door. Together
they checked that this room, facing the street, was empty, as
was another room at the rear. Rejoined by Harry, the three
then doubled up the stairs to the second floor, where between
them they kicked in doors that were shut and turned off the
gas-fires which several occupants had lit apparently to keep
their bedrooms warm in the bitterly cold night. Stewart helped
Harry break open the door of the rear bedroom, and Ernie
gave Stewart a hand in turning off a stubborn gas-tap. In the
light of their torches, which penetrated with difficulty the
thick mist of drifting smoke, they established that none of the
rooms was occupied.

As they finished doing this several other firemen – the PE
and pump crews from Clerkenwell led by Station Officer
Brown – came up the stairs. Ernie told them that the third
floor had not yet been searched; so they continued on up a
smaller wooden stair to the top floor, where the smoke was
densest of all.

'Come on, lads,' said Ernie to Harry and Stewart. 'We done
enough. I think we can leave this to them.'

Then he noticed that the surrounds of the second-floor fire-
door were not only ablaze but being sucked open by the
draught of air rushing into the flaming corridor beyond.

'Hold on,' he said. 'We'll get a jet and get to work here.'

The chance of tackling the fire could not be missed, neither
by himself, nor by the two recruits. Fire-fighting as such was
the be-all and end-all of their occupation, and here was a
great chance for the two younger men, under his guidance, to
prove themselves. It was a chance that they both also
welcomed.

They ran downstairs. Ernie Arthurs found DO Keable near
Paddington's PE and said – 'We've got the end of the fire up
there, sir, and we're going to work our way in.'

'Good lad,' said Keable. 'Carry on! I'll get a BA crew up
to relieve you.'

The three firemen put three lengths of hose together. Ernie
was out in the slip-road; Tony Stewart was on the first-floor
stairs; Harry was on the second floor with the branch. Once
the hose was charged with water the other two ran up the

stairs to join him. Ernie pushed back the swing-door with his foot, and while Stewart held it open with his helmet, Harry opened up the jet.

He edged his way into the blazing passage, backed up by the other two. All three crouched low near the walls, trying to avoid the worst of the heat, smoke, steam and spray and tumbling debris that accompanied their invasion. Ernie Arthurs continuously advised the two younger men, holding their belts in case they had suddenly to be pulled back out of danger.

'Check the floor!' he called. 'Watch the room on the right! – Keep down! – Take it easy! – On your left! – Hit the ceiling! – Watch the floor!'

Suddenly someone grabbed his shoulder.

He started and jerked around to see that Orchard had materialized behind him.

'Can I have the hook-belt?' asked Orchard.

'What?'

'The hook-belt. You're *wearing* it.'

'Oh . . . sure!'

'I'm on the TL now,' Orchard explained. 'With Jacko. Here – you have *my* belt.'

He needed the hook-belt to attach himself to the head of the TL. Ernie Arthurs had forgotten to take it off in his rush to effect the hook-ladder rescues with Harry.

'Here you are then,' he said, handing the hook-belt to Orchard and taking his in exchange. 'How's Jacko?'

Outside in the slip-road Jacko was impatiently waiting for Orchard's return. About fifteen minutes before this – after fetching the hook-ladder for Ernie and Harry on the porch and being told by Neil to do what he could to reach the people on the roof – Jacko had run back to the TL. With Ernie Arthurs already occupied, and Dyer not at that moment in evidence, he had laid hold of Orchard who was beside the pump escape.

'Can you give us a hand to re-site the ladders?' he had asked. 'I'm going up the other end.'

With Orchard's help he made up and re-housed the TL's ladders, lifted the jacks and blocks and drove out and around to the slip-road. The entrance was blocked by a parked car. But its owner happened to be standing near it, and realizing Jacko's dilemma shouted helpfully – 'Do you want it moved?' 'Yeah!' replied Jacko. 'All right. It's *my* car.' 'Get going then! Get it out of the effing way. Thanks!' But it was easier said than done, for the car kept stalling, and was still blocking the entrance when Jacko, having reversed the TL, was ready to back in. Forced to wait, he swore to himself while police and civilians offered advice to the car-driver. But eventually the car moved out of his way and he was able to back the TL up to the pavement outside number 19, just short of G25's escape.

Then another hold-up presented itself when Orchard could not find the hook-belt. Jacko swore profusely. 'It's not my night!' he cried, and indicated that Ernie must still be wearing the belt and that he was somewhere inside the hotel, probably to the right of it.

Orchard sprinted away, and in the interim Jacko put down the blocks and jacks and partly extended the ladders. By the time Orchard returned with the hook-belt, all the civilians had made their way down West Hampstead's escape and the two firemen who had effected their rescue, Sub Officer Stewart and Fireman Blair, were now themselves on the roof, making sure that no one else needed help or rescue.

'We'll leave the ladders – firemen up there,' Jacko told Orchard over the intercom, and received the metallic reply – 'I'll take a look myself . . .'

'Okay.'

'Oy, mate!' said a faint voice. 'Oy!'

Jacko looked around, and to the left and right and up. But no one appeared to want his attention or assistance. The firemen nearest him were preoccupied and on the move – as was Orchard, who had vanished onto the roof and into the smoke.

'Hey! . . . Mate! . . . Oy, mate! . . . Over here!'

Jacko's bafflement increased as the small voice repeatedly called to him through the general rumpus of machines and men at work in the slip-road.

'Oy . . .'

At last his ear latched onto the source of the voice. He looked up to his left. Ten feet away a young fellow wearing only trousers uncomfortably reclined in the fork of a tall tree.

'Can you get me down?' he called out plaintively. 'I've been here half an hour! I'm freezing!'

'All right!' shouted Jacko, controlling a desire to laugh. 'Hold on a minute – we'll be with you shortly. You're quite safe there,' he added encouragingly.

He found it difficult to believe that the youth had jumped from the roof of number 19 onto the slender topmost branches of the tree before clambering down to the fork. But such must have been the case. Then he wondered why the bloke, having thus chanced his life, was afraid of dropping the last fifteen or sixteen feet to the ground. But further consideration of this phenomenon was prevented by the descent of Stewart and Blair from the roof, followed by that of Orchard – and when a senior officer came up to Jacko and ordered him to get the TL to work as a water-tower, he forgot about the man in the tree altogether.

Jacko set to work rehousing, realigning and extending the ladders, while Orchard coupled a 100-foot length of hose to Paddington's pump. This done, Orchard then climbed to the top of the ladders and hooked on. But then yet another problem appeared – hardly any water emerged from the monitor.

Jacko was by now past swearing. He sighed, got off the TL and walked over to Acting Station Officer Randall of G25, West Hampstead. Jacko explained the problem.

'Leave it to me,' said Randall.

But it was several aggravating and progressively cold minutes later – after the hose-laying lorry's arrival and after the business of laying out the hose to a hydrant in Edgware Road and of connecting it up to an intermediary pump – before the TL's hose was charged with water and Orchard able to get to work.

Then Jacko was distracted from his concentration on Orchard by a hand on his left boot.

He glanced down belligerently at a civilian. 'Yeah?'

'Could you help me?' began the young man. 'My mate –'

'We're busy! . . . Well, all right. What do you want?'

'Could you help to get my mate down from that tree? He's got cramp.'

'Oh, Christ!' said Jacko. 'I forgot.'

He cast around for someone else to lend a hand as he could

not leave his position at the console. Randall was near him on the pavement.

'Have a word with him,' said Jacko.

The young man hurried away, spoke to the other fireman, and within minutes a first-floor ladder was brought up and the man in the tree brought down, stiff with cold and cramp and unable to stand upright.

Poor bastard, thought Jacko, and grinned. Every fire seemed to have its funny, odd or unexpected moments – this was one of them. It would make a good story for Martin and the other lads later. But now a drop in the water-power required his attention – it was only emerging at half strength from the monitor. Orchard asked if anything could be done.

'Can't help you, I'm afraid,' said Jacko sourly into the intercom. 'There's not a good volume of water from the mains.'

The matter was unexpectedly solved by the appearance of Station Officer Fred Alcock beside the TL. Without any preamble he shouted up at Jacko – 'Who the hell told you to get to work as a water-tower?'

The question was rhetorical. Before Jacko could formulate a reply Alcock continued.

'Knock it *off*! We've got crews inside there! Don't you know? – Well, knock it off. And don't get to work again unless I tell you personally!'

'Yes, sir!' Jacko replied, and told Orchard to come down. Then he shut off the water-supply as Alcock strode away.

Theoretically it was not good practice for a TL to be pouring water into a building from overhead while firemen worked inside. Not only could the power of the jet above hurl slates, timbers and debris onto the firemen below and force clouds of fiery smoke and fumes back down on them, it could also weaken the upper storeys by the weight of the water itself.

With Orchard back on the platform beside him, Jacko made up the ladders. Then the two of them made up the hose. This done they stood uncertainly by the machine, whose ladders had been left in an elevated position awaiting, as Jacko hoped, further deployment.

It was now about 4.20. All about them firemen with set expressions and jobs to do moved among the machines and in and out of the slip-road. Jacko felt despondent. He himself had not been able to contribute much: his efforts at rescue and fire-fighting having all been thwarted in various ways. But when Orchard said he would see if he could get a cup of tea from a Salvation Army canteen van parked in a side road, Jacko elected to stay with the TL – he was after all its driver and operator – in case it was required.

'I'll bring you back a cuppa,' said Orchard and moved away, vanishing among the machines lining Clifton Gardens.

On his own in the crowd Jacko paced up and down by the TL, feeling very cold and morose. Occasionally spray from jets working on the building blew down on him. But the fire, now that it had been contained, had not much more than an academic interest for him as *he* was not involved. He saw that the roof and upper floors were well alight and wondered where Martin was, and Ernie, and where and in what way the other Paddington firemen were involved. Neil he recognized in the slip-road directing fire-fighting operations off the escapes. Others he saw by the pump were Lewis, Marven, and the newest recruit, Leroy. But no one came across to him or spoke to him. It was as if he had been forgotten, like the man in the tree.

Dispassionately he watched the two other TLs further down the slip-road acting as water-towers and from their tops sending hundreds of gallons of water onto the fire.

On the second floor of number 11, Harry Pettit, Tony Stewart and Ernie Arthurs, keeping close to the charred and streaming partition-walls, had advanced after Orchard left them as far as the hallway containing the lift – despite some worries about the stability of the floor and about the sporadic blow-downs of smoke and flame and falls of water from the floor above. The little they could see in the sweltering, turbulent darkness seemed to be or have been on fire.

Although Harry had the jet full on, the column of water shooting out of it wavered now and then and was seldom at full strength. Even so, their advance was not unnecessarily cautious. What slowed them down were the swirling volumes of smoke, stinging their eyes and nostrils and making them cough and choke.

When some firemen wearing BA (Clerkenwell's ET crew) appeared behind them they welcomed the relief and respite, and staggered back the way they had come to the landing of number 9, at once sweating, overheated and thoroughly chilled by the drench of water from the jet. Harry massaged his hands, which had been stiffened by the cold and by his necessarily firm grasp on the branch.

As they stood on the flooded landing, stamping their feet, rubbing their hands, clearing their throats and the mucus from their nostrils and the sweat and tears from their eyes, Station Officer Steve Cooper passed them with Kensington's pump crew. He exchanged a brief greeting with Ernie Arthurs and ran on up to the third floor – his particular task being to make sure that no civilians of those reported missing were in fact in that part of the building.

Another face, even more familiar despite the masking of his mouth-piece and head-set, passed them on the way down – that of Pincher Martin. He had changed the cylinder on his BA set in the emergency tender before setting out to look for the rest of A21's ET crew, who he was told were in number 9. But it was Clerkenwell's ET crew whom he found on the third floor; they had by now relieved their own PE and pump crews and had taken over the fire-fighting on the second and third floors.

In less than a minute Pincher returned, running back up the dripping stairs with the news that flames were breaking through the fire-door on the first floor by the lift.

'Here we go again!' said Ernie happily. 'All right, you two? Same procedure as last time. We'll go down and try and organize another jet. Come on!'

Stewart and Harry, still highly charged themselves by the confrontation with their first major fire, were avid to do more. The three hurried downstairs and out into the street, where Ernie Arthurs again reported to DO Keable.

'We just been relieved on the second floor, sir!' he said. 'There's fire now coming through a smoke-door on the first. We'll get a jet and take it in, if that's all right with you, sir.'

'Very good,' said Keable. 'You do that. I'll get a jet on every floor and fix someone to relieve you. You're doing well.'

Ernie grinned. 'Is it all right if we take *that* one?' he asked.

A few yards away, Dave Dyer and Keith Cheal were directing a jet into a first-floor room from the pavement.

'Yes. All right,' said Keable.

'Thank you, sir!'

Arthurs ran over to Dyer. 'We've got to take that inside, Dave,' he said. 'Sorry, and all that. But you can give us a hand with another length. We'll need one.'

Dyer said nothing. He turned off the jet and set to work with Cheal, laying out and connecting another length, while Harry and Stewart took the length with the branch and nozzle into the building and up the stairs. But the young fellow's crestfallen expression prompted Ernie to be generous.

'Come on,' he said. 'You might as well come along with us and do some fire-fighting inside. Eh?'

Dyer's eyes brightened. A minute later he was kneeling behind Harry, backing him up as Harry, holding the branch once more, opened the jet on the burning corridor. Ernie and Stewart were behind them.

They had brought the hose up the stairs of number 9 to the first floor, then through the interconnecting fire-door into number 11, and so on to the fire-door linking 11 and 13 – the lift was on their right. Having extinguished the flames weaving up and around the door itself, they kicked it off its hinges and moved into the gap, with blazing walls and doors on their left and right and the false ceiling on fire above. The heat and humidity were intense, more so than the hottest sauna-bath. Occasionally they were soaked by water gushing down from the jets of fire-fighters above and seared by the occasional blow-down of fire and smoke.

'Watch the floor!' cautioned Ernie again. 'Hit the ceiling. Take it *all* off. . . . Fire on your right!'

Unsighted by the resulting dark confusion of steam and smoke that also all but obscured the flames, they were oblivious to the fact that the corridor facing them was a long one and passed straight through three houses. Down it the powerful jet of water now swept as Harry swung the branch, ducking back to avoid collapsing sections of ceiling.

'*Watch that jet!*' yelled a voice from the darkness.

'Knock it off, Harry,' said Ernie. 'Turn on the spray.'

Some muffled curses wafted faintly up the corridor from the

firemen further down who had evidently been soused by Paddington's jet.

'*Sorry!*' shouted Ernie. 'Who's that down there?'

A bout of distant coughing was followed by – 'Is that you, Ern?'

'*Yeah!* Who's that?'

'Ron Morris!' came the answer.

'Oh, it's Ron,' said Ernie and informed his crew who were continuously spraying their surroundings. 'He's with A25 – Westminster. . . . *Ron!*' he shouted. 'We got a crew here! Coming in this end!'

'Great!' replied Morris. 'You got that side. We got this. We'll meet in the middle!'

It was a cheering prospect for both crews – to be working together towards one goal, to be beating the fire and to join up with colleagues in the middle of a burning building. But the meeting never took place – although Ron Morris would before too long come across Harry on another floor, in a very different situation.

A few minutes later both crews withdrew – Ernie Arthurs and his team being replaced by Pincher Martin and Dunlop, both wearing BA sets.

They stumbled back again to the swampy first-floor landing of number 9, again gasping, coughing and retching, their faces blackened, their bodies soaked with cold water and sweat. Firemen from Clerkenwell passed them, splashing up and down the stairs, and so, once more, did Station Officer Cooper, returning to his men from below, after telling DO Keable of the body of an elderly man which he had discovered in a smoke-logged third-floor room.

Exhausted as the four Paddington firemen were, they could not but help feeling pleased with themselves. Three of them had fought the fire and contained it on two floors; two of them had earlier rescued four civilians. Ernie Arthurs also felt proud and immensely gratified by the spirit and resolution of his team of three Wombles – in particular of one of them.

He put his hand on Harry Pettit's shoulder.

'Well done, Harry,' he said. 'You done extremely well. I mean that.' He coughed and spluttered. 'The Governor will get a full report on what you done tonight, Harry. I'll see to it.'

'Leave off, for Christ's sake!' answered Harry, embarrassed. 'It's what we're paid for, isn't it?'

They walked downstairs and out into the frosty slip-road, now awash with convoluting hose and populated by busy and preoccupied firemen. Forty-five minutes had passed since the Fire Brigade's first arrival. The street beyond the trees was a mass of coloured lights, vehicles and people. Overhead reared two turntable ladders sending jets of water onto the blazing hotel.

The nearest TL in the slip-road on their left and immediately beside them was Kensington's. Drops of water and spray from the monitor nozzle at its head fell about them as they stood for a moment marvelling at the scene, exhaling deeply, their breaths swiftly dissipating in a fiery steam into the night.

Harry, recognizing the TL, peered up through the lowering smoke at the nebulous figure on top of the ladders and grinned.

'That must be Ray,' he said.

He had already been up there for half an hour. The bells had gone down in Kensington at 3.49, when ADO Rowley's message to 'Make TLs 3' was transmitted to A28 and B22 (Lambeth) by Wembley control. It was the TL's first call that night, and not until the long machine stormed up the Harrow Road past Paddington fire-station were the three-man crew fully aroused to the magnitude of the fire – when dark clouds of smoke swept over them as they approached a roundabout, while beyond them the night-sky glowed red.

As A21's TL occupied the far slip-road entrance, the driver of Kensington's TL, Phil Collins, and the Number One, Acting Leading Fireman O'Sullivan – after co-opting the help of the police who towed away and dragged out obstructive cars – were able eventually to drive into the Warwick Avenue end of the slip-road as far as Number 7. Here they parked, blocked the wheels, flaked out the hose – assisted by firemen from Lambeth's TL which had also just arrived – and connected the hose to Paddington's PE. Ray put on the hook-belt, climbed up the already raised ladders to the platform at the top, hooked on, and was shot up above roof level as Collins at the console extended the three ladder sections through the smoke, training them above number 9 and eighty feet above the slip-road.

It was Ray's first time at the head of the ladders on a shout, and the prospect he had of the fire was fearsome. Slightly below him and to his left, sheets of flame and sparks leapt skywards from the attics of three of the houses and exploded from second and third-floor windows, while voluminous masses of glowing smoke rolled up and outwards, some of it enveloping him before being blown away to his right. His senses were assailed by the multifarious sights, sounds, and smell of the burning hotel. Lungfuls of smoke which he swallowed tasted ashy in his mouth and hurt his eyes. His hands, face and body, at first warmed by the fire, were soon possessed by the freezing wind – the more so as his narrow perch, with his heels jutting out from the platform, allowed little movement, and his hands had to grasp and direct the monitor through its tight arc of fifteen degrees. But worst of all was the oscillating sway of the ladder as the water surged unsteadily up the hose and burst fitfully from the nozzle. Through the intercom he could hear Collins swearing at the lack of pressure and shouting for more water. Five minutes later the flow improved – but not for long. The rest of the time it ebbed and flowed irregularly, adding a bucking motion to the swinging of the ladders as he moved the monitor or shifted his feet. Before long the smoke and the cold and the uneven movement began to make him feel sick.

The water he was able to pour onto the attic roof nearest him seemed to have little effect. It sent some slates clattering down to the parapet. But to begin with, it was mostly consumed by the furnace-heat and turned into steam. He tried bouncing the jet off a chimney-breast at the walls which now appeared through ragged gaps torn in the roof by the flames. Sometimes he asked Collins far below and often hidden by smoke to move the ladders a little to the left or right, or to raise them, and frequently Collins' disembodied voice would inquire at his elbow – 'Are you all right?'

In his isolation the intercom was Ray's only contact with the ground. But he was never afraid. The spectacular elemental battle before him of fire, water and air completely absorbed him, overriding for a time his physical discomforts and occupying all his thoughts.

He noticed that the ladders of Lambeth's TL – it had also been ordered to act as a water-tower and its crew had reversed it into the wall as Jacko had done – had been extended up through the trees to tackle the centre of the blaze. Beyond, he glimpsed Paddington's TL, also in action. But his eyes were engrossed by the contorting face of the fire, rabid with destruction, feverishly devouring the hotel's upper rooms and roof and everything inside – until the beams and rafters, spars and joists of ceilings, walls and floors, now eaten away and weakened, began to cave in, to collapse and be re-consumed in the white-hot furnace of the flames.

Ray watched this slow disintegration unmoved, seeing each fall as a sign of victory and of the slow extinction of the fire. His view of it was unique, for from the street the process went virtually unnoticed, being so high and gradual and closely veiled by smoke.

First the roof of number 17 broke apart, sections slipping out of sight in showers of sparks, providing fuel for the fires below. Then the roof nearest him, of number 13, split open. Sections subsided, water-tanks, supports and stairs crashing down into gutted attic bedrooms, whose burnt-out floors gave way in turn, bringing new ruin to the third floor and lighting more fires in the wreck.

But the middle house of the three worst affected by the fire – number 15 – stood intact, its roof suspended, for some fatal minutes more.

It was 4.25 a.m.

Ray shivered, and wondered where Harry and the rest of Paddington's Red Watch were in the depths below.

Harry, Tony Stewart, Dave Dyer and Ernie Arthurs walked slowly up the slip-road, cheerfully weary, well-pleased with each other and with themselves, and largely oblivious to the fire-fighting activity that was still going on until Neil hailed them from an escape manned by three Manchester Square firemen.

'Hey! Ernie! Hold on a minute – and the rest of you!'

He jumped down onto the pavement and hastened towards them.

'A Paddington crew!' he said with a grin. 'Just what I need.

I bet you're knackered, gentlemen – aren't you? But have you got a job? Can you make up a crew and give these blokes a break?'

'Not these two, Guv,' said Ernie. 'They've done a lot already. We was going to have a blow.'

'Okay, Ernie. Fair enough. How about you, Dyer?'

The young fellow nodded. 'All right, sir,' he murmured.

Neil smacked his lips and glanced about for other assistance. Ernie looked worriedly at Dyer. 'I think –'

'No – leave off, Ernie,' said Harry. 'We're all right. *All* of us. Really we are.'

'Course we are!' said Stewart. 'What do you want done, Guv?'

Neil looked at their shiny besmirched faces, assessing the measure of their resolve and capability.

'Okay, then,' he said. 'I know it's been all go since we got here – and I know *I'm* knackered for one – but you can take over the levers on this escape. Right? Re-pitch it between those two windows on the second floor and work a jet off the escape into those rooms. Get going!'

'Won't be a moment, Guv,' said Ernie. 'I'm going to get my belt.'

'Your belt?' queried Neil.

Ernie explained about the hook-belt and that he was wearing Orchard's belt. He felt uncomfortable with it and wanted to pick up his own from the TL.

'Go on then,' said Neil.

Ernie Arthurs walked away while the three probationers set to work re-pitching the escape. As they did so Martin Walker emerged from a first-floor window on their right onto the balustrade, and came down the ladder leaning against the porch – the whistle on his BA set piercing the night, indicating that he had nearly run out of oxygen. He crossed the slip-road to the street, making for the emergency tender, which he entered from the rear. Inside he took off his helmet, disburdened himself of the complete BA set, which was still whistling, and slumped for a moment on a seat, wiping his face and eyes with a handkerchief. Briefly he deliberated about attaching a fresh cylinder of oxygen to the set, but decided otherwise; for although it was still very hot and smoky on the second floor, where he had left Dave, Waldron, Garner, Taylor and Gocher fighting the fire, enough of the smoke and fumes was now getting out of windows and doors for a BA set to be no longer necessary.

Blowing his nose and taking a deep breath, he adjusted his belt and put on his helmet and stepped out into the street.

In the meantime, Ernie Arthurs had joined Jacko, whom he found moodily contemplating the scene by the TL on his own, as Orchard had not yet returned. Ernie's re-appearance restored Jacko's good humour, and they amiably exchanged information about what they had done and seen – Jacko joked about the man in the tree – while Ernie retrieved his own belt from the cab, put it on and left Orchard's on the driver's seat.

On the escape, Dyer had at Harry's suggestion taken the jet up to the top of the ladders, which had now been pitched between the two second-floor windows. The frame of the one on the right was still burning and the bedroom within was well alight. The exterior wall around the left-hand window, two floors above the porch of number 15, was badly scorched and blackened; the bedroom inside had been gutted, although parts of it still burned.

Dyer was concentrating the jet, backed up by Harry, on the right-hand window when a call came from the street below.

'Come down!' shouted Neil. 'We're going to re-pitch the escape!'

He had concluded, in common with his senior officers, that at this stage the best way to extinguish the fire in the centre of the hotel, where the collapsed stairs prevented direct access, was to penetrate the building from the windows – as other crews had already done at various levels at the rear. Paddington's firemen had initiated the attack on the centre from the second-floor corridors of numbers 17 and 11. They would now make the first assault on it from the front.

Neil had discussed the matter with Westminster's station officer, Colin Searle, who had suddenly appeared beside him as the escape was being re-pitched and asked if he could be of any help. With him was a leading fireman from A24 (Soho) – Eric Hall.

Searle was thirty-four, two years older than Neil, smaller and almost as slim; he was a keen racing-cyclist in his spare time. His PE and pump crews, who had arrived at the fire at about 3.50, had been involved at the rear under ADO Baldwin and had eventually managed to enter the building via various ladders and windows. Using scaling ladders to bridge a fallen staircase, a number of them had reached the first floor. For a time Searle had stayed with his two junior officers, Sub Officer Ron Morris and Leading Fireman Peter Lidbetter, but he had left them before the incident when Ernie Arthurs' crew accidentally soaked the Westminster pair with a jet. Soon after that Morris and Lidbetter removed themselves to the second floor of number 17, where Morris met up with Griffin and took a jet into the burning rooms facing the street. Searle, meanwhile, had made his way out into the slip-road to see how matters fared at the front. There he encountered Neil.

The conclusion of the station officers' discussion was that a jet should be taken into the gutted second-floor room and that a crew should penetrate as far as conditions would allow. Providing their position was safe and tenable, they could then tackle the blazing rooms on either side. The burnt-out third-floor room *above* the window of entry posed no apparent threat, and the attic roof over all was still in one piece.

Harry, Stewart and Dyer came down. Assisted by Hall and the two station officers, they re-pitched the escape to their left, to the second-floor window framed by the blackened wall, while spray from B22's TL, working over their heads, rained down on them from far above.

When the head of the escape's ladders hit the window-sill, it was locked into place and blocks were put against the wheels.

Dyer, followed by Harry, stepped over the levers onto the ladders as Stewart manhandled the branch, which was lying on the pavement, and hoisted both himself and the charged hose over the back of the levels. He passed it up to Harry and Dyer, who began hauling it up the ladders.

At this point Neil realized that it would be unwise to let a relatively inexperienced crew, all of whom were Wombles, enter the room without a senior hand or an officer in charge, and the happy thought occurred to him that the officer might and should be himself. After all, he had been running up and down the road for very nearly an hour now – supervising various crews, assisting in the moving and pitching of escapes and ladders and organizing much of the fire-fighting at the front. Now, he felt it was *his* turn to experience the basic fireman's pleasure of opening up a jet onto the flames. It never crossed his mind that Searle or Hall might lead them in. The Wombles were *his* men. But it also struck him that three Wombles was one too many, and that a more senior fireman should go up in place of the youngest, Dave Dyer.

'Hold on!' he told Dyer and Harry. 'Can't have you going in first. Come down a moment.'

They did so, reluctantly, and as they stepped off the escape Neil stepped onto the levers and addressed himself to Searle, who with Hall had been helping Stewart pull the weighty hose over the back of the levers.

'It's about time I had a squirt,' said Neil. 'I'm going up, Colin. Take over down here for me. I'll lead them in.'

Since their discussion, Searle had said very little, as it was Neil's fire-ground and command and the firemen and escape were his. But now his sense of duty and what was right, prompted him to intervene.

He stepped onto the levers from the other side, not wishing to raise his voice in the presence of the others, and confronted Neil.

'You ought to stay down here,' said Searle, his brown eyes bright and anxious. 'It's *your* ground. You ought to remain out here at the front, Neil. Don't you think so? *I'll* take them up.'

Neil hesitated, aware at once that Searle was right, but loth to lose the opportunity of some action with a branch.

'Okay, Colin,' he said, conceding his position. 'You have this one.' He nodded at Harry and Stewart. 'You two go with him.'

'Right-ho, lads,' said Searle. 'Let's get moving! You take the branch,' he told Stewart. 'And let's get it up.'

So it was that Stewart now took the lead going up the ladders, with Harry on the levers supporting the hose, while Dyer despondently manned the levers and helped Hall.

Neil stepped back, feeling at a loss for a moment, regretting the fact that he had given way to Searle. But he had indeed been given the task of co-ordinating work at the front and had to carry it out without indulging his whims. Yet he was still slightly uneasy about two of his Wombles working with a station officer who did not know them. He resolved to find a senior hand to keep an eye on Pettit and Stewart.

Looking about for such a fireman, one of his own, Neil's eye fell on Martin Walker.

After leaving the ET, Martin had been about to climb back up the ladder leading to the balustrade when Dave Webber, emerging from the door of number 13 in the wake of Archie Waldron and Garner, the whistle on his set shrilling loudly, called over to him. 'Hey, Mart!' Dave had said. 'You're not going in again, are you? Haven't you done enough? Why don't you stop and have a fag in the ET for a couple of minutes like us? I need a break, I can tell you.' Martin paused, in two minds about what to do. Dave removed his helmet and tore off his head-set and mouth-piece. 'Come on, Mart,' he said.

Martin was about to yield to Dave's suggestion, for the thought of taking it easy with a cigarette greatly appealed to him – when Neil seized his arm.

'You got a job?' asked Neil. 'I'd like you to lend a hand over here.'

'Okay, Guv,' replied Martin, ever ready to oblige. 'I'm with you. What's to do?'

As they walked over to the escape Neil explained where the crew on it were going and what they were expected to do. He also asked where and how Martin had been involved and questioned him briefly about the fire situation within the hotel.

When they reached the escape, Neil saw that Dyer had now been rejoined by Ernie Arthurs. His presence made Neil pause, for Arthurs was a leading fireman and could not only have taken Martin's place, but even Searle's. But the die was cast. Searle was now in charge of the crew and Martin had been primed to join them.

Looking up, Neil saw that Stewart had reached the head of the ladders and was under the black hole in the wall that had been the second-floor window. Wraiths of smoke were issuing from it, dimly shadowed by fire. A flicker of apprehension crossed his mind. He stepped forward and his voice cut across Searle's instructions.

'Stewart!' Neil called. 'Stop there a moment!' He turned

to Searle. 'I want a senior hand to go up with them, Colin – just to keep an eye on the two Wombles. All right?'

Searle looked surprised. 'All right,' he answered guardedly. 'Which one?'

Neil turned to Martin. 'I don't want Stewart to be first in the room,' he said quietly. 'You go first. Check the floor, and carry on.'

'I'll go,' said Pincher.

He stepped onto the levers beside Harry, forestalling Ernie Arthurs, who had also moved forward.

Unknown to Searle and unnoticed until now by Neil, Acting Leading Fireman Pincher Martin had been helping Dyer and Hall lift the hose over the levers. Some five minutes earlier he and Dunlop, fire-fighting in a first-floor room of number 13 had been relieved by Kensington's station officer, Steve Cooper, and another crew. On leaving the building they had returned via BA control to Paddington's ET, where they had removed their BA sets. Paul Taylor was already in the ET, the whistle on his set having gone soon after Martin left the group fire-fighting on the second floor of number 17. They were joined in the ET by Garner and Waldron, whose sets were also whistling. 'I'm just going to report to the BACV, lads,' said Taylor. 'And find out what they want us for next. Won't be long.' He went out, leaving his wet and weary crew, their tunics unbuttoned, slumped on the narrow seats, drawing gratefully on a cigarette or staring blankly at the lockers. Then Dave came in, carrying his helmet and BA set, having already silenced its shrill whistle. 'Where's Martin?' asked Pincher. Dave told him, not knowing that Martin had *not* in fact returned to the second floor. 'I'm going back in to help him,' said Pincher. No one spoke and no one moved, so he left the ET on his own – to find Martin standing among the firemen in the slip-road beside the escape.

'I'll go,' repeated Pincher, and pushed past Harry.

'No – not you, Pincher,' said Neil. 'Go and put a CA set on. It's smoky up there. We might need it.'

Pincher shrugged. 'Okay, Guv.'

He stepped off the levers and trotted towards the wall to look for a CA (compressed air) set on Paddington's pump escape, parked in the street behind them.

'Martin will go with you, Colin,' said Neil. 'All right? Up you go,' he said to Martin. You know Colin. Look after our blokes – and watch what you're doing. Check the floor!'

'Right-ho, Guv,' said Martin, and by-passing Harry began climbing the escape.

Searle followed him up, pausing beside Harry to ask Neil to add another length to the hose.

'I'll see to it,' Neil assured him. 'Mind how you go. Oh – and look out for anybody still in there. You never know.'

Searle turned to Harry. 'Follow on up when we take the jet in,' he said. 'Those other blokes will take over here.' He continued up the ladders, calling out to Stewart – 'Hold on!'

'Stay close to Martin,' said Neil, laying a hand on the escape.

Harry grinned. 'Don't worry,' he said. 'I will.'

Scarcely eight minutes had elapsed since Harry, Stewart, Dyer and Ernie Arthurs had walked out into the slip-road from the door of number 9. The four of them might well have made up the crew that ascended the escape into the second-floor room. But through accidents of time, choice and circumstance, it was Station Officer Colin Searle and Martin Walker who made the fateful ascent with Harry and Tony Stewart, while Ernie and Dyer watched them from the road.

Neil and Pincher also watched the four firemen climb the escape – Pincher from the PE in the street. The rest of Paddington's firemen were at that moment elsewhere and otherwise engaged. Jim Griffin, on the second floor of number 17, was the only one of them still inside the hotel. Jacko was by the TL; Orchard at the Sally Ann canteen van; Lewis, Marven and Leroy were at the pump; Paul Taylor at the BA control van; Dave, Garner, Waldron and Dunlop inside the ET; Cheal and Wickenden on A22's escape; and Ray on Kensington's TL.

It was 4.32 a.m. – exactly an hour since the bells went down in Paddington fire-station.

In that hour, the Red Watch, Paddington, had accomplished much. They had extinguished the blazing hallways of numbers 15 and 13 and the passage between, where the first fire had been lit. They had attacked the burning stairway and first floor until ordered to withdraw. They had contained the spread of the fire sideways in the second- and first-floor corridors of numbers 17 and 11. They had fought the fire from the road, off escapes and ladders, and at the beginning had rescued nine people from the burning hotel. Harry Pettit had been involved in five rescues (one with Griffin), Ernie Arthurs in four, Dave Webber and the escape crew in three, and Jim Griffin in two. Fifteen other people were rescued by the junior officers and men of G25, A22, and G26. Three civilians made their own precipitous escapes: one down a drainpipe; one down a builder's ladder; the third down a tree.

By 4.25, most of Paddington's firemen had been relieved temporarily and replaced by a large mixture of crews from several other stations, invading the hotel from the front and rear at nearly every floor. These in turn were about to be relieved by the crews still arriving at Clifton Gardens in response to the 30 pump call.

At 4.30, Wembley control transmitted a complete list of the thirty-eight appliances attending the fire. By then, about fifty firemen were involved in some way inside the hotel, and as many were involved outside, including a crew who were firefighting from the roof of number 19.

Control of all operations had by this time been assumed by the Deputy Chief Officer, Don Burrell. He had arrived at the scene about 4.20, taking over command from DACO Pearce. Made cognisant by various officers of the extent of the fire and of what action had been taken so far, he decided that the initiative shown by those entering the hotel through rear windows should be followed by firemen at the front. He was influenced in this by the collapse of the central stairs, which prevented the basic tactic of fighting the fire *internally*, of attacking it at its source, from being employed. The assault would have to be made externally, by entering the building from the escapes. This was then initiated, each crew-leader thus engaged being urged by senior officers to ensure that every safety precaution was taken. At the same time, DCO Burrell gave instructions to the Brigade control unit from Lambeth that water should be relayed from the canal to ease the continuing shortage. This was done. The pump crew from D23 (Hammersmith), supervised by Station Officer Bowdery, and assisted by two other crews, cut through the railings beside the canal, connected four lengths of hard-suction hose to Kensington's pump, and then relayed the water through twenty twinned lengths of hose back along Randolph Road to Paddington's pump outside the hotel.

Those firemen who had been called to the fire on the first and second attendances – from Paddington, Manchester Square, Belsize, West Hampstead, North Kensington and Clerkenwell – were by now exhausted by their efforts and the enervating extremes of heat and cold. Their lungs were full of smoke; their uniforms were sodden with water, and their bodies ached with the strain of their activities, heightened by the nervous tension of fighting a fire. They welcomed the chance of a rest, of a break for a smoke or a cup of tea, or just to sit down, not thinking, trying to forget the dangers and terrors of their conflict with the fire. Some stood by, unable in the crowd of firemen present, to find anything to do. Others, with greater reserves of energy, kept going, driven by an urge for work and involvement or a special desire to help their colleagues. Like Colin Searle, several firemen from various stations, finding enough men occupied inside the hotel, ventured outside and gathered around the three escapes from which crews were now entering the building.

Among them were Sub Officer Roger Stewart and Fireman David Blair, of G25 (West Hampstead), who much earlier had rescued seven people from the roof of number 19. With Fireman Ray Chilton, of A25 (Westminster), they set about providing the extra length of hose for the crew on Paddington's escape, assisting Hall and Dyer, who were still on the levers.

On the left, A22's escape was being re-pitched. On the right, West Hampstead's escape had already been re-pitched by another mixed crew to a second-floor window above the porch of number 13. The three who entered the building here were Sub Officer Bruce Burrett, of A28 (Kensington) and the youngest and shortest of Paddington's firemen, Keith Cheal and Kevin Wickenden. They made their entry a minute after the four firemen on A21's escape vanished through a second-floor window in the house next door, into room 213 – room 13 on the second floor.

A darkness made palatable by thick smoke filled the gutted room – earlier an inferno. Now nothing remained of the furnishings but charred ruins, ashes and black amorphous heaps that reeked of fiery destruction. Nothing had definable form or colour except the little pieces of fire that still pierced the gloom from the ceiling and walls.

The room was narrow, no more than seven feet wide. Martin flashed his torch into its black interior as Stewart finished clearing the broken glass from the charred window-frame with his axe. He saw, but not clearly, that the floor was sound.

'Move over,' he told Stewart. 'I'm going in.'

Standing up on the top round of the ladder he kicked away part of the window-frame to make his entry easier, straddled the window-sill, put one foot on the floor, and then the other – holding on to the head of the escape with his left hand. Stewart and Searle, who was also now at the window, reached out and grasped Martin's belt.

He stamped on the floor.

Nothing shook or stirred except the smoke blanketing the room and the threatening points of flame. He stamped again.

'No bother,' he said. 'Okay, let's have the jet.'

Stewart and Searle passed it to him over the window-sill, clambering over it themselves as Martin advanced a few feet into the shadowy room, carrying the branch. The other two pulled the hose up the ladders and heaved it inside, where it gathered in stiff ungainly loops. Harry pushed it up from below.

'It's really going over here,' said Martin from the darkness. He could now distinguish through the open doorway ahead of him the pulsing fire-glow of a burning corridor. He swore and began coughing.

'We better have some sets,' Searle said.

'No,' replied Martin. 'It's just me. Too much smoking. . . . Hold on,' he added. 'I'll give the ceiling a wash-round.'

Stewart went towards him to back him up as Martin opened up the jet, directing the column of water at the ceiling. Spray and pieces of debris flew about, and a cloud of steam enveloped them.

'That's enough,' said Martin, shutting down the jet. He advanced to the doorway and crouched beside it while

Stewart and Searle pulled more of the hose into and across the floor. As they did so, Harry climbed up the ladders and entered the room, pausing only to drag another section of hose over the sill. He began to cough.

Searle glanced up and saw him momentarily silhouetted in the smoke against the orange glow of the street-lights. Harry moved on into the room, treading cautiously over the floor past Searle and Stewart to Martin. He crouched down in the doorway as Martin opened up the jet again, directing a short burst of water up at the blazing corridor ceiling before turning off the jet and retreating into the room as burnt-out pieces of plasterboard tumbled down in a maelstrom of steam and smoke.

Backed up now by Harry, Martin repeated this action several times, advancing out into the corridor and retreating, until the immediate vicinity was free of fire but swamped in steam. A few feet beyond the doorway was a smoke-logged landing and what appeared to have been a wooden stair going upwards. The stone staircase down to the first floor had disappeared into the dark pit of the stairwell.

Searle joined them, kneeling in the doorway. Out in the corridor Martin jerked his head. 'Smell it?'

'What?' Harry began coughing again.

'Bodies. Burning. Strong, isn't it?'

'Oh, Christ!'

Martin stepped forward, peering into the fiery darkness on their right. Harry did likewise.

'Looks like we got a couple there,' Martin said.

'God – Yes,' said Harry.

Further along the corridor were what looked like two bodies in the rubbish on the floor.

'Could be a couple of stiffs along there,' Martin called back to Searle. 'Can't see for sure. . . . And the floor's dodgy.'

'Hold on where you are,' said Searle. 'I'll get a searchlight sent up.' He turned around and called across the darkened room to Stewart. 'Hey! Give them a shout below. Get them to send up a searchlight.'

'Will do!' said Stewart. He went over to the window and shouted down – 'Get us a searchlight, will you? And bring it up!'

In the road below, Neil looked up anxiously, wondering why a searchlight was required.

'Where's Pincher?' he demanded. 'Hasn't he got his CA set on yet?'

'I'll get the searchlight,' said Ernie. He ran over to the PE, climbed on top of it and disconnected one of the searchlights there. Beside the machine, Pincher was adjusting the straps on his face-mask.

Neil frowned and smacked his lips. He felt uneasy, concerned for the safety of the four men in the room, where conditions must be worse than he had imagined – if a searchlight was needed. He made up his mind. He leapt onto the escape and began to climb the ladders. Hall, who had been pulling up hose, jumped down to let him pass.

At the top, Neil climbed over the sill and in through the window, past Stewart, who was dragging more hose into the room. He ploughed across it through shifting barricades of dense steam and smoke. Ahead of him Searle's white helmet loomed dimly out of the darkness at the door. The unaccustomed heat made him gasp. He stooped to talk to Searle.

'Are you all right, Colin?' he asked. 'How is it up here?'

'We're okay,' Searle answered. 'We're going to try to work the jet in now. Maybe a body in there. I've asked for a searchlight.'

'It's on its way,' said Neil, and his words were repeated by a distant shout from the street.

'I'll get it!' called Stewart from the window.

'Right,' said Neil. 'I'll tell Keable. Watch your step.'

He reached out and patted the crouched backs of the two firemen holding the jet. Harry looked back at him and seemed to smile.

Neil nodded, reassured. 'Good,' he said.

He turned and picked his way back across the room to the window, where Stewart was waiting to receive the searchlight. Neil climbed out onto the escape, and made his way down the ladders to the road below, by-passing Hall, who was making his way up. As he did so, Searle crossed the room to the window to take charge of the searchlight when it arrived. He leaned out to see what was happening below.

At that moment Ray Chilton looked up, and was surprised

to see his own station officer at the window, having assumed that the officer in charge of the crew was a Paddington man. He decided to go up and give Colin Searle a hand.

In the corridor, Martin turned off the jet. 'We better hold on a moment, Harry,' he said. 'We'll pull back a bit now and see what the next move is. . . . Okay?'

They retreated towards the doorway and slowly backed into the room, pulling the jet back with them.

As Neil walked away from the escape – as Pincher moved towards it, followed by Ernie Arthurs – as Chilton stepped onto the foot of the ladders – as Hall climbed up the last few rounds to the top – as Stewart in the window looked down to watch his progress – as Searle, feeling some falling fragments strike his helmet, hunched his shoulders – Harry turned to his left to speak to Martin Walker.

'I –'

*

Something snapped far above their heads. Some blackened stick of timber snapped and broke and in breaking caused other burnt-through beams, rafters, posts and joists to fracture, rend and fall. Unsupported, the attic roof caved in, crashing down on attic rooms whose charred and sodden floors, pulverized by the impact, broke apart, bringing everything above them and upon them down in chaotic ruin into the rooms below. Part plummeted down the stairwell. Some floors, the ceilings of second-floor rooms, in part upheld the avalanche. But in the downfall, a water-tank and a wooden stair, still burning, chanced to incline, keel over and fall at the same time in one direction, plunging straight through the ceiling of room 316 with all the wreckage of the attic roof. For a second the great beam running from end to end of the room supporting the floor sustained the crushing mass. Then both ends sundered, and the whole ceiling of room 213 broke loose and fell, collapsing with all above it onto the men below.

A Matter of Life and Death

The teleprinter-bells rang on and on through Paddington fire-station, their insistent shrilling resounding in every empty corridor and deserted room, and in Joe Forrest's dreams. There was no one in the watchroom to switch them off; no one bent over the teleprinter machine to read the stream of messages from Wembley, that automatically typed themselves out on the roll of paper; and as no one was there to tear off each message after it was sent, gradually the sheet of paper grew longer, jerkily unrolling until it touched the floor, and began piling up upon it.

For a time, since 3.50 a.m., Kensington's pump had been on standby at Paddington. But at 4.08 its crew were called on to Clifton Gardens as part of the 20 pump make-up. After that the teleprinter-bells rang on unacknowledged, though not quite unheard, for they wove their way into the dreams of the one fireman who was still at Paddington, growing at last in reality until they woke him up.

Joe Forrest slept at the far end of the dormitory, near Martin Walker, and as he was the van driver that night and not riding any appliance, his subconscious mind, registering this fact, had let him sleep through all the bells that had dinned out since he went to bed after closing down the bar on Jack Hallifax's departure. If he woke up at all, it was only for an instant and a glad remembrance that the bells were not for him. But when Kensington left the station, the continuous ringing eventually aroused him to the fact that something was wrong.

Grumbling and swearing he hauled himself out of his bed. He was wearing a T-shirt and denim trousers. He slipped on his shoes, plodded over to the red pole-house door and slid down the pole into the brilliant, and bitterly cold appliance-room. All the doors were open, all the lights were on, and all the machines had vanished, including the official cars and the BA control van – the Divisional van which he was driving was parked in the yard. The station was full of light and noise but void of life. He thought of the *Marie Celeste*, and the similarity was accentuated by the few pairs of shoes and slippers lying where the appliances had stood, abandoned when their owners had stepped into their boots.

Joe Forrest gazed about in wonderment, blinking in the brightness, and automatically began closing the five great doors. As he did so, he saw a distant, ghostly mist swirling about the roundabout, which only served to increase the air of unreality – until he smelled the acrid tang of smoke, redolent with disaster.

With the doors all shut, he went into the watchroom, and switched off the bells.

For some seconds the silence was stunning. Then he turned off all the lights – except for those in the watchroom which he put on a manual switch.

Picking the end of the teleprinter sheet off the floor, he slowly read the messages that told the story of the fire – from the first call at 3.32 to the latest, the 30 pump make-up from DACO Pearce, transmitted at 4.22. He learned how the fire had grown from a 4 pump call to an 8, 15, 20 pump fire and then a 30. The informatives described the building, the spread of the fire and some of the action. The lists of appliances ordered out by Wembley told him who was there. He saw that Kensington's pump crew had been on standby in Paddington for twenty minutes, that the pump from D22 (Acton) had been ordered out as a replacement at 4.13, and then at 4.21 ordered on by RT to Clifton Gardens, along with the nine other appliances making up the 30 pump call.

Even as he read this message, the teleprinter-bells sang out again and the machine sprang into life. He switched off the bells impatiently and saw that the new message was a full repeat of the 30 pump make-up. He watched as the stations and appliances were listed, and imagined how the cursing that might greet the fire-bells would change to eager exclamations when the firemen saw the size of the job.

At the completion of the message, he pressed the 'Clear' button, acknowledging its receipt, and once again had to silence the bells as another message came through from Wembley control.

This one detailed the sending of four pumps from outer stations to stand by in the all but emptied stations of 'A' Division. Two were being sent from the area under Croydon's control, one from J26 (Hornsey), and one from D25 (Chiswick) – the latter being ordered to stand by at Paddington.

The message was timed at 4.25 and was immediately followed by yet another – the informative from DACO Pearce describing the size of the hotel, the extent of the blaze, the shortage of water and that several rescues had been made. Joe Forrest swore to himself, cursing his luck. In his four years as a fireman he had attended several 20 pump fires, but never a 30 pump emergency. Now one had happened on Paddington's ground, just around the corner – involving a hotel and many rescues – and here he was, stuck in the station on his own, because he happened to be driving the van.

He wandered about the now silent watchroom, pausing only to look at the map on the wall and confirm the nearness of Clifton Gardens. The darkened appliance-room, seen through the glass wall of the watchroom, oppressed him. The sound of a two-tone horn coming up the Harrow Road and then the stirring sight of Hammersmith's pump roaring past the station only served to depress him. There was nothing for him to do. Then he realized that even if he could not be at the fire, he could *see* it.

He swung towards the door as the teleprinter's clatter burst out again. But the message, a break-down of all the thirty-eight appliances and machines attending the fire at 4.30, delayed him for no more than a minute. He left the watchroom and hurried across the appliance-room into the windy, night-shadowed yard, which he crossed at a run and came to the tower. He climbed up the fourteen short stone flights to the top, to the seventh-floor open balcony facing the fire.

High in the night he gazed towards the north across the rooftops, and stood entranced by the awesome spectacle of the distant burning hotel.

He heard no sound but the wind in his ears, and through the flames and smoke pouring from the roof saw but one sign of the many firemen there. Silhouetted against the glowing smoke he saw the tiny figure of a fireman at the head of a TL.

The night wind froze his face and body, but he stood unmoving, fascinated by his unique view of a 30 pump fire even at a distance, being free to gaze at his leisure, without being involved. For a fireman this was exceptional. Yet as a fireman he now began again to curse his luck that had kept him from being with the Red Watch on such a night.

Then he saw something extraordinary. A mushroom of flame and sparks rose silently, swiftly, out of the roof and soared like an A-bomb explosion into the sky. It vanished, and nothing seemed changed – the hotel continued to burn. But he knew there must have been a collapse.

Several minutes later he became aware that far below bells were sounding in the station.

Stiff with cold he returned down the stairs of the tower to the yard. As he moved towards the watchroom, one of the appliance-room doors began to open. A fireman stood beside it. The standby pump from Chiswick had arrived.

Joe Forrest went into the watchroom, shivering violently. The message was from DCO Burrell and timed at 4.40 a.m. It said: '*Internal stone staircases collapsed. Escapes in use at second- and third-floor level at front of building. Unknown number of persons involved. TOO 0435. AW. 0440.*'

So that's what I saw, he thought – the stairs going.

He looked up as the Chiswick pump crew entered the watchroom, after parking their machine in the second bay, in the empty space marked by the shoes of Paddington's pump crew. They were strangers to him, but they were firemen, and their presence brought the station back to life.

Before he went upstairs to the mess to make them some coffee, Joe told them what he had seen from the top of the tower – in the belief that what he had seen in particular had been the collapse of the stairs.

'I saw them go,' he said.

The collapse of the roof, the fourth floor and most of the third floor of number 15 occurred as DCO Burrell's staff officer, T/DO John Simmons, took the DCO's message concerning the collapse of the stairs to the control unit, where it was duly transmitted by radio-telephone to Wembley control, then repeated and acknowledged. When Simmons returned to the slip-road to report that the message had been sent, he saw an unusual amount of activity around and on A21's escape, and heard a fireman at the head of the escape shouting – 'They're *trapped!*'

As Simmons left the control unit, the car bringing the Chief Officer, Joe Milner, to Clifton Gardens arrived – a minute after the collapse.

Not many of those who were there when it happened saw the ball of fire that erupted from the building. The driver-operator of Lambeth's TL peering up at the fireman at the top of the ladders saw it, and swung the ladders away. The firemen on the roof of number 19, protecting the house from the spread of flames from number 17, saw the eruption and heard the collapse. But no one at the rear or at the front noticed anything untoward so high above their heads – totally preoccupied as they were with the problems and tasks at hand – and only a few who chanced to be looking upwards saw the terrible dark-red bloom that grew from the ruining house and flowered and faded away in seconds. So quickly did it flourish and die that even Ray Wade, only yards away from the attic roof at the top of Kensington's TL, saw nothing. For in that instant his reddened eyes were closed and covered by his one free hand, as he wiped away the sweat and smoke and tears.

Nor did he hear the collapse – with the general crackling roar of the fire, the hissing of the jet, and the rioting noise from the street below encompassing him with sound.

In the street itself these sounds were greater, the loudest being the throbbing of the engines pumping water onto the flames, which had caused the destruction and downfall of so much of the house already that another fall, another crash, made little impact on the ears. Even the fire-fighters in the second-floor rooms of number 17 nearest the collapse heard nothing above the commotion of their own conflict with the fire. Among them were Jim Griffin, Lidbetter and Morris.

But the men outside, on and around A21's escape, both saw and heard the collapse, though not the plume of fire and sparks that exploded above it.

Brian Hall, who was nearest the room, had just reached the

level of the window-sill when he heard a dull rumble and then a reverberating crack as the ceiling split open. He saw both Searle and Stewart half turn around, away from the window, as the ceiling and everything above it plunged into the room.

Hall ducked below the sill, curling himself up on the ladders, which shook in his clenched fists and jerked as the building shuddered with the impact. A choking cloud of smoke, ash and dust burst out of the window. Embers and burning brands shot over him and fell into the street.

The firemen nearest the foot of the escape – at first startled, then stunned and appalled as they grasped what had happened – hesitated for an instant, staring upwards, expecting the wall above them, the house itself, to shatter and come crashing down.

Ernie Arthurs, with the searchlight in his hands, and Pincher Martin, with the CA set on his back, stood stock-still, paralysed by the added realization that *they* might have been in the room. Dave Dyer, biting his lip, automatically bore down hard on the levers to steady the escape, as firemen ran towards it.

Ray Chilton, half-way up the first extension, had flattened himself and bowed his head as pieces of debris and ash rained down on him. Now he clambered on up, his heart pounding, seeing nothing of his station officer at the window, nothing but murk and tongues of fire, remembering the awful coincidence that the drill they had carried out earlier that evening at Westminster had been a mock rescue of a trapped and unconscious fireman, and that when disaster struck the rule was, as his sub officer, Ron Morris, had said – 'Drop everything, and get to him!'

Chilton needed no prompting, nor did the others below – the first of whom to scramble onto the escape were Roger Stewart and David Blair. They began their ascent as Hall shouted down from the window – 'There's been a collapse! Roof's gone!'

'Stay *back*!' yelled Neil. 'You others stand back! That's *enough*!'

He had been walking towards DO Keable – to report on the safety and intentions of the firemen in the second-floor room when a rumbling sound like a muffled bomb-blast made him whirl around. For a moment he stood transfixed by the dingy cloud spewing out of the dark hole high up in the wall, knowing what had happened and who was in there, and fearing the worst. Then he sprang forward and reached the escape with the other firemen. The four already on it were blocking his way and heading for unknown dangers. He had to reach the room first – it was *his* ground and three of the men inside were his.

Telling the other firemen to stand back, in case there was another collapse, he looked about for a ladder. Leaning against the next porch he saw a first-floor ladder – the one that Martin Walker had placed there nearly an hour before. Neil ran over, picked it up, brought it back and slammed it against the porch of number 15. He scrambled up onto the balcony, and standing under the inclined escape hauled the ladder up after him.

Above him he could hear the confused exclamations of Hall, Chilton, Stewart and Blair, but not their words: 'Check the floor!' – 'Where *are* they?' – 'I can't see a fucking thing!' – 'Move over!' – 'There isn't room!' – 'Go *on*!' – '*Jesus*! What a *mess*!'

Hall had been the first to step into the room, doing so with some temerity before the murky cloud of smoke, dust, ash and steam thrown up by the collapse had settled. For all he knew his weight might cause the shattered floor to give way under him. Nor could he see very much through the pall of darkness. But he ventured in, not stepping down but straight *onto* an obscure mass of tangled debris that snapped and sank beneath his boots. There was no sign or sound of any firemen. But with his next step a strangulated shout rose near his feet – 'Get off, you bugger! Get *off* me!' – and as he backed involuntarily away, his ears were rent by an anguished scream. Again he stepped backwards and became even more distracted by fainter voices further inside the room, beyond a high shambles of beams, like a bonfire. Someone was shouting desperately for help, and someone else seemed to be talking. He tried to move towards them, but the barricade of timbers was impassable – some of it burned – and the heat was intense. 'We'll get to you!' he shouted into the darkness. 'We know you're there!' He began to cough. Roger Stewart appeared beside him. 'Sounds like two more over there,' Hall said hoarsely. 'Do you hear them?' 'Oh, God,' said Stewart. 'I can't get

through,' choked Hall. '*Fucking hell!*' Half-blinded by the
smoke, made breathless by the steamy heat, the two firemen
swayed unsteadily on the rubble, assailed by entreaties for
help, some frantic, from the trapped men on either side of
them. But the cries from beside the window were loudest and
nearest and the firemen buried there could be assisted straightaway. 'Let's get these two out!' said Stewart, thinking this
would be accomplished in a few minutes. He moved to the
window where Chilton sat astride the sill, unnerved by the
nightmare scene, by the realization of his or any fireman's
greatest fear – to be buried alive in a burning building and
being helpless, hopelessly to die. Blair was behind him, still
standing on the escape and likewise transfixed by the fearful
situation confronting them all. But Hall, amazedly now
identifying two gasping and choking heads, one helmeted, in
the shadowy corners on either side of the window, was already
in action. He crouched down and began dragging the hot,
smoking debris off the trapped man on his right as Roger
Stewart leaned out and shouted down at the white faces of the
firemen below – 'There's four – I think four of our blokes are
trapped! There's *two* of them by the window! Two further in!
– Can't get to them! We'll get these ones out! Get some lines!
Lines!'

But the wind blew his words back into the room, and in the
general noise outside, of men and machines and of the fire, no
one heard him distinctly. No one heard him say that *four* men
were trapped – not even Neil on the porch below. He heard
Roger Stewart shouting, but gathered only the gist of his
words, that some men – two – were trapped.

Propping his ladder against the wall to the left of the escape
and over the first-floor window, Neil climbed up to just below
the second-floor window-sill. It was only by reaching up,
grabbing the sill and supporting himself with one foot on the
ladder and the other on the window-cornice below, that he
was able to pull himself up beside the head of the escape, to the
left of Ray Chilton who was half in and half out of the narrow
window, and then by leaning his forearms on the sill try to
see inside.

Not much was visible – the room was cloaked and heavily
shadowed by drifting smoke. But he saw at once that piled-up

debris immediately in front of him – bricks, wood, lathe and plaster, struts and slates – had raised the floor level by several feet to the window-sill. Charred beams jutted out of the wreckage. A few feet further in he could just distinguish that they were heaped up in a high, criss-cross, glowing mound of timbers. Some of them were on fire, and flames lit up the wall on the right. For a moment Neil saw neither Searle nor Tony Stewart – just the large dark, stooping shapes of Hall and Roger Stewart bent double close to the window, tearing at the debris on either side of it, chucking soaked and blackened bits of wood out of the window or to one side, and talking loudly yet indistinctly to each other and to Chilton and to others he could not see. Both Searle and Tony Stewart appeared at least to be alive. For he now singled out an irregular groaning coming from his right beyond Chilton, and on his left he heard someone gasping, quite close to him, and Searle's distorted voice saying: 'I'm choking! – Can't *breathe* – My helmet. . . . Get it off. And the tunic –!'

Hall reached forward awkwardly into the sodden, smoking wreckage. He seemed to wrestle with it, and suddenly Searle's besmirched white helmet appeared in his hands.

'Oh, thanks,' said Searle's voice, more normally. 'My tunic – it's caught on something. . . . Yeah.'

Hall knelt, trying to lift a beam, groping in the darkness to the left of the window a few feet away from Neil, whose growing fears, already being realized, were slightly relieved by Searle's apparent calmness – it did not sound as if he was injured. Hopefully they would soon get him and Stewart out – once the rubbish had been cleared away from on top and around them. He also hoped that Martin and Harry in the corridor had escaped the worst of the collapse, which somehow appeared to have concentrated on the one room.

Neil was about to say something encouraging to Searle, whom he still could not see, when his sensibilities were jarred by a tearing cry on his right as Chilton stepped off the escape and into the room, revealing the other trapped man.

Almost within Neil's reach and now facing him diagonally through the smoke, was Tony Stewart's head, helmetless, his eyes and blackened features screwed up in a hideous grimace of pain. He was buried in the wreckage up to his neck. When

Roger Stewart, who was kneeling beside him, tried to loosen some of the debris, his namesake gave another agonized cry and burst into a torrent of hysterical abuse – 'Get me *out* of here!' he yelled. '*Get me out!* You *bastards*! My back! – it's my *back*. It's broken! Oh, Christ! – It's *killing* me!' His face twisted again in pain and he lapsed into a semi-conscious mumbling diatribe, crying out again and cursing as Roger Stewart continued imperviously to clear the looser wreckage away, only wincing when he scorched his hands. On Neil's left, Hall had been joined by Chilton in trying to free Searle, Chilton's station officer.

'Oh, hullo, Ray,' said Searle.

'Can you get him out?' asked Neil.

'Is that you, Neil?' Searle's voice sang out from the gloom.

'Yes, Colin – I'm here.'

Neil hauled himself forward on the sill and onto his stomach. Part of Searle's blackened face streaked with sweat and water appeared beyond an obstructing beam. He was tucked in at a right angle beside the wall, lower than the sill. Only his shoulders and the top of his disarrayed and unbuttoned tunic showed above the rubble. He stared at Neil, the whites of his eyes shining weirdly through the smoke.

'You'll get me out of here, Neil,' he said, panting. 'Won't you? . . . There's something across my knees – And my arms. I can't move. . . . But you'll get me out. Are the others all right?'

'Don't worry, Colin,' said Neil. 'We'll get you out in a jiffy. How are you?' he added, almost casually, hiding his concern.

'Well . . . I don't know. But I'm caught by the legs. Can't move them. . . . Bloody hell! It's bad, isn't it? I'm sorry about this, Neil.'

'For fuck's sake, Colin – knock it off! Let's get you out first – How are you doing?' he asked Hall, who was tearing at the debris with his hands.

'I'm doing what I can, Guv,' said Hall, tight-lipped, his face already smudged and sweating. 'But there's a lot of stuff here.'

'Well, keep at it. You're doing well,' said Neil as cheerfully as he could. 'We'll get you out,' he again assured Searle. But his heart sank, and his mind was now in a fever of worry and fear.

The situation was a desperate one. It was clearly going to take some time to free both Searle and Tony Stewart, who seemed to be badly injured. Both men were much more deeply embedded than anyone had thought, pinned down by unknown masses of beams and rubble, and in the dangerously confined space there was room for no more than the three rescuers already crowding the area by the window. Neil knew, moreover, that their weight and almost certainly that of any more firemen might cause the already over-burdened floor to give way. There was also the danger of further falls from above, of chimneys and walls – even that the whole house might suddenly collapse in total ruin. But these possibilities, of further destruction and death, were too terrible to consider, and he forced them from his mind, telling himself he must concentrate on the rescue-work at hand.

A loud voice, that of ADO Gerald Clarkson, hailed him from nearby. On DCO Burrell's instruction, Clarkson had climbed up behind Blair on the escape and wanted to know the details of the situation within the room.

Neil was about to wriggle back off the sill and onto his ladder to report to Clarkson and ask that someone check from within the building the whereabouts of the two firemen who had been at the far side of the room, when a sudden fall of fiery embers was followed by an ominous crunching of timbers in the middle of the room. The five rescuing firemen by the window froze like statues, expecting the worst. A beam slid down, subsiding into the wreck, and the shrouding smoke began to glow with new fires, making ruddy the shadowed faces of the men. For an instant there was silence – then Tony Stewart gave demented voice to his fears, and those of the others.

'It's *going*! It's *all* going to go! *Get me out!* Get me *out* of here!'

'*Belt up*, Stew!' cried Neil. 'For Christ's sake!'

He jerked his hand away from the sill as a flame licked up the wall. Edging himself forward again he looked down and saw that fire was breaking through the smoking debris below the sill.

'It's getting hot,' said Searle, his eyes peering anxiously at Neil – who now saw to his utter dismay that out of sight of

Searle a line of little fires had kindled in the smoke along the wall.

Oh, God, thought Neil – it's burning up underneath – we'll never get them out in time!

Stewart's voice broke off in a sob; his head slumped to one side and he began to groan.

'Neil,' said Searle, accusingly. 'I'm getting *hot*.'

Fireman Pat Neary emerged from the front door of number 17 at the moment of the collapse.

A large, affable, balding man, aged thirty-two, he had arrived at Clifton Gardens with the PE and pump crews of G25 (West Hampstead) where he was the station mess manager. He had been driving the pump. After helping to man the escape from which his colleagues, Roger Stewart and Blair, made the roof rescues, he had been involved in the hose-laying operation from Edgware Road, and then, entering the hotel from the rear with a Belsize crew, had found a young man asleep in bed in a ground-floor room at the back of number 17. He and Fireman Stanley had taken the heavy sleeper outside, and on re-entering the building Neary had gone up to the first and second floors to see what use he could be there. In the darkness of the second floor he found five or six firemen. A couple were tackling the remnants of fire in two badly burnt front rooms; others were up an enclosed and narrow staircase trying to reach a fire situation above. They were engrossed in their tasks, and clearly not much in need of a solitary fireman's assistance. Besides, he did not know any of them – (they included Griffin, Morris and Libdetter) – and this fact more than any other decided him in favour of going outside again to find and rejoin his own crew.

He had just followed some Belsize firemen out into the slip-road when the roof and third floor collapsed in the house next door. He did not hear the crash above the noise of the pumps at work and shouted commands. But suddenly there was a commotion on his left, less than twenty feet away. Firemen crowded round an escape. Some clambered up it at speed. There was a lot of shouting, but he distinguished no words until a knot of white-hats (senior officers), standing outside number 19 – among whom he recognized the Deputy Chief,

Mr Burrell – hurried towards the escape. He heard the words 'collapse' and 'trapped' and realized that the second-floor room which was now being entered off the head of the escape could only be one room away from where he had just been. Perhaps, he thought, he could reach the room from within the building – for the head of the escape was now blocked with firemen – and be of some help.

So he turned, re-entered the building once more, and using his torch, though its batteries were fading, hurried up the dark, dripping debris-strewn stairs to the second-floor landing, where this time he encountered no other firemen, although he heard them at work on the third-floor stairs on his right. On his left was a door leading into a large room, 215, untouched by fire, with a window overlooking the back. He had been in here before (as had Dave, Archie, Garner, Taylor, Gocher and Martin Walker, a quarter of an hour before) and he remembered there was a jagged rent like a doorway, in the right-hand corner (made originally by Archie and enlarged by the others to fight the fire in the passage).

It was from this room that much earlier the hazardous hook-ladder rescue of a civilian had been made by Trotman and O'Dwyer. Much later it would be crowded with waiting firemen, including Neil, and be witness to his grief. Now it was fitfully lit from outside by the dull red glowing smoke blown down from the blazing roof.

Fireman Neary stumbled across the sodden floor of the room to the gash in the wall, and by the waning light of his torch saw in the pitch-black passage beyond that a slide of rubble had spilled on his left from a narrow, arched and door-less opening in the wall connecting the two houses. Thick vapours poured out of it. Taking a breath through his nose and crouching low, he plunged through the opening into the blackness beyond.

Cut off from all other sight and sound now except that of far-off shouting and nearby flames, he became aware of a man crying, screaming for help on his right, seeming near yet far away, like a voice from a cupboard under the stairs. Fearful of falling and of more falls from above, he inched forward up a hot pile of rubble, painfully having to feel his way, for his torch's feeble beam was useless in the blanketing smoke. '*I'm burning!*' the voice cried. 'Help! Help! *Help* me! Get me out of here! *Get me out! Get me out!* I'm burning!' Neary stopped, his hands shaking and sweating. 'Where *are* you?' he shouted. 'I don't know where you are! I can't *see!*' *'Here!'* cried the voice, seeming to come from under Neary's hand. 'I'm *stuck!* Down here! Hurry – get me out!' 'Stick your hand out!' said Neary. 'I *am!*' came the answer. 'Can't you see it?' Neary's out-stretched hand encountered nothing but darkness and rubble. Then a crunching movement of timbers beyond him and a crash on his left startled him into the realization that if he in turn was overwhelmed no one would know where the trapped man lay – they would both be entombed. It was madness also to advance into unknown dangers and pitfalls, with no back-up and no light. On his own he was as useless as his torch. He would have to get help. 'I can't reach you!' he shouted. 'I'm going to get help!' *'No! No!* Don't leave me!' 'I've got to! For a moment! I'll be back! – Hold on, mate!' 'Oh, *God!* Don't go!' cried the voice.

Neary hastily backed away, slithering back down the rubble and out of the opening. He dropped his torch. The despairing voice faded away, swallowed up by the noise of his retreat and the returning confusion of sounds in the other house. He staggered to his feet, swung around, his mind raw with the trapped man's fears and his own alarm, and burst through the gap in the other wàll, into the room at the rear. He made for the doorway and saw, beyond it on the landing, the shapes of two firemen, looking up the stairs. They jerked around when he fell upon them, grabbing their arms. 'There's someone in there!' he exclaimed. 'A bloke in there – he's trapped! See what you can do. I'm going to get some more help. Tell them outside – they don't know.' The two firemen, their youthful shiny faces half-lit by the fire above, stared at him with blank amazement. 'What?' one of them said. 'There's been a *collapse!*' said Neary furiously. 'The floor's gone! And some-one's *trapped.* In *there!*' He pointed. 'Fucking idiots! Go and talk to him. Do *something!* I'm getting help!' He stormed off down the stairs and out into the street.

[What happened next is a matter of surmise, as the two firemen whom Neary talked to – he saw no other firemen on the second floor at that time – have never been identified.

Apparently they were backing up Jim Griffin and another fireman, also unknown, who were both trying to work a jet up the stairs. At a big fire it would be usual for mixed crews of firemen not to know each other – especially if they came from different Divisions or were recruits. Griffin did not know any of the firemen backing him up at this stage. Nor did Neary know the two he told about the trapped man. Afterwards Lidbetter would remember very clearly that the two firemen who alerted him were young and wore yellow leggings – he thought they were Wombles. Perhaps they were, and ever since have understandably kept silent about their irresolution, in itself also understandable and in the circumstances not to be blamed. But although they took no further action they at least passed on the information. In any event, it was Pat Neary's discovery, unknown for many months afterwards, that probably saved the life of Martin Walker, a mess manager like himself.

What may have happened is that the two firemen, taken aback by Neary's sudden wild appearance and his words, hesitated before doubtfully entering the rear room, which was empty and undamaged apart from the hole in the right-hand corner. Passing through it into the passage as Neary had done, they would see at once by the light of their torches the outflow of rubble from the arched doorway on their left. One of them, poking his head into the deeper, smoking darkness may have heard a voice crying out, and glimpsed something of the hellish chaos within. But they dared not venture further and looked for other help. Turning about they saw another fireman pulling hose across the passage from the landing.]

Peter Lidbetter had not long teamed up again with his sub officer, Ron Morris. The latter had been busy with a jet extinguishing the pockets of fire still remaining in the burnt-out shells of the two front rooms – earlier Griffin had been working with him – when Lidbetter arrived. Almost at once the ceiling of the room they were in, next door to the room of the collapse, burst into new flame, taking them by surprise. Unknown to them it coincided with the collapse – which neither of them heard above the torrent from the jet smashing against walls and ceiling. Lidbetter heard a dull rumble, but in a burning building that was not unusual: it was also much less distinct than the crashes occasioned by the fire on the floor above them. While Morris continued to deal with the new outbreak, Lidbetter chose a quieter moment to go out into the passage and straighten the snarled-up hose on the landing.

He was thus engaged when two young firemen in yellow leggings and with frightened expressions appeared beside him. 'The floor's collapsed,' they said. 'Someone's trapped in there.' 'Where?' he asked. They showed him, directing him towards the arched doorway which he entered without a second thought, switching on his torch as he did so. Its beam penetrated the clouds of smoke sufficiently for him to see that the collapsed debris at his feet sloped up and away from him, towards his right. Because he was standing, he had a comparatively wider view than Neary, apart from a more serviceable torch. He could perceive in the darkness that on his immediate left was a fire-blackened wall, then a gap, then the dim red glow of smoke-hidden flames. Like others after him, he assumed that the gap was a doorway to the room of the collapse – as was the arched doorway which he had just entered. He was not to know that the blackened wall enclosed a stair to the third floor, that the gap beyond led to a landing and a collapsed stone staircase, and that the arched doorway had originally led directly into a cupboard-like space, about 5 feet by 2 feet, in whose opposite wall had been a fire-door, which opened onto the landing and led to the corridor running through the hotel. On the other side of the fire-door, on the right, had been the inner wall and door of room 213. The remains of the fire-door were now under his feet, and the wall and door of 213 had fragmented and disappeared under the collapse. When he took three uncertain steps diagonally to his right to mount the debris, here three feet deep, he moved over the buried wall without knowing it and into the right-hand corner by the door of what had been room 213. As he did so the smoke and steam thickened further, nullifying the effect of his torch-beam. He took another cautious step, wondering where in all the chaos the trapped man lay, and started when a barrage of frantic cries and entreaties came hollowly from the darkness at his feet. 'I'm here! *Here!* What's going on? For Christ's sake, get me out of here! I'm *burning!*'

Suspensefully Peter Lidbetter stooped and shone his torch

through the smoke and down at the rubble below him. The hairs on his neck rose on end as he gazed appalled at the vision dimly revealed in the torch-light. All he could see of the buried man was a pale hand waving at him from the ruin.

All Martin remembered afterwards was Harry turning towards him and a dark shadow coming down on them. His helmet came off and he was knocked to the floor. Stunned for some seconds by the sudden impact, by sheer surprise, his mind was a blank, not registering what had happened nor whether he was standing, sitting, upside-down, blind or deaf, badly injured – or dying. The darkness was as complete as the silence. Only by blinking his eyelids did he know his eyes were open; only by smelling pungent fumes did he know he had a nose; only by moving his features and breathing did he hear any sounds above the thudding of his heart; and only by moving or trying to move his muscles and his limbs did he discover that he was sitting in a reclined position with out-flung legs and his right arm by his side. He could not move his feet, legs, waist or trunk – only his left arm and his head. His right foot had no feeling at all. He wondered if it was broken. But although he was acutely hot and uncomfortable, he felt no pain. He thought it could not be *that* bad – that he only had to try to stand up and he would succeed, that whatever pressed down upon him was only a lathe and plaster ceiling, which could be heaved away or broken through. But when he tried to move he failed. With his free left hand he pushed at a rough wooden surface above him; he pushed very hard. But nothing moved, and he became aware that the blackness about him was not after all complete – nor was the silence. He saw points of fire, like flecks on his eyeballs, seemingly inches away. He felt a damply suffocating steaming heat that stung his nostrils and throat and eyes – and he heard someone coughing far away and sighing, and a muffled voice saying – 'Oh, God, what happened? Martin? Martin?' Then fingers touched the fingers of his outstretched right arm, and a hand grasped his and held it fast. 'Harry? You all right?' His own voice sounded harsh and high. 'Harry? . . . *Harry!*' He heard a far-off choking and a faint voice, belying the terrible strength in the hand, said: 'Help . . . me . . . Martin. Get me out. I . . . don't . . .

want . . . to . . . die. . . . Please . . . don't let me die.' The horror
of their situation overwhelmed him. He shouted, screamed,
cried for help, hearing his voice make sounds he had never
heard before. He strove with all his might and his free left
hand to rid himself of the weight upon him and the night and
silence. When he desisted for a moment, exhausted, his senses
reeling, he could feel the sweat running into his eyes; his body
prickled with heat. A distant gasping faintly echoed his own.
Then the heat began to centre and intensify around his left
foot, leaving the rest of him cold with fear and searing him
with pain. His foot was burning. Red-hot knives were skinning
his flesh. Again he screamed for help, frantically trying to jerk
his foot away from the torturing flames. But his boot was held
in an unseen vice. Yet the vision of himself being slowly burnt
to death was a torment greater than the actual flames.
Frenziedly jerking his leg, crying out insanely, insensitive to
what other pain he caused himself, he redoubled his exertions
– until all at once his foot was released from the boot. Relief
and pain contended for a moment until the pain was rein-
forced. For his burnt foot, naked but for a sock, was now exposed to all the scalding combustion of the debris impacted
around it. No longer was it in part protected by the leather
covering both his foot and lower leg. Nor could his toes find
their way back inside the boot. Every time his foot touched the
sides of its prison it burned, and although he tried to hold it
suspended, not touching anything, his strength and purpose
could not maintain it there for long. For some seconds he lay
prostrate, giddy with inhalations of unseen fumes, made mind-
less by fear and prospects of horror. Then he remembered he
was not alone, and that the hand he now grasped and had
gripped as tightly in his frenzy was not responding with its
former strength. 'Harry!' he shouted. '*Harry!* Hold on! *Hold
on!* I'll get you out – I *promise* you!' The other hand grasped
his again, as if in acknowledgement. He heard a long low
choking moan and a sleepy far-away voice whispering – 'I
don't want . . . to die. . . .' A spasm of pain shot through him
as his foot, sinking down again, sank into scorching debris. He
jerked it away, writhing about until he lodged it somehow in
an area less hot and found some temporary respite. He felt
sick and faint – but his mind came alive again to his plight

when the hand that was clasping his hand suddenly let go. 'Harry?' Reaching out desperately, he recovered Harry's hand – now clenched and still. He shook it, embraced it with his hand again. 'Wake up, Harry!' he shouted. But there was no response nor sound. *'Harry!'* he cried. Fighting back his despair his fingers reached out hopefully around Harry's wrist to feel the pulse. Nothing flickered beneath them. He lay there suspended in deathly silence, made animate by the blackness crushing his body and soul. But he would not grant it the victory, nor yield to his knowledge of death. He was *not* alone, he told himself. Harry was with him. Harry was only unconscious. There was hope. 'Hold on,' he said to himself, holding Harry's fist in his. Someone would come to them – find them and rescue them. A hundred firemen were somewhere outside. Some would have seen what had happened: they would have heard him shouting. Where *were* they? *'Help!'* he shouted, and his voice crying out in the darkness frightened him, making him sharply aware once more of his plight, and his fears, and his pain. So he cried out again in fear and pain – to let others know, and himself, that he was *alive* and wanted to live. But nobody came to his rescue. Anger seethed in him. He cursed and swore at the firemen who did not hear him, who went about their business unknowing and uncaring, who drank tea at the canteen van. At times his voice broke in despairing sobs, and he gladly would have surrendered his will for cool, insensate oblivion. But again the silence and the torment of his foot drove him to rend the darkness with his pleas and demands, while the thought of Harry, silent somewhere beside him, whose hand he still grasped, gave a purpose to his passion for life.

It seemed to him he lay under the debris for fifteen minutes or more before a voice, seeming near yet far away, said worriedly: 'Where *are* you?'

Where *am* I? he thought. That's nice. 'I'm *here*!' he yelled, suddenly finding that his left hand, stretched up behind his head, could squeeze through a gap between the wall and whatever held him down. *'Here!'* He waved his hand wildly about. But astoundingly it went undiscovered and the voice went away. He cried out in desperate frustration, and then held his breath, listening. The voice *must* return – they knew where he was. They would soon get him out, and Harry. But the next thing he heard, apart from his own stifled gasps of pain, were not voices or a voice, but footsteps that trod on top of him. Again he called out, waving his free left hand.

A muffled voice swore in incredulous amazement, and he knew that he had been seen.

Martin Walker's whereabouts were discovered by Pat Neary three to four minutes after the collapse, and not fifteen as it seemed to Martin. Peter Lidbetter reached him about a minute or so later, and seeing the hand clutching hold of a beam in a sunken position, he assumed that the trapped fireman had partly fallen through the floor and was preventing himself from falling further by hanging on to the beam. Lidbetter accordingly removed his belt and axe and lowered them down for the man to grasp, hoping to pull him up. But this failed. 'It's no good,' a voice said faintly. 'I'm stuck!' And Lidbetter realized when the fireman let go, with his hand now clutching the air, that he must be prostrate under the mass of wreckage on which he himself was standing. He began to pull the shattered sticks of charred, wet and steaming debris away from where the buried fireman's head must be, so that he could have more air and the freedom of both arms. But although Lidbetter was soon able to remove some of the surface rubbish amongst the tangle of beams, struts and rafters, a particularly heavy beam near the wall defeated his efforts. 'Get a move on, mate – for Christ's sake!' said the pained voice from below. 'It's flaming *hot* down here!' Lidbetter redoubled his efforts, expecting at any moment to be joined by other firemen, now that the alarm had been raised. But when no firemen appeared – and having no sign or sound from the two who had directed him to the collapse, he shouted across the room at voices he could hear at the far side, where he thought there must be a window. 'There's someone trapped over here! Give me a hand, will you!' But no one answered.

In his ignorance that the centre of the room was blocked by a solid interwoven barricade of timbers, that the firemen at the window were heavily engaged in rescue themselves, that *they* thought rescuers were on their way to the back of the room, that the two Wombles, seeing him in difficulties, had gone to fetch help from Jim Griffin and the other fireman on the stairs, and that Neary's message was only now spreading through the house, Lidbetter began to feel afraid. The buried fireman and himself seemed to have been forgotten. Although he was alone in fact for no more than a few minutes, it seemed to him like ten. While the voice beneath him alternately swore and pleaded, he tore at what could be seen of the debris through the swarming smoke and steam, burning his hands on the still scorching springs of a mattress whose sodden remains overlaid the fireman below.

He shouted again at the unseen firemen at the window, and this time his cry was heard, not by them but by Ron Morris, who having extinguished the incandescent ceiling of the room next door had at that moment backed out of its ruined doorway into the passage.

Morris shut down the jet and heard a shout for help coming from the arched opening. Within seconds he had worked his way through the nebulous darkness beyond and forced a path through the debris on the other side of the trapped man.

'Oh, thank Christ!' said Lidbetter doubly relieved that he was no longer alone, and supported now by his older, very experienced colleague. He explained briefly about the beam and the man underneath, who shouted out – 'Who's *that*?' 'Ron Morris. Who are *you*?' 'Martin Walker. Oh, get this lot off me, Ron! I can't hold on much longer.' 'Hang on a minute....'

Martin swore at them hysterically, not understanding why they were taking so long, agonized by his roasting foot and the vision of being entirely consumed by fire.

His cries were now heard and his voice recognized by Jim Griffin, who had struggled back down the third-floor stairs after someone shouted up them about a collapse. He was now lodged inside the arched opening behind a leading fireman he did not know (Lidbetter). In the smoky light of his torch he realized that not much more could be done than the two firemen – one of whom he now identified as Morris – were already engrossed on doing – nor was there the space. Griffin decided he could best assist by extinguishing the fires apparently burning under the debris and blatantly flaring on top of it. He seized the hose that was lying in the passage and shoved the branch towards the leading fireman. 'Here – use

this. Give him a soaking,' he said. 'Get a hose-reel!' he snapped
at one of the firemen behind him. 'And some lines. I'm going
to the room below.'

His intention was to cut away the ceiling and floor under
his colleague and put out any fire therein. He also thought
it might be possible to free Martin from below in the process.
He hastened away, pushing through the knot of alarmed
firemen. On the landing he passed DACO Pearce and some
other officers. The word had spread. More help and equipment
was on its way.

But for some moments longer, before they were joined by
T/DO Simmons and ADO Clarkson, Lidbetter and Morris
continued their fight to free Martin on their own. Between
them they managed to lift the beam that was over his head
and prop it, cautiously, against the wall, and while Morris
redoubled his efforts to dislodge and drag the ruined mattress
to one side, Lidbetter sprayed the debris about them – carefully, so as not to disturb its imbalance nor cause another
collapse, nor suffocate the buried man with clouds of choking
steam.

They heard him gasp under the wreckage as the icy water
evaporated about him.

'*Harry's* there,' they heard him say in a shrill voice, punctu-
ated by gasping and sudden groans of pain. 'I know he's there.
. . . Down there . . . I. . . . You've got to get us out. . . .'

Morris peered doubtfully through the steam and smoke at
Lidbetter. Both thought the trapped man was babbling,
delirious. For there was no sign of any other fireman in or
above the smouldering wreckage – and if anyone was under it
then. . . . But their priority was to release the man whose hand,
still sticking out of the debris, demanded their help, and this
had to be done before the room became a funeral pyre or fell
in or was buried by another fall. Grimly they resumed their
labours.

'We'll get you out in no time, Martin!' called Morris.
'Take it easy!'

'He's there!' the voice assured them excitedly. 'I know he's
there. . . . Near my legs. I had his hand. I felt it go – but I've
got it now . . . I'm still. . . .'

Under the rubble, Martin screwed up his eyes and bit his

lips, trying to stifle the torment of his mind and body. He felt a hand grasp his left hand. He thought it was Morris. 'If you don't get me out, Ron,' he cried, 'I'm a gonner.'

'Hang on, son,' said a voice he did not know. Someone else had joined the other two.

When at last they removed whatever had been covering his face and he glimpsed the dark shambles about him, and the shapes of the three rescuers above him, he realized how disastrous the collapse had been and what a desperate situation he was in. But at least he could see, a little, and breathe more freely, and he was out of the horrifying blackness below. Someone was close beside him, bending down, deflecting water off a hand onto his face.

'That better?' asked Lidbetter, loudly and anxiously, staring down at the blackened, helmetless head that had appeared in the hollow at his knees.

Martin closed his eyes. His head sank back against the wall. He tried not to remember, to forget all terror and pain and grief. Water ran easefully down his face; his mind went blank. When he opened his eyes, he remembered with wonder that he was alive. And far above, beyond the triumphant dark-red streamers and banners of smoke, beyond the high, uneven, floorless, roofless wall that towered like a monument over him, he was aware of nothing but the night.

It was three hours before Martin Walker was released – three hours of suffering, concern, endeavour, exertion and danger in nearly insufferable conditions of smoke and fire, with the ever-present risk of further and total collapse.

In half that time, Tony Stewart and Colin Searle were freed – but at the same cost to mind and body. For the *two* firemen, burnt and injured, conscious all the time and only too capable of feeling, required twice as much effort from their rescuers – and the dangers and difficulties at the window were similar to those at the door of room 213.

Outside, in the street and in the slip-road, over a hundred and fifty firemen watched and waited. Fire-fighting had almost ceased. The still blazing upper floors, where the fire had been checked and prevented from spreading, were being allowed to burn themselves out. The turntable ladders' jets were shut

down and their ladders put to other work. Only a few crews
remained on or near the roofs at each end of the burning hotel,
on 19 and in 11, to keep the fire in check and damp it down.
Rescue had become the first priority again, the rescue of firemen themselves, and to this end every effort of body and mind
and all necessary equipment was now directed.

But very few of the many firemen who were there could be
of direct assistance. Those rescuers who had reached the room
first remained there, refusing to leave until their task was
done. The rest, some of whom tried to bluff their way into the
building, desperate to help – especially Paddington's men –
had to wait outside, not knowing what was happening, or who
exactly was involved. For from the start, because of the noise
outside and the piled-up barrier of debris within, preventing
physical and verbal contact between the two teams, each of
them, working independently, believed for a time that the
firemen *they* had found were the only ones trapped. Officers
coming up to investigate the separate situations at the window
and the door – knowing only that *two* firemen were said to be
trapped and not getting a clear view of the smoke-logged
room – thought that the rescuers they discerned inside the
room, tearing at the debris, were the *only* ones involved. Nor
did the rescuers themselves know for certain otherwise. It was
when the various pieces of information were reported back to
the Chief Officer, Mr Milner, and his deputy, Mr Burrell,
that the true picture emerged. Not just two firemen were
trapped, but three – possibly four. It was not until later that
the fourth fireman became a definite figure and a tragic fact.

To begin with, only the most senior officers and the firemen
closest to the trapped men knew it was a matter of life and
death.*

Mr Milner: *My arrival just followed the partial collapse of the roof
and third floor, which buried a fire crew (a station officer and three
firemen) under a substantial amount of debris at second-floor level.
The Deputy Chief Officer had already mounted rescue operations to*

*In the italicized passages that follow Mr Milner's statements are taken from
his official report to the GLC Fire Brigade Committee, and all the others come
from statements presented to the Honours and Awards Committee in December
1974.

release the trapped personnel and, having made an appreciation of the fire-ground situation, I decided to leave him in command of the operations although, of course, retaining my responsibility for all that happened at the incident.

ACO Watkins: *Mr Burrell informed me that there had been a collapse of floor in the centre building and that members of the Brigade were trapped on the second floor where an escape was pitched and a crew working from the head. I was to supervise operations. At the head of the escape I found that Station Officer Searle and Fireman Stewart were trapped under a great quantity of flooring and joisting; there was deep-seated fire in this timber, hampering operations and endangering those who were trapped. Station Officer Wallington, of A21, Paddington, a leading fireman and two firemen were working in the room extricating those who were trapped and keeping the fire under control.*

T/Sub O Stewart: *I entered the room and found the crew injured and trapped within the debris. I was joined by Fireman Blair and other Brigade personnel and gave assistance in the release of the injured.*

Stn O Wallington: *I was able to ascertain that Stn O Searle (A25) on the left and Fm Stewart (A21) on the right were both trapped by heavy timbers and brick debris from the waist down and were both pinned under the sill in very cramped conditions. They were both conscious. There was a considerable amount of fire still present in and under all the debris. There appeared to be no other Brigade members involved at this front end of the room, although the considerable mass of the fall appeared to be in the centre. I passed this information down to other personnel below me and asked that an attempt be made to check the rear of this room from within the building. T/Sub O Stewart, Fm Chilton and T/L/Fm Hall, under my direction, had commenced to attempt to remove several heavy timber-joists from across both trapped persons, the removal of which was necessary before any further rescue attempt could be made.*

ACO Watkins: *It was immediately apparent that the work was going to be complex and of long duration, and the DCO arranged for crews to be at hand on the ground and first floors to assist and provide equipment as required.*

Stn O Wallington: *At this point a hose-reel tubing was brought up the escape and passed into the restricted area left to work around the trapped men. Additionally, Fm Blair (G25) manned the head of the escape, and later Stn O Hicks (A24) directly supported me from the ladder below.*

ADO Rowley: *I was situated outside the front of the building at the eastern end when a partial collapse of the upper floors occurred. A few moments later I was informed that an unknown number of Brigade personnel had been trapped by falling debris in a room at second-floor level. Initially, I assisted in the positioning of equipment to facilitate the rescue of the trapped personnel which was being attempted via the escape ladder pitched to the second floor. DO Keable informed me that two men were trapped near the front window of the affected room, and for whom rescue attempts were well in hand. However, it was feared that other personnel were involved further in the building and had yet to be located. I was instructed to reach the affected area from inside the building and clarify the position.*

ADO Baldwin: *During the course of fire-fighting operations [at the rear], I was informed by Stn O Alcock (A22) that there had been a collapse of the upper floors at the front of the premises, trapping two or three firemen, and I was to endeavour to reach their position via the rear of the building. I ordered further hook-ladders to be thrown up the face of the building to top-floor level and an entry to be effected. But at all levels it was discovered that due to the complete collapse of the stone staircases and part of the floor areas, a large gap existed between the rear section of the building and the front, with a fire situation that made it impossible to bridge, coupled with the fact that we were told not to use jets of water on this section in case this caused a further collapse on those already trapped and the would-be rescuers. In order to report the situation in respect of the rear of the building, I handed over my responsibilities to DACO Roundell and reported to the front. . . .*

Stn O Hicks: *I was informed by Stn O Alcock [at the rear of the building] that some men were trapped following a collapse. Both crews (from A24's PE and pump), using existing ladders, re-entered the building from the rear. But collapsed stone staircases prevented further progress. T/Sub O Macey remained at the rear with Fm Wilkinson, Fm McCarlie and Fm Temple and got a jet to work on the third floor via hook-ladders, until a collapsing roof forced them to abandon ship. . . . Fm Clay and myself went to the front of the building and saw the situation. Fm Clay got to work with others controlling the fire on the first floor immediately below the trapped men. . . . I asked the driver of A21's TL whether his safety limits would allow him to pitch immediately above the window where the two men were trapped. He said that this manoeuvre could be carried out. I informed ACO Watkins, who was on the escape pitched to the second-floor window, but unfortunately the TL had to be used as a crane, to lift and hold a twelve-by-two-inch roof-joist off one of the trapped men and could not be put to further use. I returned to the foot of the escape.*

FROM OPS ROOM BY EX TEL
FROM DCO BURRELL AT CLIFTON GARDENS
FM OGDEN ATTACHED TO A29 RED WATCH
REMOVED TO ST MARY'S HOSPITAL W 2
WITH LACERATED FINGER
TOO 0450.*

Stn O Wallington: *By now, two TLs had been trained over our heads, and a line was passed from one (A21's TL), secured around a baulk of timber over Stn O Searle and gently elevated. This allowed the baulk to be wedged against the room wall, thus giving T/L/Fm Hall and myself better access to Stn O Searle. Similarly, another line was attached to timber trapping Fm Stewart. But as this was raised, it was found impossible to wedge it, and for some time it was supported by T/Sub O Stewart upon his shoulders – he having adopted an upright stance above the two trapped men. By now, various cutting-away tools, saws, levers and crow-bars had been assembled. But with the extreme lack of working space within the front edge of the room, tools had to be stowed on the sill, or passed up the escape from below as required. Clearing of debris continued to take place by hand. Both trapped men were in some considerable pain, and the fire under them, which was tackled sparingly with the hose-reel, added smoke and steam to their discomfort. Fm Stewart now appeared to be breathing with some difficulty, and a resuscitator was brought up and applied to him.*

FROM DCO BURRELL
AT CLIFTON GARDENS
FIRE SURROUNDED
TOO 0459.

FROM DCO BURRELL
AT CLIFTON GARDENS
SIX EMERGENCY LIGHTS REQUIRED
TOO 0501.

*Ten minutes before the collapse, Fireman Ogden was pulling hose through a second-floor window at the rear when he cut himself on broken glass. He was sent to get some first aid from an ambulance whose crew insisted he be taken to hospital and the wound properly stitched. He was not detained, and returned to Clifton Gardens.

FROM DCO BURRELL
AT CLIFTON GARDENS
TWO MEMBERS OF BRIGADE TRAPPED
BY FALL OF DEBRIS
IN FRONT ROOM ON SECOND FLOOR
EFFORTS BEING MADE TO RELEASE
AMBULANCE STANDING BY
TOO 0505.'*

Mr Milner: *At about 0500 hours, while rescue, search and fire-fighting operations were still continuing, fire prevention officers reported that there was an imminent danger of massive collapse of the roof and upper walls, which might entomb personnel within the building.*

Stn O Hicks: *I was informed by Fm Joy (A24), who had come down from where he was working on the roof, that the window-arches at fourth-floor level immediately above the ladders being used in the rescue, were bulging outwards. I told him to return to the roof and give warning of any further movement. I told DO Keable, and it was obvious to us both that a wide crack had appeared in the window-arch at roof level, immediately above the rescue operations. A searchlight was trained on the bulging wall. I ascended the escape and informed Mr Watkins of the situation. I stayed at the head of the ladders and assisted the other men there in freeing the two trapped men.*

ACO Watkins: *The building had been subjected to a great deal of heat, and had lost stability through the collapse of the roof, upper floor and staircase. The brickwork of the chimney was also in a precarious position. During the proceedings I received a message that the coping above had moved some inches. I passed this information on to those involved in the extrication and asked if they would like a relief. But they elected to stay at work.*

Mr Milner: *The situation was such that, while only two or three men could work in close contact with those who were trapped, it was necessary to support their work by men on ladders pitched within the potential collapse area. It was also essential to have crews on the first floor to control the fire therein which was threatening the trapped men*

---

*Normally, information about trapped or injured firemen (like the message about Fireman Ogden) would not be sent to Wembley control by RT – in order to prevent families hearing unofficially about an accident via the Press or other firemen, who might be listening on the radio frequency. Later messages concerning the injured firemen were *telephoned* to the Ops room at Lambeth. A message concerning the death of a fireman is never sent.

and the rescuers on the floor above, and to maintain a small number of standby rescuers at third-floor level in close support of those actually engaged in the extrication work.

The reported dangerous situation of the building gave the Deputy Chief Officer and myself grave concern, with regard to the involvement of the personnel within. We decided, however, that there could be no abatement of rescue work, but that the numbers of men in close support should be reduced to a minimum, and that all personnel should be warned of the danger to which they were exposed. Instructions were given for as many men as possible inside the building to be issued with walkie-talkie radio sets, so that in the event of further collapse, they could be used to assist in locating and determining the number of men who might be trapped.

Notwithstanding the hazards to which they were exposed, officers were constantly moving through the building to maintain contact with crews, and no man exposed to these risks demurred from undertaking his duty or requested any relief throughout the rescue operations. Indeed, the most difficult task of the officers was to prevent men entering the premises to assist the rescuers.

ACO Watkins: *The situation regarding smoke and heat varied greatly. There was obviously plenty of ventilation, but working at close quarters as these men were – the use of BA was out of the question – seemed to me that they took a good deal of punishment over a long period. . . . The rescue work was carried out patiently and efficiently by those involved, and they constantly encouraged the men who were trapped. One of the more harrowing factors of the operation, particularly for the younger men, was the cries of pain as the heat increased or as something was moved affecting an injured limb. In spite of this, the work progressed in an orderly manner, using all the equipment available, including TLs.*

Stn O Wallington: *Eventually, T/L/Fm Hall, assisted by myself, was able to commence sawing through a 6" x 2" beam that appeared to be pinning Stn O Searle. Fm Chilton and Fm Blair continued to work at the debris around Fm Stewart. Minor falls of debris and burning timbers from above were a constant hazard. . . . Fm Stewart's belt was finally cut off and he was then free. With some considerable difficulty he was lifted out of the debris by Fm Chilton and passed across to me. I then passed him down to Stn O Hicks, who carried Fm Stewart down to the balcony below, assisted by Fm Blair, with further assistance from ACO Watkins, who was also on the escape below the window.*

Stn O Hicks: *After 1¼ hours' work in icy, precarious and dangerous conditions, Fm Stewart, who obviously had a serious back injury,
was freed, held upright, put across my back – and assisted by those who
were able to, I transferred him and myself from the escape to the first-
floor ladder and carried him down to the balcony.*

Mr Milner: *The first fireman (Fm Stewart) was released and
brought through the window by ladder to the first-floor balcony, and
then internally on a stretcher by an intact staircase to the ground floor.*

TL FROM OPS ROOM BY EX TEL
FROM DCO BURRELL AT WORSLEY HOTEL
ONE FIREMAN RELEASED INJURED REMOVED
TWO FIREMEN STILL TRAPPED EFFORTS BEING
MADE TO RELEASE
TOO 0556.

FROM DCO BURRELL AT CLIFTON GARDENS
8 PUMPS 4 STN OFF I DO I ADO REQUIRED FOR RELIEFS
AT 0630 HOURS
TOO 0556.

FROM DCO BURRELL AT CLIFTON GARDENS
GAS APPARATUS INVOLVED
UNABLE TO SHUT DOWN SUPPLY
REQUEST ATTENDANCE OF GAS AUTHORITY
TOO 0609.

Stn O Wallington: *Sawing of the beam pinning Stn O Searle
continued by T/L/Fm Hall and myself, with Stn O Hicks and Fm
Blair having returned to their original positions. Conditions now became extremely smoky, as fire was progressively getting worse under and
around Stn O Searle, making it difficult, even with a searchlight, to see
the timber-joist being cut. Eventually, with the aid of a sharp bolster-
chisel, the joist was parted, Stn O Searle's belt was cut off, and he was
lifted onto the sill. At this point I moved to the head of the escape.
Stn O Hicks took my place at the sill on the first-floor ladder, and
between us we carried and slid Stn O Searle down to the waiting personnel on the balcony below.*

Stn O Hicks: *Although he was badly burned down one side he was
manoeuvred onto my shoulders. I was then able to carry him down, with
the assistance of others, in a more conventional manner to the balcony,*

where he was put on a stretcher and taken to the ground floor down an
internal staircase. All personnel then vacated the area, due to the danger
of the building collapsing. All personnel involved in the rescue of these
two men were utterly exhausted following the rescues, and were unable
to take an active part in further fire-fighting operations.

```
TO WEM CON FROM OPERATIONS ROOM
FROM DCO BURRELL AT CLIFTON GARDENS
A SECOND MEMBER OF THE BRIGADE HAS NOW
BEEN RELEASED
INJURED REMOVED
TWO FURTHER MEMBERS OF THE BRIGADE
ARE STILL TRAPPED
EFFORTS BEING MADE TO RELEASE
TOO 0612.
```

Neil Wallington stood by the Sally Ann canteen van,
shivering violently with cold and delayed shock, his hands
shaking so much that his cup of tea spilled into the icy road.
Around him was a restless crowd of firemen and policemen,
stamping their feet, talking disjointedly over their sandwiches,
cups of tea and soup, which were freely provided as at every
major fire by the Salvation Army. The two Brigade canteen
vans, also parked in nearby side-roads, afforded a similar
service for the wet, cold and exhausted crews who had been
fire-fighting and also for those who had arrived too late to be
involved and were trying to keep themselves warm while they
wondered dully who had been trapped and how it had all
happened. They were now discussing the rumours that two
firemen had been released and that two were still trapped.
Among them stood Neil, Brian Hall, Roger Stewart, David
Blair and Keith Hicks – shocked, silent, aching in every limb,
their hands raw, their reddened eyes unblinking, trying to
blot out the nightmare of the past one and a half hours.

But distorted pictures still flashed across their minds through
a remembered dark miasma of smoke and steam and the
blinding glow of searchlights – of grimacing faces, hunched
uniforms, bowed helmets, grimy, cut and bleeding hands,
heaving, pulling, tearing at beams – of fire flaring up around,
beside, beneath them and continuing to blaze somewhere in

the background – of water turning to scalding steam and soaking their already sodden uniforms and filling their boots – of the freezing chill that despite the heat and their sweating exertions seized their cramped limbs whenever they paused for another breath and breathed in more lungfuls of smoke. Again they saw and heard the ominous fall of fiery fragments, suddenly showering down upon them, sharply reminding them they were in a deep pit, with stark walls unsupported for two floors, enclosing them on three sides, and that their position, on the verge of ruin itself, was two floors above the street. They felt again the fear that they would all die, and were depressed again by the dread consciousness of their own inadequacy and weakness – they could only do so much, and constricted as they were that 'much' was just a little at a time. Again the two trapped men stared demandingly up at them and held out their hands – Searle grasping Neil's hand, as if for dear life, and Stewart, Chilton's – and they heard again above their own words of encouragement, hope and reassurance, the anguished, urgent, dismaying cries and entreaties of the two trapped men. 'Oh, God – you've got to get me out!' – 'Come on, come on!' – 'I've got to get *out*!' – 'It's getting hot! – 'I can't breathe!' – 'What are you *doing*?' – 'Oh, Christ, it hurts!' – 'You've got to get me out of here!'

'Don't look so bloody cheerful,' said Stewart to Blair. Then he cried out – 'You bastards! *Bastards!*' – as the pain of his burnt and injured back, against which a smouldering beam had lodged itself, splintering his spine, screeched through him as they began to pull him out. First he was lifted, with a line around him, by Lambeth's TL high overhead. Then Chilton tried to raise him, his arms under Stewart's shoulders. But one of Stewart's legs and his belt were caught. They freed the leg and cut off his belt, then dragged him explosively screaming to the window and out onto the escape. 'My *back*! Watch my back!' he cried. But there was no time for niceties or care – they had to get him to safety. Yet as Hicks, assisted by many hands, struggled from the escape to the first floor ladder in order to reach the balcony, Stewart, agonized and upside-down, still managed to gasp – 'My watch! It's coming off. Grab hold of it, will you?' – and Hicks paused long enough to remove the watch before continuing the descent.

In the room above them, Roger Stewart with Chilton's help laid the staircase beam he had borne on his shoulders in the corner where his namesake had been buried. They remained in the room clearing debris, spraying water around Colin Searle as Neil and Hall took turns in sawing through the beam which had pinned him down in a squatting position; it lay immovable across his knees. They could hardly see. Smoke and fire increased, despite water from a hose-reel which added steam to obstruct their vision. Searle helped them by guiding the saw in the trench they had dug by his legs. 'Bloody hell,' he kept saying, his eyes wide with fearful anxiety. *'Bloody hell!'* He felt acute pain in his doubled-up legs, centring on his knees, and was conscious of a burning warmth. But the pain, he thought, was caused by the severe cramps that had seized his legs, making him wish more than anything to be able to stand. They also deadened all other feeling – fortunately, for unknown to him and his rescuers fire was slowly eating away his right leg. The others saw the unextinguishable flames curling out of the debris between Searle and the wall. But they dared not think what was burning out of sight beneath him. They had thought, as he complained less forcefully than Stewart, that he was not so seriously injured, if at all. But now they began to wonder at his fortitude. It was only when the beam snapped, when his belt had been cut, when they lifted him out, that Neil and Hall saw the seat of fire that had embraced him; and as they heaved him onto the window-sill, his right leg, horribly burnt from ankle to hip, passed before Roger Stewart's eyes, and was wincingly grasped by Hicks as he shouldered the injured man.

But all Searle knew was that he was free. He felt only indescribable relief. 'Thanks, lads,' he kept saying, grinning wildly. 'Oh, *thanks*. It's great to get out. Fucking *great*! Don't drop me. Oh, thanks, lads. *Thanks!'*

'It's Martin and Harry, Guv,' said Griffin gently. Neil looked away, his hands still shaking, spilling his tea.

'They were buried at the back of the room,' continued Griffin. 'I've checked all our crews – there was a roll-call ordered – and only Martin and Harry are missing. It's them all right, Guv. I tried to get up to them again, but it wasn't allowed. There's white-hats up and down the stairs. Rowley's in there with them, and Baldwin, and I know Ron Morris is there.'

'Oh, Christ. . . . How are they . . .?'

'I don't know. I heard Martin singing out not long after it happened. . . . I'm glad about Stewart and Searle being out.'

Neil steadied his hands and his gaze and saw in the other man's begrimed face a picture of his own exhaustion and doubt.

He did not know, for Jim Griffin never told him, that while the rescuers had dug and tore at the debris in room 213, Griffin had been in the undamaged room below with Dave, Pincher, Taylor, Waldron and Fireman Clay of Soho, hacking, cutting, tearing at the ceiling, trying to reach the trapped men from beneath. They had been there for an hour, and to begin with had worked at the rear of the narrow room, until someone shouted from the balcony outside the window, that the two men were trapped at *that* end. Lit by a searchlight and box-lamps, kneeling in turn on top of a cupboard or standing on scaling-ladders, they had had to smash through the false plasterboard ceiling before they could gouge holes in the original one. Dust, plaster and dirt rained down on them. But the ceiling and floor above were densely impacted, with rubble on top packed three feet deep. They got through the joists and floor-boards, but could get no further. A hose-reel was thrust in the holes to dampen fires in the floor. Embers fell on them. At one time they were drenched in water when the jet being used by Wickenden, Cheal and Burrett in the gutted room next door to the collapse in number 15, flooded under the dividing wall into the rubble and cascaded through the holes in the ceiling. 'Knock it off!' they yelled. 'Turn that bloody jet off!'

When Stewart and Searle were released, Griffin and the others had been among those on the balcony who had helped lift, carry and lower both men onto stretchers, before they were carried down to waiting ambulances in the street.

Jim Griffin and Archie Waldron were in fact the two firemen who carried Stewart out of the building – after which Griffin had gone around the fire-ground, checking Paddington's crews to see if anyone, apart from Martin Walker, was missing. Dave, Taylor, Pincher, Waldron, Garner and Dunlop he had worked with or seen in the building. He had seen Dyer at the foot of the escape, and noticed that Ray Wade, on standby at Kensington, was also there. The two youngsters, Leroy and Keith Cheal, he met beside the pump escape, in which they had come to the fire with Griffin Orchard, and Harry. Wickenden and Lewis were with them – as was Joe Forrest, who had brought the six emergency lights ordered by DCO Burrell at 5.0 a.m. to Clifton Gardens in the Divisional van. They told him that Marven had been ordered by Station Officer Alcock to assist him in some preventive fire-fighting on the now collapsed third floor of number 17. Beside the TL, Griffin came across Ernie Arthurs, with Jacko at the console and Orchard at the head of the ladders, which were still at that time holding a beam off Searle. All asked anxiously about Martin and Harry, of whom there was no sign.

After Colin Searle was freed, Jim Griffin found Neil at the Salvation Army canteen van. By this time, the news had reached the waiting firemen outside the building that another fireman had been discovered under the debris, and there was now no doubt as to who it was.

They looked up at the blackened second-floor window, sadly wondering what was happening in the depths of the room. But very few would ever know what it was really like.

Soon after the collapse, about 4.45 a.m., Lidbetter and Morris were joined by T/DO John Simmons and ADO Gerald Clarkson. They had been detailed to assist the other two rescuers by DCO Burrell after DACO Pearce, who had gone to the scene of the collapse, reported on the situation at the rear of the room.

The Chief Officer, Joe Milner, then decided to make a direct appreciation of the situation himself. He was shown the second-floor room where the battle to free Martin Walker was being fought. The dangers and difficulties were evident. But he saw that all was being done that could be done. He asked for standby crews to be sent up to act as reliefs if necessary. Then he went down the stairs to assess the general fire situation in and out of the building, leaving DACO Pearce to supervise and co-ordinate the rescue operation from the undamaged room at the rear. Mr Milner was optimistic – he had to be. He knew no effort would be spared to rescue the trapped men. But the fear remained that the effort would not be in time, and that even if one man was not already dead, others might die before long.

Sub O Morris: *We commenced to clear the debris from the upper part of Fm Walker's body, and were then later assisted by various senior officers and other Brigade personnel.*

T/DO Simmons: *I entered the room, finding debris immediately at the door, and thick smoke preventing any vision. I commenced pulling at the debris and burning timber, and felt the hand of the man, Martin Walker. The hand gripped mine and he cried out – 'If you don't get me out quick, Ron, I'm a gonner.' I talked to him and worked at uncovering him, breaking floorboards and thrusting debris back under me until I had uncovered his head and shoulders. I then grasped him under the arms and lifted his shoulders waist-high. He cried out in pain that his legs were trapped. I laid him down again.*

'He's down there somewhere,' Martin kept saying. 'Beside my legs. Harry Pettit. . . . I *know* that he's there.' 'Yeah. . . . Okay,' they said to him. Someone unbuttoned the neck of his tunic, exposing his yellow jersey. 'All right. . . . Take it easy.' Eventually he gave up trying to tell them what he knew. Nobody seemed to believe him, nor want to know – and neither in the end did he. For while he held the other man's hand, he was holding on to life. To die, to be dead, was unthinkable. But there were times, when he felt his mind darken, his spirit become faint, and his eyes begin to close, when he panicked and cried out – 'I'm going! I'm going! Get me out!' – it was then that no reassurance from the rescuers was as comforting as Harry's hand in his.

Early on, he was given a hose-reel, which he had asked for, and with his free left hand was able to poke it into the rubble and spray his burnt left foot and obtain some measure of relief.

T/DO Simmons: *A hose-reel appeared, brought up by ADO Clarkson. At this stage the false plasterboard ceiling on the landing collapsed onto myself and ADO Clarkson, followed by burning debris, and the whole area became thick with smoke and dust. Walker was again showered with burning material, and I squirted water over his head and shoulders and directed the water over his nose and mouth to enable him to breathe from the oxygen entrained in the water. I passed the hose-reel to Walker to play on his feet and legs. A great deal of steam came back at him. Approximately 10 minutes after entering the building, a substantial collapse occurred to the left and behind the room in which we were working, and the whole area shook. I got a jet onto the collapse behind us and knocked some of the fire out. Approximately 30 minutes after the start of operations, I moved further into the room to allow ADO Rowley in to assist.*

ADO Rowley: After a number of unsuccessful attempts, I eventually located the room in which it was feared Brigade personnel were trapped – entry into the area being via a small opening. . . . Already in this room were four persons . . . attempting to release Fm Walker, who was pinned up to his shoulders in fallen debris. Walker was conscious, and indicated that another fireman had been with him and would be quite close at hand.

'We've got one here,' Lidbetter had said. 'There's *two* of us!' cried Martin. 'Not *one*. Two! I keep on telling you!' 'All right,' they said. 'Take it easy.'

'It's Harry Pettit!' cried Martin. 'Harry!' His voice broke in sobs, and for some time afterwards he did not mention Harry's name again.

Meanwhile the four rescuers continued to pull away the entangled wreckage that had buried him, seeing little, not knowing which beam was weighing down or trapped by other beams. Whenever embers or burning fragments fell on the trapped and helpless fireman from the darkness above, the others flung themselves protectively across him. But despite these alarms and the great sense of urgency, they had to work slowly, in case they removed some vital beam supporting the floor. Testing every move they made, feeling their way, coughing and choking, their lungs, nostrils, eyes and hands seared all the time by the heat, they persevered.

ADO Rowley: Working conditions were very cramped, and whilst tenable, were made more difficult by smoke and heat issuing from pockets of fire all around and under the trapped man. The precarious condition of the surrounding structure was a major cause of concern, and it was decided that only the application of hose-reel jets to the pockets of fire and the careful removal of the debris around Walker would ensure his release without causing a further collapse.

From time to time, anxious faces of senior officers appeared in the smoke. 'How are you getting on?' they asked concernedly, never impatiently. In the nearby room of number 17 that overlooked the rear, all kinds of equipment that might be of help, lines, searchlights, boxlamps, hammers, axes, crowbars, saws, scoops and buckets were being and had been assembled. A relief crew stood by there, as well as a young doctor and nurse from St Mary's Hospital, and several senior officers. Other officers had to be posted on the landing, on the stairs and at the street-door to prevent importunate firemen, eager to help in any way they could, from crowding in, especially those who knew the trapped men. They were told, roughly, to go elsewhere, and assured that they would do more harm than good.

ADO Baldwin, whose 'A' Division office and flat were at Paddington fire-station, asked and was allowed to go up and join his colleague, ADO Rowley. When he reached the second floor, he was told by DACO Pearce to organize a fire-fighting crew to contain the fires on the floor below. This he did, delegating the task to Station Officer Alcock, and returned to assist in the rescue attempt, quite unaware, as no one had told him, that more than one fireman was trapped at the rear of the room. He began by damping down with a hose-reel the severe fire behind the rescuers.

Another senior officer with a personal connection with the two trapped men was the 'A' Division commander that night, DO Keable.

DO Keable: *When I crawled into the room, I saw that Sub O Morris and L/Fm Lidbetter (both A25), and DO Simmons, ADO Clarkson and ADO Rowley were trying to release Fm Walker. He appeared to be trapped from the waist down, with the trunk of his body in an upright position and his head just above floor level. He had a rope tied under his armpits, and I instructed that this be held taut by a Brigade member in the next room in case of further collapse.*

The rope was held by T/Stn O Brooks of G24 (Hendon) for well over two hours until he was relieved by ADO Clarkson.

DO Keable: *Ambulance personnel at second-floor level had given me a cylinder of Entonox (pain-killer gas), and I offered this to Walker and explained that this would deaden his feelings while he inhaled it and would relieve his pain. He declined the offer, preferring to remain fully conscious. The cylinder was left handy in case he changed his mind.*

Later he was asked if he wanted a resuscitator or BA set, and again he refused. Although he was suffering, he wanted to *know* his release was being achieved, to be aware of what was being done, so that he might assist the rescuers if and when he could, and let them know if any unseen fire had started up beneath him. But above all he was determined not to surrender himself to the insensate, terrifying blackness that had engulfed him and Harry when they were on their own.

DO Keable: *Conditions in the room were very smoky, due to the deep-seated fires in, under and around this room, and because of Walker's low level in the room, there was no respite for himself or his rescuers. ADO Baldwin, who was subduing fire in the immediate vicinity with a hose-reel, subsequently joined in the physical release of Walker. Other crew members were damping down as necessary at all floor levels. But a serious fire involving the remaining roof-timbers was allowed to burn more or less unchecked, because its extinction would undoubtedly have brought about further collapse onto the rescuers and the trapped personnel.*

ADO Baldwin: *The rescue area itself was completely involved in smoke, heat and steam, with fire threatening to spread between floor levels. This was kept partially under control by use of hose-reel jets. At the time of my entry into the room where the rescues were taking place, I was told that Stn O Searle and Fm Stewart were trapped under the front window and that crews were working at that point to release them, though due to thick smoke it was not possible to see them clearly.*

It cleared enough at one point for Ron Morris, lifting his head for some respite from the smoke, to catch a shocking glimpse of the head of his station officer, Colin Searle. Until then Morris had been ignorant that Searle was also trapped in the wreckage, only ten feet away. He said nothing, and bowed his head again to the task in hand.

ADO Baldwin: *I worked with ADO Rowley, Sub O Morris, T/DO Simmons and another fireman whom I do not know, attempting to release Fm Walker, who was trapped under the debris by his legs and feet.*

'I can't move my legs!' said Martin. For some time he was convinced that the hose he had been carrying when the collapse occurred was the object trapping his feet. It was fully charged with water and lay solidly across his legs. Repeatedly he asked for the water supply to be shut down or for the hose to be cut. 'Please get the water knocked off,' he said. 'Cut this bloody hose and I'll get my feet out.' But it was only when the hose was partly uncovered that something could be done.

T/DO Simmons: *Walker, helping us, said he could feel a hose-line as hard as a rock pressing against his legs, which gave him pain and was possibly trapping him. I asked for this to be knocked off. But nothing happened for some time. The sub officer cut the hose with a knife.*

When Morris did so – with great difficulty as the hose was deeply buried, and he had to cut it out of sight by Martin's leg – water flooded the debris, and the firemen working in the room below were soaked. But although, as Martin's rescuers had hoped, the fire danger was diminished by the water, and his left leg became free, his right foot was rigidly held by something else further down in the wreckage. The immediate result of the cutting of the hose was that Martin was drenched in icy water. From then on he shook and shivered continuously with cold.

T/DO Simmons: *Jets of water, working from below and outside were causing smoke and heat to waft up at us, and I asked ADO Clarkson to get all jets knocked off. ADO Clarkson, throughout this period, had worked as a runner on the stairs and provided additional hose-reel and a searchlight. Following this, he stayed and held the searchlight, passing instructions to the people on the landing and the stairs. . . . The fire behind us started to get up again, and there was a constant need to douse flames to the rear and to the left, and to put spray onto the hot debris as it was passed from the room to those in the passageway and on the stairs. All this time the leading fireman and sub officer worked with their hands and made further attempts to extricate Walker's legs, each time causing him to cry out in pain. We called for salvage scoops and buckets, and formed a bucket chain down the stairs to carry off the rubble.*

ADO Rowley: *It was only when debris had been removed from around Walker's body and attempts were made to burrow debris from beneath his leg . . . that Fm Pettit's body was located.*

ADO Baldwin: *It was at this stage of the proceedings that it was discovered that a fourth fireman was also trapped under the debris. . . .*

Ron Morris was clearing a tangle of floor-boards, carpet, timbers, lathe and plaster from Martin's legs when he saw in the debris beneath him a fireman's epaulette. He wrenched aside more masking rubble and exposed part of the buried fireman's back. ADO Rowley, working opposite him, caught Morris's eye and saw its dismayed direction. Morris thrust his hand into the rubble, under a beam. He found the collar, the edge of the helmet, and the fireman's neck. His fingers felt for a pulse there. He looked at Rowley and shook his head – and Martin, who had been watching them, cried out defiantly – 'I know what you're saying!'

ADO Baldwin: *The fireman, whom I now know to be Fm Harry Pettit (A21), was lying face down, with his feet towards the front of the room, some eight feet into the room from the front window. The lower half of his body was completely covered by heavy debris; the upper half, from waist to shoulders was clear and visible. But the head, with the helmet still in position, was bent forward down through a hole in the floor-boards and was covered by debris and wooden rafters.*

ADO Rowley: *He was face down in the debris, with his head trapped under the same beam pinning Fm Walker's leg. . . . Both Sub O Morris and I checked but failed to detect a pulse-beat in Pettit's neck, and as a result of the surrounding conditions and predicament of Pettit, it was apparent that the man was already dead.*

ADO Baldwin: *With the above factors in mind, the personnel endeavouring to release him and Fm Walker concentrated all their efforts on Fm Walker, who was conscious and suffering severe pain from the burns he was receiving from the fire.*

'I told you,' said Martin, shivering with cold. 'I've known all the time. . . . Look!' He removed his right arm from the rubble lodged by his leg. 'Look. . . .' His hand had hold of another hand. 'It's Harry. . . . I've known all along.'

Ron Morris disengaged the two hands. 'You won't want that, Mart,' he said. 'Not now.'

The rescuers bowed their heads and their minds again to their labours. They covered Harry Pettit with a salvage sheet, to hide him from Martin's eyes and their own. But the knowledge of his death was a terrible burden, sapping their already weakened strength and clouding their resolve, which were soon demoralized further by the realization that the beam and Harry's head were inextricably wedged against Martin's right foot. His release, which should have become more easy, was going to be even more complicated and prolonged. For they dared not cut through the massive beam, on which much of the wreckage rested, in case it caused the floor to collapse. They would have to burrow underneath it, without disturbing the dead fireman or causing Martin more pain. Doggedly they set to work again in the depths of the wreckage and amid the densest smoke.

Unknown to them, the other end of the great beam that had trapped both Harry's head and Martin's leg lay eight feet away, across Colin Searle's bent knees. Yet although the beam had brought death to one of them and endless minutes of pain to the other two, the miracle was that when it fell it did not kill them all. The wonder also was that the walls of the house, unsupported by two floors and the roof, continued to stand.

DO Keable: *During the rescue operation, conditions progressively deteriorated. A large crack opened up in the centre of the window-arch immediately over the head of the escape ladder into the affected room, whilst the party-wall and chimney-stack had a very definite lean towards the scene of the rescue operations. These two factors, plus the continued burning of the well overloaded second floor, placed everyone concerned in a position of the greatest possible danger, and this point cannot be emphasized too much. All personnel continued to work undaunted by this certain knowledge, and it was a hard task to keep the number of persons exposed to this risk to a minimum. Station Officers Powell (A27), Alcock (A22), Cooper (A28), and DACOs Pearce and Roundell were all involved inside the affected section of the building, plus other unknown members.*

Dave Webber was one. He had been among the helping firemen on the balcony when Stewart was freed and brought down and had guided Hicks' feet and supported Searle when he was released. Despite Dave's earlier strenuous involvement in the three perilous third-floor rescues, in the initial fire-fighting on the second floor of number 17, mainly with Archie and Martin, and in the frustrated assault on the ceiling below the collapse room, he still had the energy of a twenty-one-year-old and the will to put his desire to help Martin and Harry into action. He knew they were somewhere in the second-floor room above him. So he waited until the exhausted rescuers of Stewart and Searle had been ordered out of the room before he climbed swiftly up the escape and into the window as they climbed unsteadily down.

One rescuer had remained – Ray Chilton. He emerged, coughing from the smoke and steam, carrying a bucket full of rubbish which he emptied out of the window. After Searle's departure he had broken a way around the central pile-up of beams and had begun helping to remove the rubble dug out by Martin's rescuers. Dave gave him a hand for several minutes. But when some firemen from Soho entered the room from the escape, he seized the opportunity to realize his original intention of joining in the actual rescue of his colleagues and advanced further into the room beside the wall.

He found Martin in a halo of diffused light, surrounded by the indefinite shapes of four white-hats and two firemen who, wreathed in smoke, knelt around him like devotees at a shrine. Becoming aware of him, they looked up blankly, their faces as black as their helmets. He recognized Rowley and Baldwin who nodded. Another white-hat said: 'Who are you?' 'He's from Paddington,' said Rowley. 'Like Walker.' 'Oh – pitch in,' said the white-hat.

'We've got a mate of yours,' said Simmons to Martin, who squinted through the searchlight's glare at the standing figure at his feet.

'Hallo, Martin,' said Dave.

'Who's that?'

'It's Dave – Dave Webber.'

'Oh, hallo, Dave.'

'You'd do anything to get out of doing the mess,' said Dave as a joke.

Martin seemed to smile, but he said nothing. Dave saw that the sub officer, Ron Morris, whom he recognized, was holding Martin's right hand in both of his.

T/DO Simmons: *Two firemen came up the escape and in through the window as the rescues at that end of the room had been completed earlier. We then, together with ADO Rowley, lifted the remains of the staircase, which was seriously hampering rescue, through the window and dropped it to the ground. This then allowed better access and more of the larger pieces of debris to be cleared and dropped from the window.*

The ruined wooden staircase had lain at an angle by the wall near Martin's feet. Earlier, near the window, one end of it had been borne on Roger Stewart's shoulders. Its removal gave them more room and also took some weight off the floor and freed other debris beneath it. Dave, cornered where he stood, and still uncertain where to put his feet, was not at that moment in a position to help Simmons and Rowley.

They were assisted by Chilton and four Soho firemen – T/Sub O Macey, Fireman Clay, Temple and McCarlie – who had joined Chilton in chucking rubbish from the room out of the window. 'No one else!' said Simmons. 'Don't let anyone else in here.' There were now twelve men in the narrow room, excluding the two trapped men.

'That's Harry down there,' said Martin to Dave, indicating the salvage sheet with his eyes. Dave looked at it, not wanting to believe the obvious. 'Yeah, I know,' he said, meaning that he knew Harry was trapped with Martin; he did not want to know any more.

Telling himself that if he worked very hard Harry might still be saved, Dave knelt down and now threw himself with his hands and all his boundless energy into assisting both his colleagues' release.

First, working mainly with Rowley and Lidbetter, he uncovered as much as possible of the beam pinning Martin's right foot.

T/DO Simmons: *The medical team were now with us and examined Walker – the doctor wishing to put Walker out with an injection. This I would not allow, as Walker was assisting us, and in such a smoky corner, I was concerned that he should respond when I talked to him, so that I knew he was still breathing. ADO Rowley cut Walker's sleeve to allow an injection when required.*

The doctor was young and oriental in appearance. Martin looked up at him with weary gratitude. Any respite from the pain he had endured for two hours now, would be a relief. But when he saw the needle that would bring him oblivion, he changed his mind – he had to remain conscious, to know what his rescuers were doing, to help them, and know when at last he was free. A fit of trembling seized him. 'No, I'll hang on,' he said, and Simmons backed him up. The doctor returned to the rear room.

Martin gritted his teeth. He now began to wonder and worry how and when his wife Wendy, his daughter and his mother, would be told about what had happened to him.

T/DO Simmons: *I asked ADO Clarkson to have a rescue-line lowered from the TL, which might be used like a crane to lift the beam which was trapping Walker. When it was in position, the projection was not sufficient. Nevertheless, we kept hold of the line for an emergency.*

A21's TL was now being operated by another crew, who had relieved Jacko and Orchard after the release of Stewart and Searle. But Jacko had remained protectively by the appliance, nervous that the other crew might either open up the monitor or accidentally touch the building with the ladders and cause it to collapse on Martin and Harry below. Then a senior officer asked the crew if the TL could be re-angled further over the room, with a rescue-line hanging from its head. They re-pitched the TL, and when the man at the top said over the intercom – 'I can *see* them' – Jacko could restrain himself no longer. Seizing the rescue-line and slinging it over his shoulder, he speedily climbed the ladders, going higher and higher above the street and into the smoke until, at the heels of the fireman at the top, he could see straight down.

The ladder shook with their weight and the force of the wind. Despite the weaving smoke and sparks flying upwards, he could see that a chasm like a hell-mouth had been made in the ruined house by the collapse. Roofs and floors on either side of it burned. In the depths of the pit, four storeys below him, Jacko saw the diminutive prostrate figure of Martin surrounded by small, intensely active people – looking like a distant picture of the death of Nelson. He knew it was Martin, for even at that height, he could see the yellow jersey exposed by the unbuttoned tunic – the jersey Martin had worn that night for the first time. The sight distressed him greatly. He gripped the ladder, feeling desperately helpless.

'Martin!' he roared into the depths. 'It's *Jacko*! Get out of there! Do you hear me? You'd do *anything* to get Christmas off! *Wouldn't* you just? *Martin!* Some cunts will do *anything* to get out of a beating at *squash!*'

He rested his forehead against the trembling ladder.

Far below him Martin turned his head. He could not see who had shouted down at him out of the night. But he knew who it was, and he smiled.

T/DO Simmons: *Some of the debris being cleared allowed the leading fireman and ADO Rowley to take it in turns with the floor-saw.*

It had now been decided that an attempt must be made to cut through the beam on both sides of Martin's foot. Time was running out on the rescuers. A message had reached them that fire prevention officers below had estimated it would not be long before the chimney and walls collapsed. There was talk of evacuating the building. In the rear room the possibility of amputating Martin's foot was discussed – a suggestion that DCO Burrell, in the street outside, refuted when it was put to him. He said it was to be avoided at all costs. But although he

was painfully aware that more lives might be lost, he gave no
instruction to clear the building, certain that such an instruction would never be obeyed, and believing that the tenacity of
the rescuers would be rewarded. He had the greatest faith that
all concerned would do their best. 'Just get them *out*,' he said.

TO WEM CONTROL FROM OPS ROOM
FROM DCO AT CLIFTON GARDENS
DIFFICULTY BEING EXPERIENCED IN RELEASING
TRAPPED PERSONNEL DUE TO CONFINED ACCESS
AND FALLEN DEBRIS
SLOW PROGRESS BEING MADE
TOO 0721.

By now all the rescuers were suffering badly from the strain
of their efforts and their prolonged exposure to heat and above
all smoke. Spasms of coughing racked them. Increasingly often
they had to pause for a moment to rest or clear their vision.
Several times they were asked if they wished to be relieved, but
no one nodded assent. Morris and Lidbetter in particular were
obsessed with the idea of freeing Martin and continued com-
pulsively to dig alongside Dave in the rubble around the beam.

ADO Rowley, feeling sick and faint, was forced at last to get
some fresh air. He left the room by the window and stumbled
down the escape to the slip-road, where he reported to DCO
Burrell – as did T/DO Simmons some minutes later, having
left Clarkson and Baldwin to supervise the now desperate
attempts of Lidbetter, Morris and Dave to free the trapped
man.

They were joined now by Fireman David Harris, of D22
(Acton), who had stepped forward when DACO Pearce asked
for a volunteer from the standby crew in the rear room.

Both Rowley and Simmons returned to the scene of the
collapse after a brief rest, reaching the room via the internal
staircase of number 17, which was lined with tensely waiting
firemen, as was the second-floor landing. Among those in the
rear room were Jim Griffin, Pincher Martin, Keith Orchard,
Malcolm Garner – and Neil, who had been prevented by his
senior officers and by his own admitted exhaustion from taking
any further part in rescue operations. Ernie Arthurs, Archie

Waldron and Paul Taylor were on the stairs. For a time Keith Cheal was in that part of the building, as was Leroy, who had been ordered to bring some box-lamps up.

He had found his way into the crowded, flooded rear room, where a young nurse was filling a syringe with fingers trembling with cold. Heavily oppressed by the harsh realities of the fire, Leroy returned to the noisy street and the cold night air and the companionship of his contemporaries, Wickenden and Cheal, stunned by the thought that *this* was what it was like, being a fireman, and that he himself was actually there.

Most of the other Paddington firemen in the building had used the order for an ET crew to bring up heavy cutting and lifting gear, porto-power and spreaders, as their excuse to enter the building with the equipment. Once in, they stayed, refusing to leave, saying that they were from A21 and it was *their* mates who were trapped. But there was nothing they could do to help, and some became frustrated and angered by the apparent inaction and the officiousness of the white-hats.

ADO Rowley, who worked at Paddington, like Baldwin, recognized the men from A21 and spoke to them when he returned, although there was not much to say. If they asked about Harry, he was guarded, answering if pressed that Harry was in a bad way. The truth he could not admit, even to himself, for he vividly remembered how alert, how alive Harry had been when he had gone to be interviewed by DO Keable, at the start of the Red Watch's duty that night. Rowley returned to the rescuers, now more sick at heart than in body, and ordered Morris and Lidbetter out, telling them forcefully that their exhaustion made them more of a hindrance than a help.

'We've got to have a *fresh* crew!' he told them. 'Go and get a breather. You've done enough.'

Lothfully they acquiesced, acknowledging at last their weakness, making their way out of the window and down the escape, hardly able to stand, see or breathe. They were taken to the control unit to rest and given cups of tea, while Dave and Rowley were joined by Fireman Temple of Soho, three of whose colleagues were still shovelling rubbish out of the window. In the face of this continuous avalanche, two other firemen, sent up to replace Morris and Lidbetter, now entered the room – Jacko and Dave Dyer, both of whom had been waiting at the foot of the escape for such a moment.

To begin with they helped the Soho firemen – Jacko astride the window-sill. Then when Jim Griffin called up to him from below, warning him that the front wall above him had cracked, he told Dyer to take his place and worked his way past the other firemen to where Martin lay.

'Hallo, Mart,' he said. 'Still taking it easy? How are you?' Martin smiled. 'I'm all right, Jacko,' he said.

Someone thrust a searchlight into Jacko's hands – 'Hold that!' – and he directed its glare into the ragged hole under the beam and onto Dave's bloody hands. He caught Dave's eye. Where's Harry? he mouthed, and looked down at the salvage sheet at which Dave had nodded and on which he was standing. He moved off it, steadying his hands – Martin was staring at him. Then Dave began to swear.

'It's no use! I can't get *under* it. We've got to either move the beam or *him*, his helmet's caught as well!'

The building shuddered again, the floor trembled, as another mass of debris collapsed and crashed behind them.

None of us are going to get out, thought Jacko. He looked around at Dave, Baldwin, Rowley, Martin, Temple and Harris, at the other firemen dimly seen in the room, and realized they were mostly from 'A' division. They'll give us a mass funeral, he thought, and wondered who would carry his coffin. Then he had a sudden feeling that no one else would or could be killed. One victim was enough – there would be no more.

'Give me a knife!' said Rowley.

'Mind how you go,' said Martin as Rowley began cutting through the leather of his right boot. Harris stood astride him. 'Hold on to my belt.' 'Hold his arms.' 'Get hold of his boot.' 'Martin – turn on your side.' 'Oh, Christ!' 'I've split it down to the ankle.' 'Twist your foot to the right.' 'To the *right*!' 'Give him a hand.' 'Oh, Christ!' 'Hold him.' 'Now pull!' 'Help him!' *'Pull!'* 'Go on!' 'Pull! *Pull!*' 'Oh, *Christ!*'

He cried out as the burnt flesh of his right foot tore away and his tendons burst. But suddenly, agonizingly, his foot was plucked from the trap of his boot and the beam – and he was free.

Many hands carried him out of the room, put him on an ambulance-chair and carried him down the stairs to the ground floor, where they laid him on a stretcher, under a sign that said 'Fire Exit'. Many faces greeted him, happily, joyously, making jokes. People touched him, slapped his arms, his shoulders, saying: 'You're okay, Martin!' – 'Good to see you!' – 'You'll be all right now!' – 'Good luck, son.' Some he recognized. But he could not smile, he could not speak, trying to control his emotions and the shivering that still assailed him so much he had to hold onto the sides of the chair and the stretcher. His body was frozen; his feet still seemed to burn. But his mind hurt more – some greater pain oppressed him, half-remembered. Then the cold early morning air hit his face, and he saw bare branches of trees, street-lights, stark against a dark grey sky as he was carried through a mob of firemen in the slip-road.

Suddenly a face that he wanted to see appeared beside the stretcher, beside the white crash-helmeted head of an ambulanceman. Jacko smiled at him, encouragingly. 'You're all right, Mart. You're all right now.'

Martin struggled to speak, to be heard above the noise of voices and machines. 'Do us a favour, Jacko,' he whispered. 'Don't let Wendy know until Lisa's gone to school.'

'Don't worry about that, Mart,' said Jacko. 'I'll tell her.'

'You a mate of his?' asked DCO Burrell. 'It might be a good idea if you went to the hospital with him.'

Jacko nodded. 'Thanks. But don't let anyone tell his wife, sir. None of the HQ blokes. *I'll* do that.'

'All right,' said the Deputy Chief. 'We'll sit on it. Go on – get inside.'

'Thanks, Guv.'

The ambulancemen laid Martin's stretcher in the bright interior of the ambulance. A coloured nurse made him comfortable, covering him with blankets. 'I don't suppose you remember me,' said one of the ambulancemen, removing his white crash-helmet. 'But I was in your squad at Southwark – nine years ago.' 'Oh, yeah,' said Martin, slowly recalling his face. 'I'll see you,' said the ambulanceman. He grinned, and stepping outside, shut the ambulance doors.

Jacko sat on the bed opposite Martin, convulsively clasping

his hands together, their agitation betraying his steady smile. The nurse was talking soothingly and cheerfully to the patient.

'All right to go now?' asked a voice in the front.

'No – you can't go yet,' called the nurse. 'There's another casualty to come.'

Jacko stared at her back. 'No. We got to go *now*!' he protested. She turned around. 'The – other person won't be out for some minutes yet. *He*'s injured.' Jacko nodded at Martin. 'He needs attention.'

'Well, I was told there were *two* of them coming out,' she said.

'There is. But I – I really think we should get going straight away.'

'What for? It won't hurt if we wait a minute.'

'But –'

Jacko knew that Martin was listening, though his eyes gazed at the ceiling. He stood up, caught the nurse's arm and inclined his head towards hers, facing away from Martin. She frowned.

'We don't need to wait,' he whispered. 'The other one's dead . . .'

'I know what you're saying!' cried Martin.

'Oh,' said the nurse. 'Oh, okay. Off we go. You can go now!' she called to the driver.

As the ambulance pulled away from the kerb, from the scene of the fire in Clifton Gardens, from the still burning hotel, the unbearable pain in Martin's mind exploded. He was out of the room – no longer trapped – injured, but alive. He was free. But Harry had been left behind – Harry, whose hand he had held until he died and long after that.

Harry was dead.

Martin turned his face to the wall and began to cry.

'Oh, no, Mart!' pleaded Jacko. 'Don't. . . . You're all right, Mart. You made it!'

He knelt on the floor and grasped Martin's hand, holding it as tightly, as desperately, as Harry had done.

TO WEM CONTROL FROM OPS ROOM
FROM DCO BURRELL AT CLIFTON GARDENS
THIRD MEMBER OF BRIGADE INJURED RELEASED

FOURTH MEMBER OF BRIGADE STILL TRAPPED
EFFORTS BEING MADE TO RELEASE
TOO 0742.

Ray Wade watched the ambulance go. 'There was four of them trapped up there,' he said. 'I seen three come out. The fourth is my mate, Harry. He's still in there.'

He was talking to some men from the London Salvage Corps, with whom he had worked for five years before achieving his goal of becoming a fireman. The Salvage men, waiting for the fire to end, had asked him what was going on.

'I don't know nothing else,' said Ray and moved on towards the ET.

Ever since coming groggily down from the head of A28's TL, where he had hung on for nearly an hour until, nauseated by the smoke and the swaying, he had had to descend, he had wandered up and down the road, lost in the crowd, knowing hardly anyone, not knowing what had happened in the second-floor room, nor to begin with who was in there.

The Kensington leading fireman in charge of the TL had taken the hook-belt off him – the driver had said: 'You done well.' And Ray had sat in the TL's cab for ten or more minutes recovering, smoking a cigarette and getting his breath back. Then he went to fetch a cup of tea for the TL driver.

On his way up the slip-road he had noticed some extra activity on and around an escape. He had commented on it to Roger Lewis whom he met beside Paddington's pump. 'There's someone trapped in there,' said Lewis. 'Supposed to be a fireman.' 'Oh, Lord,' said Ray. 'Who is it?' But Lewis didn't know.

Later, after bringing back cups of tea from the Sally Ann van for the two Kensington firemen, Ray had stood beside the TL watching the action in the slip-road. He had been smoking a cigarette and drinking his tea when another fireman asked him for a light. 'There's four blokes in there,' said the other man. 'Cor, bleeding hell,' said Ray. 'Are they all right?' 'Don't know,' returned the other fireman. 'No one seems to know anything. Did you ever see so many white-hats in your life? It's like a fucking blizzard!'

An ambulance backed into the slip-road, and stretchers

were taken out. Not long afterwards a fireman, crying out in pain, was brought out of the second-floor window and disappeared into the one below. He emerged in a minute from the front door on a stretcher, and an ambulance took him away. Ray recognized the injured man as Tony Stewart. Then a sub officer from the BA control van came over and asked A28's TL driver if all his crew were present. 'Yeah – one's up, one's down.'

Ray wandered away to Paddington's pump. 'You all right with your crews?' he asked Cheal, who replied: 'We don't know. We can't find Harry.' 'I hope he isn't in *that* bleeding lot,' said Ray. He then went back to A28's TL, and when its crew were relieved, he joined the group on the levers of Paddington's escape.

When Searle was released, Ray was inside the hotel, in number 11, which he had entered to find a toilet. He noticed that off the hall, in a flooded billiards-room, several firemen, wearing BA sets and plainly worn out, were resting on chairs and on the floor; one was abstractedly rolling snooker balls around the table. When Ray came out, he saw the ambulance containing Searle go past him, its two-tone siren sounding. He then rejoined the group at the bottom of the escape and stood there for an hour and froze, while rubbish from the room above was continually emptied out of the window into the basement area.

He had heard now that Harry and Martin were in that room and he wanted to be of some help. But no more firemen were being allowed up the escape and there was nothing he could do. So when a fireman from Soho offered to give him a break, after first refusing, he agreed. He wandered away, and so missed the chance to enter the room when Morris came out and down the escape – a chance that was seized by Jacko and Dyer. Unaware of this, Ray stood silently by Paddington's pump for a time with some of Paddington's Wombles – Cheal, Wickenden and Leroy, who were all sadly subdued. He was ten years older than two of them, but he was also a Womble, as was Harry, and was glad of their company.

When Martin was at last released, Ray watched from the back of the crowd as the injured man was put in an ambulance, with Jacko for company. He was pleased about that. No one had been killed, and no one appeared to be badly injured. He could not help but be optimistic about Harry. He was worried – but believed everything would turn out all right in the end.

So when he went to the ET after talking to the Salvage Corps team, he could not believe that the tears in Dave Webber's eyes were anything other than tears of sweat and exhaustion. Dave was slumped on a seat, smoking a cigarette with a grimy, bleeding hand. Joe Forrest was with him. They stopped talking when Ray appeared at the ET door.

'Have you heard anything?' asked Ray. 'Do you know how Harry is?'

'Sorry, Ray,' murmured Joe. 'Can't help you.'

'I suppose he's all right,' said Ray. 'Even supposing it's *him*. No sod's said anything, have they? I mean, it mightn't be him at all.'

Dave turned away, to hide the grief he had first felt when Martin had been carried out of the second-floor room and he had stood by the salvage sheet on his own. He had felt such a sense of black despair and loneliness that he had had to escape, get out, before it overwhelmed him. And he had stumbled back across the room to the window, looking for light and air and companionship and life.

'I'll be back with you tomorrow,' remarked Ray.

'Oh, yeah,' said Joe. 'You been at Kensington. What with?'

'The TL. I had a go with the monitor – the first time in my life.' Ray grinned at them, showing all his teeth. 'Cheers.'

He walked away up the road from the ET, feeling strangely alone among the many firemen. Yet it was interesting being there, at such a fire, and although he worried about Harry, the worst could be that he was badly injured. Ray hoped it was not that serious. But why were they taking so long?

He came to the TL, which he saw had been taken over by Bob Dunlop, who was sitting at the console and looking very cold. 'Can you get me a cup of something hot, Ray?' he asked. 'Sure!' replied Ray, glad to be of some use. But another fireman said *he* would go and told Ray not to bother. He shrugged his shoulders and ambled slowly over to the pump to rejoin the Wombles there. But a senior officer, coming out of the building, forestalled him.

'Right, you blokes!' the white-hat said to the firemen nearest the door of number 17. 'Gather round. When we bring out the next one – I want you to crowd round the door, round the stretcher. Understand? We don't want any photographer taking photos. Okay. Stay close.'

Dutifully the firemen gathered around the porch and in the doorway, asking each other who the fireman was and whether he was injured like the other three.

'Do you know who it is?' a young fireman asked Ray. 'They say he's from Paddington.'

'So am I,' said Ray. 'Yeah. . . . It appears to be my mate, Harry. He's the only one we haven't accounted for.'

'Oh. Is he – all right?'

'I'm sure he is,' said Ray, hopefully. 'They would have said otherwise, wouldn't they?'

They brought him out of the second-floor room and passed him awkwardly, carefully, through the narrow arched opening between the houses. They carried him into the rear room where the Chief Officer and other officers and firemen were waiting. Among them was Neil, and among the many hands which held and helped to carry the body of the dead fireman were those of Jim Griffin and Pincher Martin. Keith Orchard dragged a mattress onto the flooded floor, and gently on it three station officers, Cooper, Powell and Wright, laid Harry Pettit on his back, at the feet of his station officer. Neil looked down without moving as the doctor, in a blaze of boxlamp light, knelt and made a brief and knowingly useless examination before looking up at the Chief Officer and shaking his head. People sighed, murmured wearily, and spoke in saddened whispers. Someone spoke to Neil – but he stood unmoving, staring incredulously at the face below him and the form as immobile as his.

Harry lay like a fighter knocked to the ground, unmarked, except for a graze upon his forehead. His eyes were closed. His fists were clenched; one leg was bent. He was helmetless and without his belt; his hair and uniform were wet. His features were empty of any expression. But his lips were parted as if he were about to speak.

An order was given: 'A21's crew away.'

'Come on, Guv – we can't do any more for him.'

But Neil continued to stand – unseeing now, unhearing, fighting to control his feelings in the face of death – until someone brought a red blanket to cover the mattress, and hide Harry from his view.

Then everyone was ordered out of the room, and he forced himself to move, to go down the stairs to the ground floor and out into the street, following the silently crying figure of Jim Griffin.

Outside, he saw that the sky was light and a pale fresh blue in the dawn. He pushed through the firemen gathered round the porch, not noticing Ray, and saw his sub officer, Paul Taylor, near Paddington's pump, talking to the station officer from Southall. Taylor was saying – 'I heard they had just given him an injection. I hope he's all right.' Neil took him aside. 'How bad is Harry?' asked Taylor.

'He's gone,' said Neil. 'He's gone. . . . Gather the lads together, Paul – we're going home.'

He walked on out of the slip-road into Clifton Gardens, past the young, unhappily inquiring faces of three of his Wombles – Cheal, Wickenden, and Leroy, who more than the others was by now completely dazed by all that had happened that night at his first fire.

The tree-lined road was awash with water and lines of hose; firemen stood in scattered groups among the red machines; pump-engines whirred in the background. But no one shouted now. Civilians passed by on their way to work, looking askance at the chaotic scene and the spectre of the scorched, smoking, still burning ruin of the Worsley Hotel behind the trees.

Outside number 17, the assembled firemen crowded round the stretcher as it was carried out. The red blanket covering Harry must have been spread like that, thought Ray, to prevent any photographs being taken. But he knew he might be wrong about this, and so, just to be sure, he diffidently spoke to a large, bespectacled ambulanceman who was closing the vehicle's doors.

'Excuse me,' he said. 'But how is he? He's . . . a mate of mine. . . . I was wondering if he was all right.' 'Couldn't tell you,' said the ambulanceman. 'We don't know if he's dead or alive.'

The doors slammed. Ray moved away, believing that even if Harry was badly injured, there must be a fifty-fifty chance he would pull through.

'Come on, you lads!' said an ADO. 'No hanging about. If you've nothing to do, you can make up some of the hose and clear up the area generally. Lend a hand, lads.'

Before doing so, Ray stood for a minute watching the ambulance speed noisily away from him up the road.

Suddenly the orange street-lights went out.

The siren-sounding ambulance passed by Neil as he reached the ET, where he had hoped to find some privacy and in which he might yield to the overpowering emotional pressure building up within him. But at the rear of the ET were Ernie Arthurs, Malcolm Garner and Pincher Martin. Garner was sitting on the rear step, sobbing, his head in his hands. Pincher had just broken the news to him and Ernie.

The sound of the ambulance's siren died away.

'Is it true, Guv?' asked Ernie miserably.

Neil nodded. 'Tell everyone –' he said, controlling his voice 'Tell them to wait here, Ernie. We're going home soon.'

Then he turned away from them, to contain his own grief and to keep command of himself by busying himself in the routine matter of retrieving the nominal-roll boards for each appliance before the Watch went home.

But the Chief Officer, Joe Milner, who walked by the ET some moments later, had nothing to distract him from his thoughts and feelings. His deputy, DCO Don Burrell, was formulating the Stop message, ordering men and machines away, and initiating various relief and clearing up procedures at the control unit, where newspapermen's demands for information were being met by T/DO John Simmons. It was DCO Burrell's command. But the ultimate responsibility was the Chief Officer's, and it weighed heavily on him. His last task had been to ensure that DACO Clisby had been sent for, and he now walked blindly up the middle of the road, oblivious of the men and machines he passed, mindful only that one of his men had died – a young man, a probationer fireman, who had apparently showed much promise – and that the only time he had seen the young man and known him had been in death.

Then, unexpectedly, DACO Charles Clisby appeared in the road in front of him.

For the last three and a half hours Clisby had been at Wembley control, watching how the VDU mobilizing system dealt with its first major emergency.   Well satisfied with its performance and with that of its operators, he had decided to pay a quick visit to the scene of the fire on his way home. He was already more than half-way there when a call came over the car's radio-telephone telling him to report to the Chief Officer at Clifton Gardens; he thought it would be about him acting as a relief for another DACO. Unexpectedly, the first person he encountered when he arrived at Clifton Gardens was the Chief. Even more unexpected were the tears running down his face.

Joe Milner spoke with difficulty. 'One of my lads has been killed, Charles,' he said. 'I want you to do your usual. . . . Report to Mr Burrell, Charles – he'll give you the details. . . . Thank you.'

He walked on up the road.

When Clisby found the Deputy Chief at the control unit, he learned what had happened and what he was expected to do.

Don Burrell grasped his hand and took him aside.

'Fireman Pettit of Paddington has been killed. There's only one job I want you to do, Charles. Go and see Pettit's wife.'

A21 A22 A29 A28 A24 A25 A26 A27 A DIVISION
G24 G25 G26 G28 G29
C25 C27 C28 C30
D22 D23 D24 D25
B22 J26
STRATFORD CROYDON LSC OPERATIONS ROOM
FROM DCO BURRELL
STOP WORSLEY HOTEL CLIFTON GARDENS
HOTEL FIVE FLOORS AND BASEMENT
150 X 50 FEET
HALF FIRST FLOOR WHOLE SECOND THIRD
AND FOURTH FLOORS
DAMAGED BY FIRE ROOF OFF
TWELVE JETS BREATHING APPARATUS

ALL PERSONS NOT YET ACCOUNTED FOR
SAME AS ALL CALLS
TOS 0802

*

'It looks like you've been busy,' said a passer-by.

'What?' Ray glanced at the man.

'Looks like a really big fire.'

'Oh, yeah,' said Ray. 'It was a thirty pumper.'

'Was there anyone hurt?'

'What? Oh, yeah. Four of our blokes. They were in there when the roof come down. They're injured.'

'Oh. Not badly, I hope.'

'Well – it seems that some of them are.'

'Oh. I'm sorry. . . . Well . . . bad luck.'

'Yeah . . .'

Friday 13 December

She was woken as usual at 6.30 a.m. by the ringing of the alarm clock's bell. But unusually she fell asleep again. Hamish was away at work, and their little boy, Stephen – he would be two in two months' time – was silent in the other bedroom. So she turned over in the double bed, secure and warm, and closed her eyes for a drowsy moment that became an hour of un-remembered dreams.

She was twenty-four and her maiden name, before she married Hamish Harry Pettit in July 1970, had been Patricia May Hewson. They had been living in the small maisonette in a council block of flats in Longley Road, Rochester, for seven months, since May that year when Hamish became a fireman. It was only his mates and colleagues who called him Harry.

She got up just before 7.30, put on her dressing-gown and came downstairs to the front room, where she switched on the central heating and the radio. As she pulled back the curtains, the news headlines on Radio Medway told her there had been a big fire in London, at a hostel for hotel staff in Maida Vale. Nineteen people had been rescued, said the radio, and two firemen had been injured and taken to hospital. One fireman was missing.

She went into the kitchen, leaving the radio on, and while she made herself a breakfast of cereal, toast and tea, she worried about what effect the fact that firemen had been injured would have on Hamish. Maida Vale, she knew, was on his fire-station's ground. But it never occurred to her that he might be involved.

By the time she brought Stephen downstairs to the front room, the radio's breakfast show had moved on from the national and local news at 8.0 a.m. and was dealing with traffic problems and the weather. Wishing to know more about the fire, and to talk to Hamish, she telephoned the fire-station. But the number she was calling, a telephone coin-box in the mess, went unanswered. She replaced the receiver, concluding that the Watch must all still be occupied at Maida Vale or somewhere else, and started preparing Stephen's breakfast, which he ate in the front room. The radio, an old-fashioned set which Hamish had renovated, was near him on a book-shelf.

At 8.30, while Stephen tackled his cereal, it was announced on the news headlines that the missing fireman had been found, and that he was dead. She sat beside Stephen, who prattled away regardless, now more than ever concerned for the distress the death of a fireman would bring to Hamish, and she was about to telephone the station again when the door-bell rang.

It was Hamish's mother. She had come as usual to look after Stephen while Pat was away at the hairdresser's where she worked, and to see to the little boy's lunch and that of his father. Hamish's mother, small, grey-haired and doughtily Scottish – she came from Oban – was known to her three sons, daughter and daughter-in-law as Daisy.

Pat said someone had been killed in a fire in London. 'What fire?' asked Daisy. 'Haven't you heard?' asked Pat. 'It was on the radio.' 'No, I haven't. What fire?' 'There's been a big fire at Maida Vale. That's Hamish's patch.' 'Oh, God. . . . No!' 'I hope it's not someone at Hamish's station,' said Pat.

Not much more was said about it, for Stephen soon demanded his grandmother's attentions and Pat had to leave for work – which she did after washing up some of the breakfast things and telling Daisy what she had prepared for Stephen's and Hamish's dinner. Hamish would usually, after a night-duty, be home about 10 a.m.

At Rita's, the hairdresser's – a smart, blue-painted and converted corner shop in an older terrace of houses in Castle Avenue, a few minutes away across the council estate – Rita herself, her black hair carefully coiffeured, her square, brown spectacle-frames firmly on her nose, said, Yes, she had heard the news and wasn't it dreadful? She reassured Pat, of whom she was very fond, by saying that if anything had happened to Hamish, Pat would have been told by now. There was no time to say much more, as it was 9 o'clock and the customers were waiting in the little salon. Fridays were always busy days.

As Pat, in her gaily coloured nylon overall, set about tinting her first customer's hair, her thoughts in between the female chatter kept reverting to Hamish. She could not help worrying about him – but there seemed no point in trying to telephone Paddington again. As Rita had said, if anything was wrong they would surely have got in touch with her, and besides, Hamish would be already on his way home.

She remembered the last time she had seen him, the day before. She recalled that at about 2.0 p.m. he had called at the hairdresser's to talk to her – something he had never done before. At noon he had had a driving-lesson and then his test. But the car, a Viva, in which he had been taught, broke down, and he was transferred to another car which had an unaccustomed, awkward clutch, and it rolled back when he parked on a hill. So he failed the test. He came to tell Pat about this before going back to their flat for a late lunch and then going off to work – Ray Wade would pick him up at 3.45 at Star Hill. 'I've failed,' he told her. 'But I'm not going to do it again. That's it. I've given it up.' He explained what had happened, and having got it off his chest and received her sympathetic consolation, he went away. 'See you tomorrow,' he said. He would never say good-bye, thinking it sounded too final.

But it was not the last time he spoke to her. That night she telephoned the fire-station after *News at Ten*, just to talk to him, something she usually did when he was on night-duty. No one answered her call. She tried again later, again without success.

Unknown to her, most of the Watch were then enjoying a drink with Jack Hallifax around the bar. But a few minutes later, at 10.46 p.m., the PE and pump were called to the so-called 'explosion' in the Ryder's Terrace mews. As soon as Hamish – he was with the PE – returned about five past eleven, he telephoned his wife.

It was not usual for him to do so. But he wanted to tell her that he had changed his mind about taking another driving test. He would have another go, he said, as it was a waste of time and money not to see it through. Besides, it was the car's fault, not his. Then he asked her if she had heard on the news about the pillar-box 'explosion' earlier that evening or about the one from which he had just returned.

Neither had been caused by bombs, but the element in them of unforeseen, unprepared-for danger, of blind chance and fate, must have made him very much aware of his own love for life and for his family and home. For although he was seldom demonstrative about his feelings or sentimental, he chose that night to tell her what she needed to hear and know, and would never hear again.

'I love you, Pat,' he said. 'I always will. Please be careful. Look after yourself and Stephen. Good-bye.'

'Bye, bye,' she said.

Charles Clisby arrived in Rochester with DO Bainbridge, whom he had picked up at Brigade HQ to back him up in the breaking of the news of Fireman Pettit's death. They drove in a staff car, Clisby at the wheel, speeding down the A2, with blue lights flashing, using the horn when necessary, and with a police escort part of the way. The morning was cold but clear and there was less wind. Clisby moodily smoked his pipe. His task was not one he relished, but as he had performed this particular duty six times over a period of twenty years and had a system for informing the next-of-kin, he had been the natural choice as the Brigade messenger sent to inform the dead fireman's family before they heard the news from newspaper men or other firemen. The nine o'clock news, which he and Bainbridge heard on the car radio, had the basic facts of the fire, but fortunately mentioned no names. While Bainbridge double-checked the Pettits' exact address and the wife's name over the RT – he had already been given route directions by the Ops room – Clisby brooded over the difficulties ahead of him. He had no idea if there were any children, if the wife worked, if anyone else would be in the house or flat, how many relatives would have to be told, and how helpful the neighbours would be. It could be that both the wife and the neighbours were out or away and that she could not be located.

They drove to Rochester police station, where they acquired the services of a police constable to direct them to the Pettits' home. They found the flat on the long second-floor verandah of one of four council blocks of flats, all with military names. A young woman hanging washing on the communal

green below gave Clisby a bad moment, for she could have
been the widow and would have been unduly alarmed by the
sight of three uniformed men approaching her front door. The
confrontation had to be quick, direct and formal – that was
Clisby's way. But the girl never looked up, and turned out not
to be the widow – for when Clisby rang the door-bell of the
flat next to the Pettits', he was told that she was at work. The
neighbours, a young married couple, Margaret and Bill, with
a daughter who was getting ready to go to school, were
stunned by Clisby's news, but agreed to help in any way they
could. They were able to tell him that Hamish's mother was
in the flat next door – they had seen her pass their kitchen
window – and would be on her own. The little boy usually
spent the morning, they said, playing in another neighbour's
flat.

Clisby asked Bainbridge to go next door, with Margaret, and
tell the mother: he was to try to calm her, make her a cup of
tea and telephone for a doctor. Margaret's husband, Bill, was
to direct Clisby and the PC to the hairdresser's and help
identify the wife. She would have to be told there and then,
for there was no point in prolonging her distress by sending the
PC or Bill to fetch her; it was also right her workmates should
know and support her with their sympathy and concern.
Clisby felt that the announcement should be ritualistic and
made with dignity, so that afterwards the occasion would be
well-remembered – in sorrow, but not in woe.

Bainbridge rang the bell next door, with Margaret beside
him, as Clisby, Bill and the PC walked along the verandah
towards the stairs. As they ran down them they heard behind
them the mother's anguished scream.

The three men got into the car and drove the short distance
around the estate to Rita's. Without any preamble they
entered the shop, alive with female voices behind a white
partition. A young girl at a reception desk turned pale at the
sight of them and fled into the salon. The voices died away.
Rita appeared, saw Clisby, gasped and put her hand to her
mouth. With tears already in her eyes, Rita called out –
'Pat . . .' Bill approached the partition, looked beyond it and
beckoned. No one spoke.

She walked slowly towards the men, twisting the wedding

ring on her finger, saying to herself – Oh, please – please God
– let him only be injured. . . .

Clisby saw a very pretty girl in a coloured overall, with
dark brown hair and violet eyes that were wide with fear.

He took her hand and led her to a chair.

'Please sit down,' he said. She did so and looked up at him
like a terrified child.

'Are you Patricia Pettit?' he asked, solemnly and gently.

'Yes . . .'

'Are you the wife of Hamish Pettit?'

'Yes,' she whispered.

'My name is Charles Clisby, of the London Fire Brigade,
and I regret to have to tell you that your husband, Hamish
Pettit, whilst carrying out a gallant rescue at a hotel fire in
Maida Vale, has been killed.'

Her eyes remained fixed on his, unblinking; her mouth
opened slightly, but she made no sound other than whispering
'No, no . . . no.'

They put her coat around her and led her out to the car. She
cried a little on the journey home, but asked no questions and
said nothing at all.

When they arrived, Clisby led her by the hand up the stairs
and along the verandah to her front door. They went inside,
to the front room, where Hamish's wife and his mother fell
crying into each other's arms on the settee. There Clisby left
them alone for a while, letting them grieve in private for the
loss of both husband and son.

Many tears were shed for Hamish Harry Pettit that day –
for his loss, for the wasteful, tragic end to his life. His family
and his widow's relations mourned him most, and gathered
one by one in his home to protect and comfort her and his
mother and share their grief. It was the third death in the two
families in two years. Hamish's father had died seven months
earlier and Pat's father the previous year. Now her mother,
uncle, sister and brother came to Longley Road from their
houses and places of work in response to Clisby's telephone
calls – as did Hamish's sister, Margaret, and his two younger
brothers, Ian and Perce. The latter was nineteen, and as long-
haired as Hamish had been before he became a fireman. His

particular grief was that there had recently been a quarrel; now no one could ever say to Hamish – 'I'm sorry'. The only way he might make some amends was to become a fireman himself, as he had intended, and this is what he now resolved to do. But Ian, who had been closer than anyone else to Hamish – two years younger, he had become an electrician in the dockyards like Hamish and had married a friend of Pat – would not and could not cry. He could not believe that Hamish, whom he resembled in many ways (they even looked alike) had gone, was dead. It was unbelievable, for *he* lived.

Such a belief had also possessed Ray Wade. Even when young Dave Dyer, left behind at Clifton Gardens by Paddington's ET, and helping Ray uncouple hose from a hydrant, assured him Harry was dead – 'I *saw* him!' said Dyer and burst into tears – even when Ray, having left Dyer at Paddington and returned in A28's TL to Kensington fire-station, was telephoned during breakfast by Alan Williams at A25 with the news that the radio said a fireman had been killed and Ron Morris and Peter Lidbetter knew it was Harry – even then Ray said disbelievingly: 'Oh, no. They told me it was fifty-fifty.' And although he then told the other firemen in the mess: 'It seems my mate, Harry, got killed last night – it seems it was him,' it was still something he could not believe. It was only after the long drive home with Alan Williams, but without Harry – when he entered his safe and warm house in Rainham, when he remembered his small twin sons would be at play-school, when he saw his wife, Sheila, making tea in the kitchen, when she said, in ignorance of what had happened: 'You're a bit late' – it was only then, when he had to tell her: 'We had a fire, and Harry got killed,' that he knew what he had said was true and that his mate was dead. He fell into an armchair and wept inconsolably, while his wife knelt beside him and held his hand, grieving for him and Harry's widow, and painfully, thankfully aware, like the other wives, how lucky she was that morning to have her husband home again.

Those of the Watch who were married and had children, who had more to lose, were more affected by Harry's death than the young single men, who felt the terror of its finality and were made shockingly alive for the first time to the random, fatal element in their work. Leroy went home, overwhelmed by the most traumatic experience of his young life, by thoughts, feelings, sights and emotions unknown to him until now and not capable for a time of proper assessment. He sought out his mother in the pub where she worked, to acquaint himself again with the reality of his own existence and her reassuring presence. She asked him if he felt like going back to work that night for his second night-duty. But there was never any doubt, among all his confusion, about that. Being a fireman was clearly something special, and had brought a new though as yet imperfectly perceived significance to his life.

As much and more was evident to Dave Webber, whose first thought after wearily divesting himself of his fire-gear and washing the smoky grime from his face and hands, though not its stench from his nose, was to organize a breakfast for the sadly depleted Watch. He was mess manager now, in Martin's absence. He made his way to the deserted mess and saw the breakfast that Martin had prepared. No one, he thought, sick to the heart and stomach as each man was, would want a cooked meal. Tea and toast would be enough. The mess telephone rang and went on ringing, insisting on being answered. Reluctantly he picked up the receiver. It was Wendy, Martin's wife. He could hardly speak to her, having no words to express what he felt. 'Is Martin all right?' she asked. 'Now look, Wendy,' he said roughly, 'there's *nothing* to worry about!' 'Is he there?' 'He's in hospital.' 'I *knew* this would happen!' she cried. 'As soon as I heard it on the radio, I knew it would be Martin! Is Jacko there?' 'When he comes up, I'll get him to ring you.' Dave rang off, and reminded of his own family found some coins to telephone his brother and his father, whom he asked to tell his mother that he was all right. This done, he set about mechanically preparing tea and toast for the Watch.

When Jacko arrived at the station – he had been taken in an ambulance back to Clifton Gardens and then brought back to Paddington by Joe Forrest in the Divisional van – he telephoned Wendy to tell her how and where Martin was. It was later arranged – and similar arrangements were made for the wives of Tony Stewart and Colin Searle – that she and Martin's mother were brought in a staff car to Paddington, where Dave then took them and Jacko to St Mary's Hospital in Praed Street. Dave waited outside, unable to cope with the emotional scenes he imagined would take place in the casualty ward. He took the weeping women and Jacko back to Paddington and then drove to his fiancée's place of work, while Jacko, in Martin's car, drove the mother and Wendy back to their homes. Jacko stayed with Wendy all the afternoon – unable to contact his own wife as their phone was out of order.

On their way back to Martin's house, they had briefly visited Jack Hallifax and his wife, Louise. Jack had been woken that morning about 8.15 a.m. by a phone-call from Jim Griffin, who asked for Martin's home telephone number. 'I don't know why you're asking me,' said Jack. 'Martin's on duty.' 'I know – I want his phone number.' 'Why don't you ask Jacko? Isn't he there?' 'Just do me a favour, Jack – give me his number.' 'Oh, Christ, something's wrong.' 'Yes. But I can't tell you.' 'For Christ's sake, let me know what's happened!' 'I can't,' said Jim, stubbornly faithful to the Brigade ruling that no one else must know about a fireman being injured or killed until his next-of-kin had been informed. Jack gave him the telephone number. But when Jim telephoned Wendy he found her number was engaged. In the meantime, Jack heard on the radio at 8.30 that one fireman had been killed at Maida Vale and others injured. He waited for five minutes and then could contain himself no longer. He telephoned the office at Paddington and was answered by Neil, who outlined what had happened that night.

'Not Harry!' cried Jack. 'Not *him*.'

It was the first of many telephone calls Neil answered and made that day, the busiest and blackest of his life.

He had returned to Paddington from Clifton Gardens in the emergency tender soon after 8 o'clock, with the shattered remnants of the four crews that had left the station less than five hours before – Paul Taylor, Jim Griffin, Ernie Arthurs, Pincher Martin, Orchard, Waldron, Lewis, Marven, Wickenden, Cheal, Leroy and Dave. Crowded together in the cramped interior they had stood or sat, evading each other's eyes, each sunk in solitary misery, their wet uniforms reeking of smoke, their bodies aching, their feet frozen, their hands raw, their faces blackened masks of shock, exhaustion, and grief. Malcolm Garner drove, draining the last of his strength to turn the heavy wheel.

Their dawn return to the bare, familiar surroundings of the station through the rear gates into the yard and then into the appliance-room, accentuated the tragic change in their fortunes and their numbers. Apart from those of the Watch who had been left behind – Jacko, Dyer, Forrest and Dunlop – two others were in hospital and one would never return.

Silently the remainder stumbled from the ET and went their separate ways.

Neil trailed across the barren, day-lit appliance-room whose empty spaces left by the still absent TL, pump and pump escape were marked by discarded slippers and shoes. At the rear stood the standby pump from Chiswick. He heard teleprinter warning-bells ringing on unheeded until they were silenced by an unknown fireman in the watchroom, while another message clattered out on the machine to be added to the many about the fire already transmitted onto the long, unfolding roll of paper that had piled in profusion on the floor.

The warning-bells clamoured again as he trudged upstairs to the office. An early arrival from the Blue Watch, who would take over at 9.0 a.m., was answering a telephone call and looked up in silent sympathy and respect as Neil crossed the outer office. In the inner room, a senior 'A' Division training-officer, ADO Vic Vandenbergh, put down a receiver and seized Neil's arm.

'I know what you want,' he said, and pushed the younger man towards the station officer's bedroom. 'Go in there and get it out of your system,' said Vandenbergh. 'I'll stand guard.'

He shut the door behind Neil as the telephone rang again.

With slow, shaking fingers Neil unbuttoned his tunic and removed both it and his helmet, dropping them onto the floor. Still in his T-shirt, boots and leggings he staggered to the basin to wash. He inclined his head to turn on the tap and in doing so the will-power that had kept his head erect and his feelings in check failed at last.

With his hands holding onto the basin and his head bowed before the mirror, he cried uncontrollably, wretchedly, until he could cry no more.

Then he washed, showered and changed, and re-entered

his office to fulfil his duties as the station officer of the Red
Watch, Paddington, two of whose men had been injured in a
fire on his own ground and one of whom had been killed.

There was much to do. But the first thing he did was to
answer Jack Hallifax's telephone call. Then he went upstairs
to the mess, to talk to those of the Watch who wanted to talk
and show them he shared their sorrow. They were his first
responsibility, their state of mind his major concern. But
fatigued beyond words and thought, they found no consolation in anything, except that their homes and families awaited
their return.

Neil revisited the office, where the Blue Watch under Acting
Station Officer Nobby Hall had taken over, and answered a
few of the dismayed, grief-stricken telephone calls from other
firemen. One was from Chris Reynolds. Others that morning
came from those of the Watch who had happened not to be on
duty that night – including Martin Nicholls, whose twenty-
first birthday it was. But Neil's main responsibility now was
to go and visit the injured men in hospital.

Uniformed, although he was now officially off-duty, he
drove in his car to St Mary's Hospital, Praed Street, where he
made it his business to be the first to see Martin, Stewart and
Searle, so that he could inform them officially of Harry's
death, of which neither Searle nor Stewart was aware. He
saw each of them individually in the casualty ward. Each bed
had been surrounded by screens. Saline-drips were being
administered to all three, and although they had been partly
washed, the smell of the fire was still strong upon them and
soot still oozed from their hair. Searle wept quietly when
Neil told him about Harry. Stewart was too shocked to speak.
Martin cried again. Their burns were as yet undressed and
distressing to behold. But despite their pain and sorrow, all
three were only too thankful to be alive. When Neil left them
he encountered the Chief Officer, Joe Milner, in the corridor.
He had come to the hospital on his own and was still in uniform.
Neil introduced himself and they talked together briefly. But
it was not the time or place for much else other than simple,
understated expressions of sympathy and care.

Neil then returned to Paddington, where the yard was now

full of lines of hose being washed and scrubbed and equipment being cleaned, while the pump escape, back home again, was being tested and its tanks refilled. The tang of smoke was still thick in the air. Telephones and teleprinter warning-bells still rang.

Messages from Clifton Gardens, transmitted by Wembley control, continued to clatter out all day. Relief appliances and crews were sent to the ruined hotel to assist in the clearing up of gear and the damping down of pockets of fire which still existed. At 12.30 the charred remains of two civilians were found in the ruins of the third floor. Another body was found an hour later and a fourth body soon afterwards. The fifth and final civilian victim – the body of Albert Simpson had been removed at dawn – was discovered at 3.15 p.m. But the turning over of the wreckage, the searching and damping down, continued for another twenty-four hours while scaffolders stood by, ready to shore up the burnt-out rooms and roofless walls. Relays of pump crews, two at a time on three-hour shifts, kept watch in Clifton Gardens all night. It was not until 4.45 p.m. the following day that ADO Baldwin was able to send the final message from the scene of the fire: '*Tell the Chief Officer that all pockets of fire have now been extinguished. All safe areas of the building have now been thoroughly searched for missing persons. Duty has now been passed over to local station visits. All persons accounted for . . .*'

Still unexplained was the cause of the fire. But the as yet unconfirmed suspicion of the fire prevention officers, police officers and insurance men, who had already begun a careful investigation of the ruins, was that they were dealing with a case of arson – which if confirmed would mean that the deaths of all seven who died in the fire could be classified as murder.

But this grim fact – for so it proved to be* – was not in Neil's

---

*A kitchen porter, Edward Mansfield, aged forty-one, was charged at the Old Bailey on 10 July 1975, with three cases of arson (one at the Worsley Hotel on 13 December and two at the Piccadilly Hotel on 19 and 29 December 1974) and the murders of seven people, including a fireman, at the Worsley Hotel. He pleaded not guilty. On 23 July the jury failed to reach the required majority verdict and were discharged. The re-trial of Mansfield at the Old Bailey on the same charges began on 12 November 1975. John Mathew was again the prosecuting counsel. It ended on 1 December. Mansfield was found guilty of the manslaughter of seven people, including Fireman Pettit, and of three charges of arson. He was gaoled for life.

mind when he reported to DO Keable in the Divisional HQ offices alongside Paddington's yard. Keable and Station Officer Fred Alcock had already begun formulating what arrangements should be made for Fireman Pettit's funeral – Neil would have to see to the details concerning the Red Watch. They discussed these and other administrative matters arising from the fire, and when Alcock left, Keable and Neil answered questions from an *Evening News* reporter. The newspaper also despatched two reporters to Rochester, and the afternoon editions of the paper carried a front-page story in banner headlines – 'DEATH OF A HERO'. 'FIVE DIE IN LONDON INFERNO', said the *Evening Standard*, and both papers had dramatic pictures of the rescues of Stewart and Searle. The following morning all the national papers carried the story, some emphasizing the sensational aspect and some the issues relating to fire regulations at the Worsley Hotel, though as it was a hostel these in fact were better than required by law.

When the reporter's questions ended, Neil gratefully accepted Keable's invitation to a makeshift lunch in his flat above the station, and then went back to his office, which Nobby Hall had vacated for him, to deal with the continuing telephone calls and the reports and forms that had to be filled in and made. The newspapers, national and local, who rang the station now, were referred by him to Brigade HQ at Lambeth. The calls from firemen were given more of his time. Among them were calls from the Kent Fire Brigade and from DACO Charles Clisby, letting him know the Pettit family's situation in Rochester and their reactions to the news of Harry's death. He also heard that the Divisional Commander, DO Colenutt, had cancelled his leave and was coming back to London. Neil also had a visitor, DCO Don Burrell, who wanted to show his sympathy for the younger man and assure him that everything would be done for the widow. 'I'm glad to see you're working,' said DCO Burrell. 'I know how you feel. . . . But whatever happens, Brigade life and that of the Watch goes on – it must go on.' 'I know,' said Neil.

The afternoon wore on. In between the ringing of telephone-bells, and warning-bells, and fire-bells – for the station was still operating under the Blue Watch – Neil found time to look through a file of correspondence relating to the funeral arrangements for the last 'A' Division firemen who had been killed on duty – Fireman Brian Hutchings and Colin Comber. He had known them both, for at the time, in March 1968, they had been with the Red Watch, A27 (Chelsea) he had been with Chelsea's White Watch. They had died in a flash-over in a restaurant, when heated vapours, confined in a hallway, had ignited in a flash of roaring flame. He remembered it had taken them three days to die.

Outside, the daylight faded. Coloured lights on Christmas trees in windows shone through the gathering dusk.

Try as he might he could not concentrate on his reading. For over thirty-six hours now he had only had about an hour's sleep, and his mind, whenever he fixed on an image, a word, a thought, kept drifting back to the fire in sad, bemused consideration of what had happened and *why*. Could any of it have been prevented? he wondered. Should Harry have ever died or the others been injured? Was he in some way to blame? Why were those particular four firemen in the room when the roof collapsed, a minute after he had left them? Why was it them and not him as well? Why was it them at all?

Nobby Hall came into the office and switched on the lights, thus reminding Neil that the Red Watch's second night-duty was approaching. He sighed; he hoped it would be a quiet night with not too many shouts.

There was just one more thing he had to do before the Red Watch returned. As he had been the first to welcome Harry Pettit on board seven months ago, so now he had to be the first to mark his departure from the Watch.

Neil went down to the watchroom and removed Harry's name-tag from the personnel board. He put it in his pocket. Later he would hand it to the widow, with Harry's helmet, belt and axe. Then he returned to his office, closed the door and sat down again at his desk. With a ruler he carefully drew a black line through Harry's name on the roll-call board and another through his name in the duties book.

Finally, with the accident book in front of him, and with a deep sense of right, regret and duty done, he carefully recorded the details of the passing of Harry Pettit in the approved, official way.

Whilst engaged in rescue and fire-fighting activities, Fireman Pettit H.H. was a member of a team working in a second-floor room. A collapse of roof above caused an amount of debris to fall into this room from above, and Fireman Pettit H.H. was buried by debris. Upon being released from this debris he was certified dead by a doctor at the scene of the fire and his body was then removed from the building.

Neil signed his name – *N. Wallington* – and closed the book.

*

At 6.0 p.m. the Red Watch in full fire-gear lined up in the appliance-room for roll-call.

Paul Taylor read their names. Neil Wallington stood behind him, his back to the three machines the men would ride that night – the pump was off the run.

It was a very emotional moment, for not all the names that were on the list were called out, and not all the firemen down for duty were there.

The rest stood at attention – some with tears running down their faces.

The roll-call finished, Taylor told them to stand at ease.

'Riders for tonight,' he said.

Then at 6.01 p.m., the warning-bells and the fire-bells rang throughout the station.

The line broke – and the Red Watch went back to work in Paddington once again.

'For initiative, skill and perseverance'

Six months later, on 5 June 1975, at 6.0 p.m., there was a ceremony in the Council chamber of County Hall, an impos- ing civic building on the south bank of the River Thames by Westminster Bridge. It was the presentation by the Chairman of the Greater London Council of awards for bravery to members of the London Fire Brigade.

Forty-three firemen of all ranks and from stations all over London were to be honoured that day and presented with Royal Humane Society Certificates, or with the Chief Officer's Certificates of Commendation and Letters of Congratulation for the exceptional initiative, skill, and perseverance they had shown at incidents requiring their services over the previous year. Twenty-two of the firemen so honoured had attended one incident, the fire at the Worsley Hotel, Clifton Gardens, W.9.

It was the first time many of them had met together since Harry Pettit's funeral on Friday 20 December 1974, a week after the fire.

The Red Watch at every London fire-station were off duty that day, and in the morning three hundred firemen from the London and Kent Fire Brigades, including the whole of the Watch at Paddington, assembled in fire-tunics and undress uniform at Strood fire-station, whose appliance-room was a mass of floral tributes and wreaths. At 10.45 the hearse carry- ing the coffin, draped with the Union Jack and crowned with Harry's helmet and axe, arrived at Rochester parish church for a private family service. The coffin was carried into the church, up a path lined with a guard of honour, by six pall- bearers – Ernie Arthurs, Norman Wooldridge, Paul Marven, Chris Reynolds, Frank Nice and Ray Wade. Neil Wallington followed behind, preceding Harry's wife, his mother, brothers

and sister. After the service, the coffin was placed on Paddington's TL, which was decked overall with flowers. Jacko was the
driver; Jim Griffin was the Number One. With Ray and Frank
Nice standing on either side of the coffin on the platform, the
TL led the funeral procession to the Medway crematorium,
up a long avenue lined with over two hundred firemen.

The Chief Officer, Joe Milner, and DCO Don Burrell were
also present at the funeral, as was Jack Hallifax, wearing a
uniform borrowed from DO Keable. He met the Chief at a
reception in Strood fire-station afterwards, when the Chief
enquired what Jack was doing in uniform, as he thought Jack
had retired. They met again, in St Mary's Hospital on
Christmas Day, when it seemed that every pump in the 'A'
Division went off the run for a while to visit the injured men,
and to drink to their good health from the crates of beer
stored under their beds. 'We can have you for impersonating a
fireman, Jack,' the Chief remarked with a smile. 'Well, sir,'
said Jack, grinning broadly. 'I've been doing that for twenty-
five years!'

Neither Joe Milner nor Jack were at the ceremony in
County Hall. Both were ill that day. But for the first time
since the fire all the rescuers and the rescued met together at
the same time. With them were their wives and relatives and
Hamish Pettit's family – his wife, mother, sister, brothers,
sister-in-law, with Pat's mother, sister, brother, and Rita.
They gathered in the lofty main entrance of County Hall, and
after the forty-three firemen who were to receive awards had
been ushered up the ceremonial staircase to the Council
chamber and shown to their reserved seats at the front of the
amphitheatre, their relatives and friends came up to join
them, filling the higher rows of raised seats all around the
blue-carpeted chamber, from whose vaulted dome hung a
tracery of microphones and wires. People spoke in whispers,
looking around them expectantly, nervously, waiting for the
Chairman and Council officials to take their seats on the high
dais facing the assemblage.

Among the rows of uniformed firemen at the front sat Pat
Pettit, not knowing as yet which of the firemen were those who
had been at Clifton Gardens; the only one she recognized was
Neil. Dave Webber sat behind her, and beside her was

Hamish's brother, Perce, in his new uniform as a fireman in the Kent Fire Brigade. She was wearing a brown wide-brimmed hat, a white open-neck blouse and a pale green outfit with a dark brown flower on the lapel. Martin Walker and his wife and mother sat nearby, higher up. Two weeks earlier he had returned to full duty at Paddington, after being on light duties for six weeks and before that in hospital for three months. Tony Stewart was also back at Paddington, on light duties, having been in hospital and then convalescing for four months. He sat with his wife in the top tier, not far from Colin Searle, who had arrived late and stood with DO Keable at the back. Searle, who had suffered the most severe burns, mended quickest. He was out of hospital on 5 February and back on full duty on 5 May, a month before the ceremony in County Hall. It was the first time that he, Martin and Tony Stewart had come face to face with all their principal rescuers in the same room since the fire.

At 6.0 p.m., the GLC Chairman and the presiding officials entered the chamber. Everyone rose to their feet. The Chairman that year was a woman, Dame Evelyn Denington, the first the Council had ever had. With her was the Chairman of the GLC's Fire Brigade committee, John Henry, and the Deputy Chief Officer of the London Fire Brigade, Don Burrell.

When everyone had sat down again Mr Henry, once a fireman himself until he was badly burned in a fire, welcomed the Chairman, the recipients of the awards and the guests and called upon Dame Evelyn to speak. A small, slim woman, she addressed the assemblage in a clear vigorous voice, hardly referring to her notes.

She said: 'I feel very honoured and privileged to have been asked to present the awards this evening. . . . We live in a mechanized society. We must never forget that we are, nevertheless, dependent on human initiative, on the skills, judgement and bravery of people for the direction in which society develops and for our very survival.

'The London Fire Brigade is a magnificent force, and we in the GLC are very proud of it. You, Mr Henry, who are presiding at this ceremony are, I know, very proud to be its Chairman. The Brigade is highly trained and very courageous.

Its members always put the demands of the service, however hazardous, before thoughts of personal safety. In an emergency, it is the quality of human beings that counts. A man's unhesitating response is what is needed; quickness of reaction is imperative; his selfless bravery is of overwhelming importance.

'The GLC could provide the most sophisticated and up-to-date equipment devised, but without men of the right calibre to operate it, able to rely in the end on their own physical powers and their own brains and courage, it could be of little use. It is *men*, fine men, that we are gathered today to honour.

'On behalf of the GLC and the people of London, I will have great pleasure in presenting the awards.'

Dame Evelyn and Mr Henry then descended to the well of the Council chamber. She stood in front of a table laden with rolled-up certificates, broad envelopes and commendations. Photographers on either side of the dais raised their cameras. DCO Don Burrell stood, put on his glasses, and prepared to read out the list of citations from a lectern on the dais.

'Station Officer Graham Walter White,' called DCO Burrell, and Graham White, of the White Watch, A21 (Paddington), stepped forward and stood at attention opposite Dame Evelyn, while DCO Burrell related how White had saved an elderly woman's life at a fire by rescuing her and reviving her with mouth to mouth resuscitation.

'For this work,' said DCO Burrell, 'Station Officer White has been awarded the Royal Humane Society's Resuscitation Certificate.'

There was applause as White moved forward to receive the certificate from Dame Evelyn and her congratulations. He then returned to his seat.

This procedure was followed by all the recipients. They stepped forward, stood at attention – sometimes in pairs when more than one fireman's bravery at an incident was being honoured – and listened impassively, hiding their embarrassment at the public recitation of what to them was all part of the job and had happened long ago, and staring blankly at the dais. The other firemen listened with interest, assessing the difficulties of the situations described. But the rest of the audience heard DCO Burrell's straightforward delivery of each citation with wonderment, glancing at the man or men standing before them, who had actually performed such deeds, and letting their imaginations work on the stories that were being unfolded. They heard of the lives of men, women and children being saved by resuscitation, by intrepid rescues, by perilous ascents into burning rooms and buildings, by hazardous descents into water-filled pits and collapsed workings and shafts, and in one instance by a most dramatic rescue of three workmen, one of them injured, from the top of a disused, crumbling chimney-stack, 180 feet above the ground.

By the time twenty-one awards had been presented, the atmosphere in the Council chamber was highly charged with a build-up of suppressed excitement and emotions – even the firemen themselves had responded to the cumulative effects of the calm, measured account of their colleagues' endeavours, courage and skill.

Then the ceremony reached its climax with the presentation – a unique occasion – of twenty-two awards arising out of one incident, the fire at the Worsley Hotel.

As DCO Burrell read the long list of names, each man left his seat and came forward and lined up in a series of rows across the well of the chamber according to rank and alphabetical order. In front of the firemen stood Pat Pettit, with Perce at her side and Neil immediately behind her. Dame Evelyn faced them, already moved by the presence of the young widow in front of her and by the massed rows of uniformed men beyond.

DCO Burrell adjusted his glasses and the papers in his hands before embarking on the citation. The assembled company, both seated and standing, listened intently as he began to read the official story of the fire – none more so than those who had been there and remembered what it had been like.

He said: 'On 13 December 1974, the brigade were called to a fire at the Worsley Hotel, Clifton Gardens, W9. The premises comprised eight large intercommunicating terraced houses of four and five floors and a basement, which had been converted into hostel accommodation for hotel staff. On arrival, Station Officer Wallington found the area heavily smoke-logged and a severe fire in progress at ground-floor level, spreading to the upper floors. People could be seen to require assistance at all floors. The exact number of persons involved or who escaped by abnormal means has not been established, but a near estimate is that some thirty residents were rescued or assisted by various means from the building by Brigade personnel. Initially, all crews were fully involved with rescue and fire-fighting operations and many composite crews evolved as the need for different tasks became apparent.

'Much good work was carried out; and much initiative was displayed by all personnel in attendance at this tragic incident, at which a member of the Brigade lost his life. However, the following two rescues are considered worthy of special mention.

'One. T/Sub Officer Stewart and Fireman Blair provided a first-floor ladder as an extension from the head of a fully extended escape, to negotiate a parapet in order to reach seven persons trapped on the roof. The people were extremely agitated and attempted to climb on the ladder before it had been secured. Fireman Blair was able to climb the ladder whilst it was held by T/Sub Officer Stewart and pacify them. The ladder having then been lashed, all seven persons were assisted down to safety.

'Two. A/L/Fireman Trotman and Fireman O'Dwyer were involved at the rear of the premises in assisting a man trapped at a window on the third floor. A/L/Fireman Trotman pitched a hook-ladder from an external staircase to a narrow balcony at second-floor level from where he was able to pitch, with some difficulty, a second hook-ladder into the third-floor window. Fireman O'Dwyer, who provided the second hook-ladder, joined A/L/Fireman Trotman and they both held the hook-ladder as the man climbed out of the window and down to the balcony, from where he was assisted onto the first hook-ladder down to safety. Conditions throughout this rescue were made extremely uncomfortable due to the smoke and flames from adjoining windows.

'Part of the third and fourth floors and the roof collapsed whilst a composite crew of four were searching and fire-fighting. All four members were completely buried in a front second-floor room, in varying positions, by hot burning debris and brick rubble, heavy timbers and part of a wooden staircase. The task of extricating and removing the trapped men was extremely difficult and hazardous, and rescue crews, calmly disregarding their own safety, worked for several hours in confined and cramped conditions.

'After about one and a half hours' work, two of the trapped men were released and carried to the front of the building to rescuers working from an escape and a first-floor ladder. Station Officer Wallington, T/Sub Officer Stewart, T/L/ Fireman Hall, Fireman Blair and Fireman Chilton were all directly involved in this part of the operation.

'The rescue of the remaining two men took approximately three hours, and they were removed down the inside of the building, using one of the sound staircases. L/Fireman Lidbetter and Sub Officer Morris were directly involved in this rescue work for a very long period, and were later joined by T/DO Simmons and ADO Rowley, both of whom were subsequently involved for some considerable time. A number of other officers and men took part in this rescue work and in supervisory duties to a varying degree.'

DCO Burrell paused, cleared his throat and tried to steady his voice and hands.

'The late Fireman Pettit – a probationary fireman with some seven months of operational service – became involved in a number of tasks before being trapped on the second floor. These tasks included: fire-fighting on the ground floor – two hook-ladder rescues from the second floor – searching the building and arousing a man from sleep to remove him to safety. For the excellent fire-fighting and rescue work displayed prior to his entrapment, the late Fireman Pettit has been posthumously awarded a Chief Officer's Certificate of Commendation.'

Don Burrell paused again, much moved, remembering the last time he had seen the dead fireman, in a rear room on the second floor of the hotel. He found his voice and his place in the script and continued.

'For the initiative and perseverance in the escape and first-floor ladder extension rescues, and the later involvement in the extrication of those members of the Brigade entrapped at the front of the second-floor room, T/Sub Officer Stewart and Fireman Blair have each been awarded a Chief Officer's Certificate of Commendation.

'For the initiative and skill in the hook-ladder rescue at the rear of the premises, A/L/Fireman Trotman and Fireman O'Dwyer have each been awarded a Chief Officer's Letter of Congratulation.

'For the initiative, skill, and perseverance in the extrication of those members of the Brigade entrapped at the front of the second-floor room, Station Officer Wallington, T/L/Fireman Hall and Fireman Chilton have each been awarded a Chief Officer's Certificate of Commendation.

'For the initiative, skill, and perseverance in the extrication of those members of the Brigade entrapped at the rear of the second-floor room, ADO Rowley, T/DO Simmons, Sub Officer Morris and L/Fireman Lidbetter have each been awarded a Chief Officer's Certificate of Commendation.

'For their involvement in the extrication of the entrapped personnel, ACO Watkins, ADO Clarkson, ADO Baldwin, Station Officer Hicks, T/Sub Officer Macey, Fireman Clay, Fireman Harris, Fireman McCarlie, Fireman Temple and Fireman Webber have each been awarded a Chief Officer's Letter of Congratulation.'

Don Burrell removed his glasses and wiped his eyes. The citations were at an end. He nodded at Mr Henry for the presentations to begin.

But Dame Evelyn raised her hand. She took a step forward, towards Pat Pettit, whose eyes, like hers, were full of tears.

'Just a moment!' she said. Controlling her voice she addressed herself to the assemblage.

'What you have heard is magnificent!' she said. 'It's a terrible, magnificent, and moving story! . . . What *can* one say?' She looked at the firemen standing in front of her. 'All I can say is that you were *marvellous* – it was marvellous what each one of you did! We owe you all our thanks . . . Thank you very much!'

Then one by one the twenty-two came forward to receive their awards and first of all, in Harry's place, Pat Pettit.

The Chairman of the GLC clasped Pat's hand. 'I can't say how sorry I feel for you,' Dame Evelyn said. 'But so proud – as you must be. Thank you, thank you.'

'Thank you,' whispered Pat. 'From me – and him.'

Epilogue

After the ceremony in County Hall, everyone gathered in the great blue and gilt Ceremonial Suite, where a buffet and drinks had been provided. Councillors, firemen, relatives and friends mingled together. People relaxed, conversing more cheerfully, recalling old associations. In a corner of the room, Hamish's brother, Ian, sat hunched on a chair, protectively surrounded by the women of his family. With a hand over his eyes, he silently wept for the first time for his brother's death.

Later, he told me: 'My wife's not keen – and my mother doesn't know – but I'm going to be a fireman.'

He had a long time in which to reconsider his decision, soon accepted by his mother and wife. In the months that followed, his first two applications to join the London Fire Brigade were turned down. For as a result of the economic recession and the reorganization of the Brigade's establishment, no new recruits were taken on for over a year. But his third attempt succeeded. Two years after Hamish joined the Red Watch, Ian Pettit reported to Southwark Training Centre to learn the basic tasks of being a fireman. He was posted to 'A' Division, to the White Watch at A27 (Chelsea), on Monday, 11 October 1976.

The youngest of the three brothers, Perce, had already carried out his resolve to be a fireman and had been able to do so earlier than Ian, as he opted to join the Kent Fire Brigade, which he did in March 1975. He went to Thames-side fire-station, near Gravesend, in June. By chance, on Friday, 12 December 1975 – exactly a year to the day since the Worsley Hotel fire –Perce, on duty with the Blue Watch, who had been called to an incident involving a spillage of chemicals on Denton Wharf, Gravesend, was overcome by toxic fumes, along with ten other firemen. They were taken to hospital. Fortunately neither he nor the others suffered any ill-effects.

Perce continued to live with his mother, Daisy. Pat Pettit and her small son, Stephen, moved into a new semi-detached house

near Gillingham, not far from Ray Wade. Its garden was laid
out for her by Paddington's Red Watch, who also took on most
of the heavy work involved in her move from Rochester. The
LFB Welfare Fund and the NFS Benevolent Fund came to her
aid financially, and ensured that Stephen would get a proper
education. In addition, Pat received a pension as the widow of
a fireman. She kept all Hamish's books for Stephen's use when
he grew up, and collected in a large book all the newspaper
cuttings, photos and magazine articles relating to Hamish and
the fire at the Worsley Hotel.

In due course, the Red Watch that Harry Pettit knew began
to split up, some of those who had fought the fire with him
being transferred to other Watches and to other stations; some
were promoted. Replacements arrived for Harry and Tony
Stewart, whose back injury caused him to be hospitalized once
again. He returned to Paddington on light duties, but was
eventually given a medical discharge and left the Brigade in
March 1976.

Before this and other changes in the Watch came into effect,
there was a get-together, a commemorative three-course dinner,
in Paddington's mess on 26 November 1975, a few weeks before
the first anniversary of the fire, and not long after Ron Morris
attended the Man of the Year Lunch. The occasion also marked
the completion of my writing of the story of the fire.

It was a convivial evening, though somewhat restrained: the
second trial of the arsonist, Mansfield, was now in its third week,
and most firemen, if they spoke of it at all, expected an unjust
acquittal. During the dinner, presentations and speeches were
made, despite jocular interruptions. I gave the Watch a framed
photograph of Captain Shaw, and a Chris Reynolds' cartoon,
signed by everyone, was their gift to me.

The following week, on 1 December, Mansfield was found
guilty of the manslaughter of seven people, including Harry
Pettit. No one at A21 rejoiced. But I was pleased. For after the
first inconclusive trial I had presented the investigating policemen and the prosecution with the typescript of the chapters
detailing the activities of the fire-fighters in and around the
Worsley Hotel. As a result, several of them were called as
witnesses for the prosecution (none had given evidence at
Mansfield's first trial), and a conviction was obtained.

In his defence Mansfield had claimed that he was asleep in his first-floor bed (in room 106) until two firemen awakened him. A young man, not a man aged 41, *was* woken up in room 103 by two firemen, Ernie Arthurs and Harry Pettit, and taken downstairs. A few minutes before this, when Ernie Arthurs checked room 106, he found it to be empty. It is more than likely that the short, stout man, aged about 40, whom Ernie and Harry assisted down from the first-floor porch of number 11 – outside room 106 – was Mansfield himself. In doing so Harry helped to rescue the man who caused his death.

The following year, other awards were presented to some of the firemen who had fought the Worsley blaze. On 17 February 1976, it was announced in *The London Gazette* and reported in the national press that eight firemen would receive awards for their actions in the Worsley Hotel fire –the highest number of decorations ever awarded arising out of one incident.

Four of the awards, Queen's Gallantry Medals, were presented to Peter Lidbetter, Ron Morris, Roger Stewart and David Blair on Tuesday, 9 March at Buckingham Palace. In the State Ballroom, at the end of a long ceremony involving the presentation of about fifty honours and awards to men and women from all walks of life, the four firemen entered in line, turned, bowed their heads, took three steps forward and stood before the Queen. She said: 'I am pleased to see you here,' and talked to each fireman in turn, asking them, as she attached the medals to their lapels, about the fire. She shook hands with each man, and they stepped back, turned right, and left the red and gilt magnificence of the room.

The four other awards were presented in County Hall three and a half months later, nearly a year after that first ceremony there, at which twenty-two of the fire-fighters at the Worsley Hotel had been honoured by the GLC. A similar ceremony took place in the same Council Chamber on the afternoon of Monday, 2 June. At the end of the presentation of twenty-one medals and commendations to policemen and civilians by Her Majesty's Lord Lieutenant of Greater London and Marshall of the Royal Air Force, Lord Elworthy, Don Burrell, Deputy Chief Officer of the LFB, read a citation concerning the actions of four firemen at the Worsley fire, after which Lord Elworthy presented the Queen's Commendation for Brave Conduct, a silver oak-leaf, to Neil Wallington, Ray Chilton and Eric Hall.

A fourth Commendation, awarded posthumously to Hamish Pettit, was received by his widow, Pat.

*

'You know, Gordon,' said Neil one day. 'I can't help remembering his last words, what he said before he died. He didn't want to die, did he? And he won't, because he'll always be remembered. Not just by us, but by everyone who reads the book. Harry would be pleased about that.'

Printed in the United Kingdom
by Lightning Source UK Ltd.
123458UK00001B/338/A